D1156026

Hazard or Hardship

Hazard or Hardship

Crafting Global Norms on the Right to Refuse Unsafe Work

Jeffrey Hilgert

ILR Press

AN IMPRINT OF

CORNELL UNIVERSITY PRESS

ITHACA AND LONDON

Copyright © 2013 by Cornell University

All rights reserved. Except for brief quotations in a review, this book, or parts thereof, must not be reproduced in any form without permission in writing from the publisher. For information, address Cornell University Press, Sage House, 512 East State Street, Ithaca, New York 14850.

First published 2013 by Cornell University Press

Printed in the United States of America

Library of Congress Cataloging-in-Publication Data

Hilgert, Jeffrey, 1974–
   Hazard or hardship : crafting global norms on the right to refuse unsafe work / Jeffrey Hilgert.
      p. cm.
   Includes bibliographical references and index.
   ISBN 978-0-8014-5189-8 (cloth : alk. paper)
   1. Industrial safety—Law and legislation. 2. Employee rights.
3. Labor laws and legislation. I. Title.
   K1830.H55   2013
   342'.0684—dc23   2013004467

Cornell University Press strives to use environmentally responsible suppliers and materials to the fullest extent possible in the publishing of its books. Such materials include vegetable-based, low-VOC inks and acid-free papers that are recycled, totally chlorine-free, or partly composed of nonwood fibers. For further information, visit our website at www.cornellpress.cornell.edu.

Cloth printing   10 9 8 7 6 5 4 3 2 1

Contents

ACKNOWLEDGMENTS

This book would not have been possible without the support of many people. My sincere appreciation goes to James A. Gross who has been both a great academic mentor and friend. I extend my genuine thanks to Lowell Turner, Risa Lieberwitz, Clete Daniel, Lance Compa, Robert Hebdon, and Bob Sass; the staff of the Catherwood Library at Cornell University including Gordon T. Law, Stuart Basefsky, Suzanne Cohen, and Susan LaCette; and Nilgun Tolek and Michael Shanker at the Office of the Whistleblower Protection Program at the U.S. Occupational Safety and Health Administration. The Interuniversity Research Centre on Globalization and Work (CRIMT) and the Canadian Industrial Relations Association provided a forum for discussion and feedback on part of an early version of this manuscript at the 2010 conference Employee Representation in the New World of Work. My reading of the international law in this book is mine alone, but I express my gratitude to the many experts at the International Labour Office who informed this research indirectly by their participation in courses at Cornell University's School of Industrial and Labor Relations including, among others, Catherine Brâkenhielm Hansell, Karen Curtis, Lee Swepston, Jean-Pierre Laviec, Jukka Takala, Seiji Machida, Michele Nahmias, Martin Oelz, Jane Hodges, and Chris Land-Kazlauskas. Two anonymous reviewers gave invaluable advice for developing the manuscript. My thanks also extend to Fran Benson and Katherine Liu at Cornell University Press for their support in this project. I reserve my deepest debt of gratitude for my family, Gioconda, Arthur, and Elena.

Abbreviations

AFL-CIO	American Federation of Labor and Congress of Industrial Organizations
CEACR	Committee of Experts on the Application of Conventions and Recommendations
CESCR	Committee on Economic, Social and Cultural Rights
CFA	Committee on Freedom of Association
CFR	Code of Federal Regulations
CSST	Commission de la santé et de la sécurité du travail
DOL	Department of Labor
ECOSOC	United Nations Economic and Social Council
FIR	final investigation report
ICESCR	International Covenant on Economic, Social and Cultural Rights
ILC	International Labour Conference
ILO	International Labour Organization
IRS	internal responsibility system

NCB	National Coal Board
NDP	New Democratic Party
NIOSH	National Institute for Occupational Safety and Health
NLRA	National Labor Relations Act
NLRB	National Labor Relations Board
OCAW	Oil, Chemical and Atomic Workers
OECD	Organisation for Economic Co-operation and Development
OIG	Office of Inspector General
OSHA	Occupational Safety and Health Administration
UDHR	Universal Declaration of Human Rights
UFW	United Farm Workers
UN	United Nations
USWA	United Steel Workers of America
WEP	World Employment Program

HAZARD OR HARDSHIP

Introduction

Commodified Workers and the International Response

Colonel Nicholson had again reassured his Japanese captors that the British soldiers under his command could construct their railroad bridge before the deadline. In the classic World War II film *Bridge on the River Kwai*, the exacting commander touts the organizational efficiency of his captive battalion, eventually beaming at the sight of the bridge as it nears completion. Hesitantly, near the end of the enormous construction project crafted entirely from jungle lumber, a young major approaches Nicholson and dissents, saying the soldiers—now Japanese prisoners of war—must be given permission to slow down or openly revolt, given the importance of the railroad bridge to enemy supply lines. Nicholson immediately snaps, indignant at the thought of any insubordination. Glancing at the massive structure he thunders in all his sweaty servitude, "We are prisoners of war! We haven't the right to refuse work!"

Even in the absence of barbed wire and the pointed rifle of a prison camp, millions of workers around the world are averse to raising one's voice at work, let alone using open resistance such as refusing unsafe work.

The prospect of meaningful improvement of working conditions seems so unlikely that the common suggestion for action is "Find another job!" rather than challenging management, asking questions, raising concerns, or stopping work. On the surface, "find another job!" may be a wise choice, if a person can find other employment. From a global policy viewpoint, however, there are fundamental drawbacks to this defeatist path of action.

Whether in economics textbooks or neighborhood cafes, people often erroneously see work as unfolding in a simple labor market where buyers and sellers exchange human labor and work for a price. Each government, however, constructs, shapes, and institutionalizes systems of labor and employment. Societies define different boundaries for rights at work and determine how workers can struggle to achieve social justice. Decisions of this nature encompass a variety of constitutions of the right of employees to dissent and struggle to improve their working environment. These issues relate closely to the protection of the freedom of association and collective bargaining. Occupational health and safety laws also define these boundaries. Each of these labor rights institutions shapes work and employment, making "labor markets" more a function of deliberately organized laws, habits and practices rather than the free-for-all open exchange that a "market" metaphor implies.

When workers are resigned to "find another job!" as the only option, both workers and societies ultimately lose. What is lost is the exercise of basic citizenship rights at the workplace. Citizenship, as I use it here, means not the traditional status granted by a government but rather the act of possessing certain inalienable rights and privileges that make possible real participation and representation in the governance of society. Workers have rights that are to be exercised and enjoyed, making each workplace a site of citizenship and government in a free society. When workers quit their jobs because they feel they have no other choice, society loses a degree of freedom and an avenue for voice, representation, and governance in the workplace. Taking a strict "labor market" view thus marginalizes notions of citizenship rights at work and undermines the basic idea of freedom, democracy, and fundamental human rights at the workplace. Such advice is akin to being told to "move to another country!" rather than struggle for social change.

If workers, conversely, disregard the all too common advice to "find another job!" and exercise citizenship rights at work, a particular set of problems immediately surfaces. Will society's labor and employment system offer protection? Will changes be made to correct the original problem? If the problem is a safety and health concern, government inspectors may be called upon to enforce specific regulations. Will those regulations be enough? What regulations apply? What happens after the health and safety inspector leaves? If I try to organize to push my concern, will I be fired? If we all cause too much "trouble" will the company close and move elsewhere? Each of these uncertainties raises key questions about the boundaries of workers' rights and the distribution of power in the governance of the workplace. The answers are an indication of how each society defines and shapes the role of workers as citizens.[1]

Decisions about the constitution of workers' rights do not unfold in a vacuum; quite the opposite. History plays an important role. Legislators, judges, policymakers, and other key decision-makers possess different value systems that they transpose onto various institutional practices. Ideas and the value systems that certain ideas represent are shared, adopted and at times imposed across national borders. Globally, particular labor and social policy models are exchanged and advocated. The International Labor Organization has since 1919 gathered delegates from around the world to discuss and adopt international conventions on particular labor and employment policies. These norms as ideas shape national and local choices and strategies for protecting workers' rights. The international human rights treaty system is yet another international venue for the advocacy, negotiation, and setting of labor and employment rights standards.

Taken together, the decisions made in establishing citizenship rights at work—their underlying values and moral paradigms, their real world effectiveness on the ground where people work, and the history and politics behind their development—form an important object of study for both the citizen-worker and the labor scholar. This book is an in-depth examination of a narrow but essential citizenship right at the workplace, the rights of workers to refuse unsafe, hazardous, or unhealthy work. The employment relationship in all its divergent and precarious forms is a global phenomenon. Studying how employees are empowered to dissent and the models of protection on the right to refuse is, therefore, a question of international importance.

Across the contemporary globalized workplace, a "right to refuse" is exercised when one or more workers decide not to perform some task or assignment at work for fear of a health and safety risk—even after being ordered to do the job by a supervisor, manager, or some other superior. Where such refusals are safeguarded effectively, there are systems of protections for the worker with avenues for redress. These may include legal protections against retaliation or discrimination and systems to ameliorate the workers' health and safety concern. Where refusal rights are not well protected, this book asks why this is so. The diverging ways this unique citizenship right has been respected, exercised, and protected in law and in practice is the focus of this book. It is the story of how human society has shaped and restricted the global norms that define the workers' right to protest and in turn how society defines social justice and human rights in the struggle for a healthy and safe work environment.

The story of "the right to refuse" moves back and forth from local grievance to international political negotiation. The diversity of questions raised by this subject are equally legal, political, economic, social, and indeed philosophic. Refusal rights strike at the heart of employment in a capitalist society, defining how workers are protected when they fear for their health and safety. This book is about how society has decided to treat people willing to risk their livelihood to protest a concern about their basic working environment. The issue is not an abstract legal debate but rather a series of poignant and unnerving human experiences. The choices made define social justice, determine the degree of risk faced by people and communities, and delineate the line between a dignified and undignified human existence. Attention is paid to the North American experience for the instructive qualities of its labor history but also because this experience has influenced the global norms. This book is the history of the right to refuse unsafe work under international labor standards, a global legal framework and jurisprudence that fails workers seeking social justice by refusing unsafe work.

When Workers Refuse Unsafe Work

Duane Carlson was a cement truck operator employed by Arrowhead Concrete Works, a major concrete supplier in northeast Minnesota. When a mechanic and the company safety director verified his safety concerns about the truck he was driving, he refused to drive until repairs were made.

Court documents filed in his 2003 wrongful dismissal lawsuit attest to the pressure workers can face when they decide to refuse unsafe work. The company owner told him to "keep your mouth shut and do what you are told" because "you don't get to dictate demands to me. I tell you what to do or you get the hell out of here." When Carlson, a member of the Teamsters union, continued to refuse despite the threats, management's commands escalated into a full-throttled verbal assault. "Listen you little cocksucker," the owner screamed, "get in that truck right fucking now and get it ready. I am sick of your whining. Some fuckers are going down the road and getting laid off. You're going to be the first one you son of a bitch."[2] Carlson was not called back to work after a seasonal layoff and ultimately lost his discharge case in 2008 after five years of litigation and appeals.

Minutes away on U.S. Interstate Highway 35, Deborah Scott had made a similar decision in a different kind of workplace, six years earlier. Scott refused a routine job assignment to a dialysis unit of the Miller-Dwan Medical Center in Duluth. She had been working with the chemical sterilant Renalin as a dialysis assistant. Told by the sales representatives of the company producing the chemical that it was so safe "you could practically drink it," she learned from another employee that exposure to the chemical should be avoided by pregnant women. Scott was six months pregnant and experiencing preterm labor. According to court documents in her health and safety retaliation case, three other dialysis technicians had also reported problems with their pregnancies while working with Renalin. After Scott's obstetrician ordered her to avoid exposure, she refused to return to her job. Management placed her on "unpaid leave" during her pregnancy, forcing Scott's family into economic hardship.[3]

Like Scott and Carlson, Richard Gizbert, an ABC News correspondent based in London, England, had a similar experience. Gizbert was fired after he refused to accept a third war zone assignment weeks before the Iraq War in 2003. Terminated despite a voluntary war zone policy, Gizbert sought £1.5 million for lost compensation with the Central London Employment Tribunal. He was awarded £98,781 after the tribunal found his dismissal unfair and based on his refusal to go to Iraq. ABC News appealed the decision, reducing the award to £60,000 while establishing jurisprudence under U.K. safety law that no right to refuse had occurred. "His place of work was London," said the tribunal. "He chose not to visit the war zones. He was thus in no danger, let alone imminent danger, nor could he, in the circumstances, reasonably believe otherwise." Gizbert later found work reporting with the al-Jazeera network.[4]

About five kilometers across the border from Trieste, Italy, is the Slovenian port of Luka Koper on the Adriatic Sea. Once operated as a socially owned enterprise by a workers' council in the former Yugoslavia, the port would become one of the first free-trade zones years before the fall of the Soviet Union. Today, Luka Koper handles more than sixteen million tons of cargo annually and is an important logistics hub for the region. As traffic has increased with global trade, however, worker health and safety has become an important concern for the port workers. In August 2011, a small group of less than two dozen crane operators walked off the job to protest deteriorating working conditions. Individual contract workers, some reportedly on the job for several shifts in a row, wildcatted sporadically to protest "brutal growth in tonnage at the port" and "accidents happening almost every day." These refusals to work led to new health and safety protections in a collective agreement, including health and safety protections for some of the most precarious workers at Luka Koper.[5]

China has become Africa's biggest trading partner, boosting employment and "providing more loans . . . to poor countries than the World Bank."[6] As investment has grown, however, reports of hazardous working conditions have surfaced with workers facing retribution for refusing unsafe work. Workers at the Chinese-owned Chambishi Copper Mine in Zambia told Human Rights Watch that they are routinely threatened for raising the prospect of refusing to work in unsafe areas. "Speak about safety, stop working—you're dismissed," say the managers, according to the underground miners. "I will say 'This is unsafe, we should not go ahead,' but the boss will say, 'No, go work,' and threaten to dismiss me. If you don't go along, you don't keep your job." Hazardous work has created the "mixed blessing" of employment in Africa.[7]

As in Chambishi and Luka Koper, the question of refusing unsafe work is also faced by people working in illicit and unregulated occupations. Sex workers across Asia, for example, have campaigned for regulation and occupational health and safety, including the right to refuse unsafe sex.[8] One sex worker in Blackburn, Australia, a Melbourne suburb, was found assaulted by a man who "aggressively grabbed her, flipped her onto her back and attempted to rape her" before pulling a gun on her when she protested. The woman had "persistently refused to have sex with him without a condom" and went on to file a claim for injured workers' compensation. Her lawyer argued "whether you work in a bank or a brothel, everyone has the right to feel safe and work."[9] Like workers in other types of illegal employment, from child laborers to undocumented migrant labor, working in the underground economy compounds the challenge of protecting safety and health, including the right to refuse unsafe work.

Workers in emergencies have also struggled to refuse. Kathleen Blanco, the governor of Louisiana, called in hundreds of National Guard troops "fresh back from Iraq" and granted shoot to kill authority to "restore order" in New Orleans in the wake of Hurricane Katrina.[10] As tensions rose and people realized the magnitude of the disaster that displaced three hundred thousand residents and caused damages in excess of $100 billion, a crew of private security guards reported for duty at a fifty-one-story private office building downtown.[11] The crew was ordered to take SWAT action to remove vandals said to be taking advantage of the electrical blackout. Concerned about working in the tense environment, the employees requested more training and bulletproof vests. The crew was terminated on the spot for insubordination. Their wrongful discharge case was investigated by health and safety inspectors and was dismissed without merit.[12]

Where work hazards stop and environmental hazards begin is not always clear. Testifying before a congressional committee investigating the Deepwater Horizon oil rig explosion in the Gulf of Mexico that killed eleven workers, Lamar McKay, chairman and president of BP America, argued all employees "anywhere at any level" had the ability "and, in fact, the responsibility to raise their hand and try to get the operations stopped." Steve Newman, president and CEO of Transocean, another company on the same rig, reiterated that all of the employees had "stop work authority" to call "a time out for safety."[13] This authority had failed, however. Ten hours before the explosion and ecologic disaster, an argument unfolded among the workers about safety. "The company man was basically saying, 'well, this is how it's going to be'," Douglas Brown, a rig mechanic, told federal investigators.[14] Similar attempts to refuse unsafe work were also reported in another of the world's worst industrial accidents, the Union Carbide leak of methyl isocyanate in Bhopal, India, in 1984.[15]

Reports of workers refusing work due to safety and health concerns are found around the world and across occupations. Teachers, agricultural workers, retail clerks, nurses, and truck drivers have refused work for safety and health reasons. Prison guards have refused work due to inadequate staffing levels, workers at nuclear power plants have refused work due to production speedup, and airline pilots have refused to fly due to mechanical concerns. The right to refuse unsafe work has involved individual work hazards, dangers to groups of workers, and risks to broader communities beyond the workplace. Work refusals for safety and health reasons may be isolated actions by one worker acting alone, or they may be group actions taken by any number of workers.

Despite differences in the particular details, there are commonalities shared across all work refusals. When workers face a hazard as they see it, they encounter a critical decision. If avenues for the redress of grievances exist, the decision may not be difficult. Safety and health can be secured via institutional means at the workers' initiative. Where workers are afforded no role in governance at work, however, or where their employment is so precarious the worker does not see any alternative, the decision may not appear to exist at all: Continue work. Be quiet. Keep your head down. Don't get fired or not called back. Loss of income. Unemployment. Ruin. For millions of workers around the world the choice is simple: hazard or hardship.

The right to refuse unsafe work is a global policy question that confronts all nations. Around the world, every society and government must decide how to protect, or not to protect, each worker from retaliation and termination. This involves not just drafting a progressive antidiscrimination law; it also involves the regulating of work and employment relations on a more fundamental level. Each country defines the rights of workers differently, but each national labor policy rests on a framework of laws and regulations that defines how workers who refuse work for reasons of safety and health will be treated. This "individual" decision by workers is thus an individual decision that is the result of a larger social process. The larger social process, namely how a nation writes laws and structures its business and employment systems, is found in every country of the world. From the social democracies of northern Europe and the informal workplaces of Africa, to the immense factories of East Asia and the export processing zones of Central America, to the vast agribusiness farmlands and the declining industrial towns across North America, individual worker decisions are encased in a broader institutional framework regulating each society's economies.

The right to refuse unsafe work—silently contemplated or actively engaged in—is ultimately a moral question for society. It is the worker that must face the greatest burden of occupational injuries and illnesses. If society crafts institutions, laws, and regulations that expose workers to hostile supervisors and managers without effective recourse, a moral choice has been made. Such a moral choice finds it acceptable that workers are forced to choose between two unthinkable alternatives: their physical health and safety or their economic livelihood and basic subsistence. Under this type of moral system, laws and regulations make a worker's safety and health nothing more than a commodity to be bought and sold for a price. Where a society offers no means of protecting the right to refuse unsafe work, workers themselves hold no more standing than their monetary value to the company. Here, workers are commodities. Health and safety—and thus the worker—become marketable commodities to be sold for a profit while workers assume the private burden of "their" injuries and illnesses.

The problem with this moral choice is that human beings are not commodities; human beings—people—are not mere objects to be bought and sold in a marketplace. Each human being has intrinsic worth. Slavery is widely seen as an affront to morality; slave markets have become prohibited institutions. As the question has become buying worker health and safety versus the whole human being, this moral logic, somehow, breaks down. The rights of workers in a globalized economy, especially those rights that protect safety and health, are limited. The "modern" imperative gives a higher priority to ongoing production, the authority of corporations, and making a profit. Despite weak systems of workplace rights, however, the underlying moral dilemma remains unchanged: if human beings as workers do not have the right to refuse unsafe work, they are nothing more than a commodity upon a global stage.

Labor Is Not a Commodity

At the dawn of the modern human rights era, after the wreckage of the Second World War, the idea that a worker is not a commodity was recognized and accepted internationally. Founded in 1919, the International Labor Organization was reconstituted through the Declaration of Philadelphia, adopted in 1944. "Labor is not a commodity" became the first

fundamental principle of the ILO. This was followed with the solemn obligation to advance policies and programs to achieve "adequate protection
for the life and health of all workers in all occupations." The ILO had,
since its beginning, served as a global forum for the negotiation and supervision of treaties on labor standards. The new Declaration of Philadelphia was an international recognition that "labor was not a commodity"
and connected this principle to the aim of improving working conditions.

Franklin D. Roosevelt remarked at the time how the new declaration
"was an historical document on a level with the U.S. Declaration of Inde-
pendence in 1776."[16] The text "sums up the aspirations of an epoch," the
U.S. president noted, "affirming the rights of all human beings to material
well-being and spiritual development under conditions of freedom and
dignity." He implored "attainment of those conditions must constitute a
central aim of national and international policy." "Indeed," he concluded,
"the worthiness and success of international policies will be measured in
the future by the extent to which they promote the achievement of this
end."[17]

That labor was not a commodity had gained acceptance in the postwar
years of social protection. Although "labor market" as a phrase was applied to systems of work and employment—a place where "buyers" and
"sellers" exchange work and pay for a price—all were not in agreement
with this metaphor. Notable writers such as Karl Polanyi[18] described labor
as a *fictitious* commodity. The economy was organized by institutions that
enforced labor's unnatural commodification. Labor as a *fictitious* commodity was contrasted with *genuine* commodities such as basic material
goods. Polanyi and others argued that new institutions could be built to
provide social protection, enough social protection to *decommodify* labor
and employment. This *decommodification* required knowledge of institutions. As the Cambridge economist Ha-Joon Chang later noted, following
Polanyi's logic, economics was itself the study of institutions and how the
various institutions constitute "rights-obligation structures" throughout an
economy.[19]

In the decades after the Declaration of Philadelphia was adopted at its
twenty-sixth general conference, the ILO advocated labor and social policies for a postwar world based in social justice. The ILO was awarded the
Nobel Peace Prize in 1969 in part for the idea *Si vis pacem, cole justitiam*—
if the world is to achieve peace, it must cultivate justice. Led by a tripartite

(unions, employers, and governments) system of decision-making, the ILO directed its actions at the formalized and predominantly male labor force. This focus was critiqued but would remain amid a backdrop of "reduced labor-based inequality" in the 1960s. Social justice required direct engagement with employment relations and macroeconomic planning. The ILO led the effort to transform the principle of labor, decommodified, into reality.[20]

The ILO's social justice efforts in the postwar decades were most innovative in the work of the World Employment Program of the 1960s and 1970s. Recognizing global economic disparities, the WEP advocated policies seeking full employment and a human needs-based model of economic development. This required creating diverse state interventions beyond classic market-based policy. The ILO's WEP advocated redistribution and broad national economic planning. At one point, ILO experts were assisting national governments in developing five-year plans. Through the 1960s and early 1970s, a global macroeconomic alternative had even emerged in response to neoliberalism's "failed policies of the counterrevolution." Such strategies eventually met the ire of U.S. government leaders, U.S. trade union leaders, and employers from both the United States and Europe. Each of these key national and social actors voted against the WEP agenda when the issue came to a head at the World Employment Conference in 1975.[21]

The 1970s and 1980s was a period of "intellectual shrinkage" for the ILO. The United States stopped its dues contributions to the ILO in 1970, suspending its membership in November 1975. Various reasons were given for the U.S. withdrawal, but the most direct impact on the ILO was an immediate reduction on the annual ILO budget:

> The strident letter sent by Henry Kissinger, U.S. Secretary of State, to the Director-General was in fact written by Harvard Professor John Dunlop, the doyen of American industrial relations theorists. The suspension created immediate difficulties for the ILO, since the USA, which contributed a quarter of the ILO's regular budget, had also failed to pay its huge backlog of financial dues.[22]

As globalization and the decline of industrial unionism challenged the ILO's tripartite governance, the U.S. withdrawal placed the ILO on the defensive. The ILO offered no response to the World Bank's structural adjustment strategies that proposed "a dismantling of protective regulations and a substitution of pro-individualistic, pro-market regulations." The labor market flexibility debate grew yet when the ILO had "came up with evidence of the adverse effects of the new pro-market policies, efforts were made to keep it quiet to avoid alienating key governments," especially key states that were promoting neoliberal reforms. Intellectual shrinkage after 1980 meant the pace of standard setting would slow, the content of labor conventions would become more voluntarist and favorable to employers, and ILO supervision would be weakened.[23]

The disintegration of the Soviet Union and the spread of capitalism created a new opportunity for the ILO. The World Bank, the International Monetary Fund, and the Organisation for Economic Cooperation and Development (OECD) all challenged the historic ILO role of institution-building for social justice. Popular unrest would keep social justice afloat yet pro-market critics argued against the "proliferation" of labor conventions.[24] One of the ILO's post–Cold War responses was *The Declaration of Fundamental Principles and Rights at Work*, a statement that defined four "core" issues as fundamental rights. These included the right to freedom from forced labor, the right to freedom from child labor, the right to equality and freedom from discrimination, and the freedom of association. What was lost, aside from work safety and health listed as a fundamental right, was a more expansive consciousness of the ILO as a forum for advancing broader systems of institutional governance through labor and social policy, not just silos of particular rights at work.

Today, the ILO estimates about 2.3 million workers are killed by work-related injuries and illnesses annually[25] and the figure is not declining.[26] Another 270 million nonfatal work-related accidents occur annually, in addition to about 160 million new cases of work-related disease identified each year.[27] Global capitalism today exacts an incalculable human toll on society and the planet. The financial toll is estimated to be between 2 to 11 percent of gross domestic product, stark figures that if halved would in some countries eliminate all foreign debt.[28] The reality that work-related illnesses and injuries have become a leading cause of adult morbidity is the tragic backdrop to the strategic weakening of the ILO over the last generation.[29] More people are killed at work today than by warfare. Workers' rights continue to be challenged not only by a hypercompetitive global economy but also by increasingly precarious work arrangements and the failure to address the many new economic realities challenging human rights at work.

Complicating this picture today is how occupational health and safety hazards have become more complex. The "old" occupational health problems such as cotton dust and brown lung have resurfaced in areas of the world with weak governance and regulation—forcing workers "to replay history, despite the availability of information and knowledge transfer unthinkable just a generation ago."[30] New varieties of workplace hazards are also emerging. This includes the explosion of new synthetic chemicals and their global trade. Whereas health hazards such as asbestos, lead, and white phosphorus were once the most serious causes for alarm, now one thousand new synthetic chemicals—two to three per day—are introduced into the global marketplace every year, bringing the number of synthetic chemicals in use to over one hundred thousand and growing. Other types of occupational hazards unknown a few years ago include occupational risks from products manufactured with nanoparticles, genetically engineered organisms of one variety or another, a list of hazards related to climate change, and workplace-based social hazards such as violence, psychological trauma, and mental health issues.

How workers are empowered (or not empowered) by society to protect health and safety is a central question in labor and employment policy. With the weakening of the international response through the ILO, workers are placed at risk and bear the burden of weak institutional protections. The typical response, when safety and health receives attention, is to strengthen the classic labor inspection model. As new hazards emerge while regulatory regimes often remain captured by business, however, new strategies are needed in response. Returning the question of occupational safety and health to the realm of workers' rights and the role of labor rights in the working environment is a step of fundamental importance for labor policymakers and workers at risk worldwide.

This reexamination requires studying the institutions of worker representation and governance in the working environment. This study focuses on one dimension of worker representation, the right to refuse unsafe work. Among the characteristics that define commodified labor is that management holds the institutional freedom to hire, fire, and exert control over workers. Gradations of this freedom exist across different societies, but the freedom remains. The OECD summarizes employment dismissal protections for all member states and the Anglo-American countries top the list in the freedom to dismiss workers. The United States, with its employment at-will doctrines, ranks first among OECD member countries, with Canada and the United Kingdom claiming the second and third most "flexible" labor market policies on dismissal protection.[31]

Refusal rights law defines both the rights of workers as well as the termination freedoms held by employers. Just as some societies limit employers' right to dismiss employees on grounds such as racial or gender discrimination, employee dissent and the right to refuse unsafe work forms a similar moral limit on the termination of the employment relationship. Labor policy in general—the body of laws and regulations controlling work and workers—is the vehicle whereby such moral imperatives are implemented. Labor policies are found in every society.

Where employers hold liberal freedoms of termination, refusal rights become rights that are very difficult to exercise and enjoy. Oftentimes labor policies turn the right to refuse into a case of employee disloyalty and insubordination, placing additional burdens of proof upon the worker. Where workplaces confront a globally competitive environment, or where work itself is organized in a precarious fashion, seemingly insurmountable burdens are placed upon workers exercising the right to refuse. Yet the right to refuse unsafe work may be the most empowering way that workers represent themselves on the question of health and safety in the working environment and remains a ubiquitous question across workplace relations. This book details how workers lost the right to refuse under international labor and human rights norms. It is an in-depth look at how our global society has decided to resolve—and failed to resolve—the protection of any fundamental human right to refuse unsafe work.

1

Human Rights and the Struggle to Define Hazards

Protecting basic refusal rights where workers face the most dangerous working conditions has had wide public support generally. Definitions of workplace hazards, however, are socially contested; meaning workers and employers often disagree about the definition of workplace hazards. The right to refuse typically has been wedded to some threshold, defined legally, that describes the degree of occupational hazard a worker may refuse. The phrase "imminent and serious danger" is one such legal standard that is used to determine when a worker can refuse unsafe work.

One can argue over the specific hazard threshold that will be covered by the right to refuse. At a more fundamental level, however, is the question of *who should have the right to define* hazardous work in the first place. The typical decision makers are the legislators, regulators, and ultimately judges. An alternative view is that the workers themselves should be the ones to decide. Many people have a visceral negative reaction to the idea that a single worker should be empowered to define the very nature of a workplace hazard to which they are exposed. It runs counter to a host of deeply held values. This is especially the case in the United States, where worker commodification is the norm in law. Arguments against this worker freedom range from an objectivism rooted in scientific rationality to the view that workers are not capable of making such important decisions. Indeed, the scientific infrastructure erected around occupational safety and health in the last generation plays into a basic logic that a technocratic view has the capacity to solve all health and safety concerns. This perspective also views power relations at the workplace as less important, believing instead that if objective science can identify a hazard to human health, a broad social consensus necessarily follows in response.

Labor history is instructive on this point. Where commodification is strongest, as in Anglo-American countries, workers have struggled to refuse unsafe work on their own terms and according to their own definitions of hazardous work. Workers have held a different idea about the right to refuse unsafe work compared to not only employers but to progressive policymakers, regulators, and judges. The struggle for the right to define the nature of a hazard has, therefore, been as much a struggle as have those against particular hazards. These are two sides of the same coin, indivisible throughout labor history. In recounting this rich heritage, I open the debate about who gets to decide the nature of a hazard and thus when society protects the right to refuse. Although the aim of this book is a detailed examination of international labor rights norms, I use Anglo-American labor history to elucidate this key question underlying the global debate, namely, who decides the definition of a hazard at work?

Empowerment to Define Hazards at Work

As a subject of struggle by unions in collective bargaining, the right to refuse was protected as early as the Jellico Agreement of 1893, which covered eight Appalachian mines and was at the time "one of the most advanced agreements of any miners in the country." It allowed a miner "to refuse to work if he thought the mine was dangerous through failure of the bosses to supply enough support timber."[1] James Grey Pope has called conflicts where workers had unique ideas about their rights *constitutional insurgencies*.[2] Militant strikes by miners in the 1920s clashed with the Kansas Industrial Court, an early U.S. experiment in industrial relations law. Progressive middle-class reformers maintained that "constitutional rights in the economic sphere blocked adaptation to change" and strikes "amounted to 'industrial warfare' that should give way to peaceful administration" as fundamental principles "interfered with pragmatic bargaining."[3] The miners disagreed, as did other workers. Quoting Carter Goodrich's *The Miner's Freedom*, these workers were active self-advocates:

> They develop informal rules governing such matters as the distribution of coal cars, the 'proprietary' rights of the miner to his own space on the seam, and the principle that a man 'ought to know when he is tired' and therefore decide for himself when the working day is done. . . . Violations of the code were adjudicated and punished by co-workers, applying sanctions ranging from sour comments to ostracism and, occasionally, physical assault. At the core of the most successful, pioneering industrial unions were groups of workers with especially strong traditions of informal jurisgenerative practice: Deep shaft miners in the United Mine Workers, tire builders in the United Rubber Workers, and the skilled metal trades in the United Automobile Workers.[4]

This "effective freedom" originated from a "popular rights consciousness" that was distinct from the prevailing legal norms, labor's professional legal representation, the business community, and Progressives who sought to advance their own politics.

After the enactment of the U.S. National Labor Relations Act of 1935 (the Wagner Act) and adoption of Wagner Act principles in Canada in the 1940s, the right to refuse unsafe work gained ground as a viable subject of collective bargaining in North America. Collective labor agreements would become the only way to circumvent the strict common laws on the termination of employment that had commodified workers in the United States and Canada. Refusal rights were not effectively enforced before agreements with labor unions and the passage of new labor laws that facilitated collective bargaining.[5]

By the 1960s and early 1970s, collective bargaining had strengthened the right to refuse in the United States and Canada. Some labor arbitrators—although not all—had stepped back from a "work now, grieve later" standard, often with the aid of explicit contractual language protecting the right to refuse. Just cause termination in labor agreements also altered the common-law rules for terminating employment, affording more protection to workers refusing unsafe work. These trends did not extend the right to refuse to all, but they did protect against liberal discharge norms for millions covered by collective agreements.

How collective bargaining affected the right to refuse unsafe work is seen in the breadth of these protections. In a survey from the early 1970s of 1,724 labor agreements, each covering more than one thousand workers, health and safety was addressed in 93 percent of the agreements. Agreements covering over 1.9 million employees recognized "the right to refuse to work under unsafe conditions or to demand being relieved from the job under such circumstances." A smaller group of agreements gave the union the authority "to remove a person from the job."[6]

Canadian provincial labor law began requiring that collective bargaining agreements include clauses that discipline could only be for just cause.[7] Canadian labor arbitrators slowly were becoming more and more comfortable with independently using the language available within a labor agreement to protect a worker's right to refuse unsafe work:

> A more expansive right to refuse unsafe work has been fashioned by arbitrators from several basic elements of the law of collective bargaining. . . . Arbitrators are empowered to reinstate an employee who has been wrongfully discharged, to award back pay and to substitute a lesser penalty for the one imposed by management. Shaping this legal raw material into an elementary right to refuse was an easy task. Disobeying an order, even an improper one, is generally cause for discipline. An employee must comply with the maxim "work now, grieve later," because the grievance and arbitration process, not the shop floor, is the preferred forum for dispute resolution. A refusal to perform unsafe work is recognized as an exception to this rule.[8]

The first published arbitration decision in Canada to recognize the refusal exception to the "work now, grieve later" standard was in 1963 in *B.A. Oil Company*.[9] The leading case after this jurisprudence became *Steel Company of Canada* in 1974, a case that was cited favorably throughout the 1970s.[10] Some Canadian arbitrators at the time adopted an undue imminent hazard standard. More conservative arbitrators used as a yardstick "risks which are normal for a grievor's workplace" and gave those risks "the arbitrator's stamp of approval."[11] As Richard Brown noted, with *Steel*

Company and other decisions labor arbitrators exercised more discretion in protecting workers against health and safety discrimination:

> Blind acquiescence in risks normally associated with a job is wrong because the production process is largely controlled by management with little input from workers. In addition, the practice of a single employer may fall below industry standards. The *Steel Company* award recognized the danger of relying exclusively upon management's judgment and found that a procedure which had been consistently followed by a foreman was not acceptably safe. The grievor had been instructed to use a poker to dislodge debris overhead, but had refused when a falling brick struck his partner's arm. After the grievor was suspended, the other members of his crew were taken to the roof to complete the task from that location with the aid of extensions on their pokers. The arbitrator's conclusion that a danger existed was supported by evidence that a safer procedure was possible . . . and that a minor injury had occurred.[12]

Such arbitration decisions posed threats to the common law and, therefore, threatened management control of the workplace. Labor arbitration moved the right to refuse toward what could be called a basic "status protection" for workers, where the exercise of the right to refuse could be enjoyed based on the class status of being a worker in an employment relationship. The assessment of risk in Canadian arbitration was interpreted based on an arbitrator's judgment and not a legislator's interpretation of hazards at work. Arbitration decisions were imperfect and still focused on the evaluation of the hazard that workers faced before protection against termination was granted, but they represented a new and important trend to protect the right to refuse. Arbitral labor jurisprudence was in one sense becoming a more effective protection of worker refusal rights. This trend was more pronounced in Canada than in the United States, where arbitrator values also continued to treat refusal cases as basic employee insubordination cases.[13]

Although important, arbitration had its limits. As a general rule, arbitral jurisprudence places the burden of establishing the justification for discipline on the management. In cases of the right to refuse unsafe work at arbitration, however, an employer "need only prove disobedience before an employee is called upon to show that a refusal to work was proper in the circumstances."[14] Rarely was the management called upon to demonstrate that the work was safe for the worker as a justification for an insubordination charge.

By the 1970s, a substantial North American jurisprudence had developed. This jurisprudence, although it did not always protect the right to refuse, at least attested to what could be called a radical consciousness of health and safety held by workers and their organizations. Not bound by a narrow conceptualization of occupational safety and health, worker activists held unique interpretations of safety and attempted to exercise refusal rights while at the same time negotiating for improved workplace governance. Between 1966 and 1975, safety related work stoppages grew by 385 percent in the United States while the overall rate of stoppages increased more slowly, from 14 percent to 38 percent of all work stoppages in the base year of 1966.[15] Labor conflict over health and safety was on the rise, and unions were becoming an outlet for environmental health and safety concerns.

Across North America, health and safety emerged a top issue in collective bargaining as labor inspectorates were failing in their mission to protect workers from hazards. Unions chided the U.S. health and safety inspectorate for "attitudes that show a priority compassion for the problems and inconveniences of management."[16] One OSHA official responded positively to displeasure from labor and management. "Since the criticism of the OSHA program is about equal from all sides," he said, "we are probably steering a right course toward accomplishing the objectives of the act."[17]

A team of labor researchers observed that this odd reaction from early OSHA leaders implied "the [OSHA] mission is to find a middle ground in an area of class conflict, rather than to achieve a working environment free from recognized hazards."[18]

Even as OSHA came into force in the United States in 1971, union collective bargaining provided the only effective means by which workers held a voice in their working environment. It was thought that OSHA would protect workers better than decentralized collective bargaining, but even though the new agency did raise the profile of safety and health, which was at times helpful in bargaining, it was quickly disappointing for labor. It would take no longer than the first OSHA labor complaint to shatter any illusions.

Allied Chemical employed two hundred members of Local Union 3-586 of the Oil, Chemical and Atomic Workers at a plant in Moundsville, West Virginia. Charges of widespread mercury contamination, including mercury seeping through the cracked floors, were forwarded to state health officials after plant managers refused to meet a union health and safety committee to discuss the problem. Inspectors from the West Virginia Department of Health confirmed the contamination in February 1971 and in March a Walsh-Healy federal contractor health inspection also justified the workers' concerns. Allied Chemical openly contested the findings. One month after OSHA became law, the Oil, Chemical and Atomic Workers acted on behalf of their local affiliate and made history with the first OSHA complaint.

The OSHA inspection failed to order the immediate abatement of the mercury contamination. The Labor Department ruled that health hazards were not to be considered "imminent dangers" under the Act, despite a clear legislative intention otherwise and evidence from a survey collected at the time of the OSHA inspection that revealed 67 percent of workers were experiencing signs of mercury poisoning. Two weeks later, OSHA issued its first citation in history to the Allied Chemical Company, fining it $1,000 and issuing a lengthy, nonbinding cleanup order. The company paid the fine to OSHA and made no legal appeal. The lessons from the first OSHA citation were later chronicled as an historic "first" in several ways, revealing "how the government would respond to complaints about health hazards . . . and how it defined 'imminent danger'."[19]

Labor unions argued that worker health and safety could be protected only when workers are empowered. "The question becomes one of power," noted the health and safety activist Tony Mazzocchi of OCAW on the need for labor rights. "Those workers who are the potential victims ought to regulate. . . . It should be the worker who carries out the mandate of the law, the right to inspect, the right to cite, the right to bring about change based on what is known, the right to be notified, the right to know." Only by thinking of the subject "in terms of empowerment" could a difference be made.[20]

That OSHA was to take a "hands-off" approach to regulation was evident when MIT professor Nicolas Ashford interviewed the first leaders of OSHA and the National Institute for Occupational Safety and Health (NIOSH), the new federal agencies established by the U.S. Congress.

Marcus Key, director of NIOSH, and George Guenther, the first assistant secretary of labor for occupational safety and health, voiced strong agreement with the sweeping new findings of the Robens Committee. The Robens Committee's high-profile parliamentary inquiry into worker health and safety policy in Britain had argued for fewer legal restrictions on business and advocated partial voluntary self-regulation of worker health and safety. Key summarized the principles of the Robens Report in a speech to the American Public Health Association in 1972, noting curtly that "not all problems can be solved 'by the strict language of a standard' " before he recommended flexibility in developing worker health and safety standards.[21]

In remarks at the Kennedy School of Government that would foreshadow later debates on worker health and safety at the ILO, George Guenther said the new OSHA should follow the underlying values embodied in the Robens Report. Ashford reported:

> George Guenther, former Assistant Secretary of Labor for Occupational Safety and Health, agreed with the appropriateness for the United States of the following Robens Report conclusions: (1) there is too much law; (2) the law is not relevant to the workers' situation; (3) the various administrative agencies are unnecessarily fragmented. It should be remembered, though, that it is the British system that is characterized by fragmented legislation; this is not the case in the United States. Guenther was misusing the Robens Committee's observation that 'there is too much law' to justify *not* developing regulations.[22]

Guenther made these comments less than two years after OSHA's enactment, giving little credibility to his argument, which criticized OSHA's work when the agency was barely up and running. Voluntary compliance was the mantra from day one of OSHA. The values and the belief system behind this "total operating philosophy"[23] were likely lost on the people showing signs of mercury poisoning who were working at the Allied Chemical Company's plant in Moundsville, West Virginia.

Business Week reported that unions had become increasingly concerned about the working environment, especially hazards that caused disease. "Unions heretofore never dreamt that such situations might exist," noted George Taylor, director of occupational health and safety for the AFL-CIO.[24] "Everybody is being forced into looking at this question," said Mazzocchi. "If you critically examine what each union does, you see that people are at different places. But they are in motion, whether it is a hard run or a walk."[25] Likewise, a number of collective bargaining agreement gains in the 1970s addressed the working environment and out-of-plant environmental damage. These efforts placed workers and their unions in a position of contesting the nature of production itself with an increasingly sympathetic public willing to legitimize new environmental labor rights.[26]

Collective Bargaining for the Working Environment

Safety and health in the working environment became more important to the collective bargaining of a number of major unions in this period, including the United Auto Workers, OCAW, the United Farm Workers, the United Mine Workers, and to a degree the United Steelworkers of America. An entirely different conception of safety and health in the working environment was emerging and being advocated by workers directly.

After holding union conferences around the country entitled "Hazards in the Industrial Environment" in 1969 and 1970, OCAW surveyed 508 local unions on safety, health, and environmental concerns. The UAW surveyed over four hundred local unions. Fifty-nine percent of the local unions knew their workplaces were contributing to air, water, and land pollution, including 79 percent of those with over one thousand members. Thirty-seven percent reported members being assigned job tasks resulting in air or water pollution, including nearly half of the locals with a thousand or more members.[27] These concerns would be prominent in labor campaigns in subsequent years and demonstrated how effective an in-plant local system of collective bargaining was in raising the issue of hazards and in advocating change.

One of the first conferences organized by labor and environmental groups, the Urban Environment Conference of 1971, allowed urban reform groups, environmental groups and advocates, and organized labor to meet and work together to protect on-the-job and community health.[28] This was part of a broad-based movement with labor union activism at center stage. Labor unions, however, would find themselves in the unfavorable position of leading a budding social movement while ensconced within a weak collective bargaining and labor law system that provided little strategic leverage for what were fast becoming major structural challenges from economic globalization.

Collective bargaining, despite passage of the law authorizing OSHA in 1970, continued to be the vehicle affording workers the most protection when shop floor resistance to worksite environmental damage occurred. A good example is the refusal of Gilbert Pugliese at the Jones and Laughlin Steel facility in Cleveland. Pugliese "refused to push a button" to rush hundreds of gallons of oil into the Cuyahoga River. He was suspended for five days while his supervisors considered permanent suspension but decided against it in consideration of a revolt of the workers. Two years later, with OSHA in operation, a company foreman again insisted that Pugliese push the button. Local media embarrassed the USWA into fighting his impending discharge for insubordination. Pugliese kept the job he had held for eighteen years and the Jones and Laughlin Steel Company was forced to find alternative means to dispose of the Cleveland plant's waste oil apart from their practice of dumping it into the Cuyahoga River and the Lake Erie watershed.[29]

It was collective bargaining that afforded protection against insubordination charges; OSHA had ignored the right to refuse. Protection against "imminent danger" was left in the statute but did not explicitly enable any refusal rights. This would be a topic for later regulatory rulemaking. The best protection of the right to refuse would be protections from at-will employment through a collectively bargained just clause contract provision. As with Gilbert Pugliese, for many there was but little difference between the legal right to refuse unsafe hazards at work and an unsafe hazard at work that would later damage a community's environment.

Although self-interest of a sort could characterize such claims, the actions of many workers at the time also represented a much broader set of values that could not fully be described as simply self-interested; at times, they held a stronger moral dimension. Political expedience at a time of growing ecological consciousness may have been the case in some bargaining relationships, but this does not by itself disqualify the moral dimension of this labor activism, especially with the growing backdrop of precarious employment relations under increasingly competitive globalization.

Numerous cases can be found across North America illustrating how workers struggled to expand the definition of unsafe and hazardous work. Health and safety issues figured prominently in the sixty-seven day strike against General Motors in 1970. Management at forty plants agreed to nearly two thousand worker demands on health and safety, over one-third of which addressed "onerous, dangerous" and "uncomfortable" conditions in the plant environment[30] Better ventilation, reductions in noise pollution, and the removal of oil and debris from factory floors were among the gains. This did not change the polluting automobile (changes that were advocated in bargaining), but these proposals advanced by workers and agreed to by management resulted in immediate environmental improvements through collective bargaining.[31]

OCAW was prepared for a prolonged confrontation for health and safety committees in the 1972 negotiations with leading U.S. oil producers. Labor's demand was "the right of workers to control, at least as decisively as their employer, the health and safety conditions in the factories and shops."[32] A nationwide industrial confrontation was averted when the American Oil Company agreed to the demands. By January 1973 twelve of the fourteen major oil companies accepted similar terms. The campaign then turned to Shell Oil Company, a holdout. Shell workers walked off the job and launched a national boycott of Shell Oil in what newspapers called "the first time in American labor history a major strike has started over the potential health hazards of an industry."[33] Nearly every major environmental group supported the strike, including the Sierra Club. Environmentalists began to study labor relations, with detailed strike news appearing in scientific journals such as *Science*:

> The strike is about a health and safety clause in a new, 2-year contract covering some 5,000 OCAW workers; it has already been accepted by more than 15 other oil companies. The clause would establish a joint labor management committee, with each side equally represented, to approve outside surveys of health and safety conditions in the plant, make public reports, recommend medical examinations where necessary, and determine what changes should be made if hazards are found to exist. Should disputes arise within the committee, normal grievance and arbitration procedures can be followed. Barry Commoner, of Washington University in St. Louis, regards the clause as highly significant. "By working for environmental quality at the workplace, and developing new ways to improve it, these joint committees will help control environmental pollution at its source," Commoner has said.[34]

What was happening was the development of a broad-based coalition where workers' freedom of association and collective bargaining were paired with and at the center of a cross-class movement to regulate the unilateral corporate management of production. In some ways labor was on the cusp of what had proven strategically effective in both the women's and civil rights movements, the convergence of a downtrodden, socially excluded class and a more established, gentrified social class that began to see value in the aims of the mass movement. Labor law would be at the center of this movement.

As labor law reform returned to the agenda with the Carter Administration in the late 1970s, *Business Week* described the argument made by OCAW:

> Because workers are exposed first to substances that eventually reach the environment, they are the "first line of awareness on environmental issues.". . . Unorganized workers will not have the courage to complain about harmful work conditions. Labor-law reform is an environmental issue after all.[35]

Strengthening workers' rights would be a logical place to start for workers, unions, and other environmental health and safety advocates seeking concrete change.[36]

Other unions brought forward similar claims in bargaining that contributed to this general social movement to varying degrees of success. UFW leader Cesar Chavez argued that "we have come to realize . . . that the issue of pesticide poisoning is more important today than even wages."[37] Fighting sweetheart agreements between the growers and the Teamsters Union, the UFW negotiated contracts restricting the most dangerous pesticides, without the backing of national leaders such as AFL-CIO president George Meany. UFW alliances with environmental groups were strained when growers moved to organophosphate pesticides, a change favored by environmentalists for its ability to break down quickly after application, despite being more deadly for farmworkers. Teamsters president Frank Fitzsimmons led a raid on the UFW's 150 grape contracts in 1973 and ignored pesticide control at the bargaining table in favor of a policy of "strict compliance with all federal and state laws . . . for the health and safety of employees."[38] Regardless of setbacks like these, the movement did exist as a central concern of the UFW and a dialog unfolded with other unions such as OCAW. Ongoing financial difficulties exacerbated efforts at coalition building, however; the UFW was unable to send any delegates to key health and safety conferences, one of the many roadblocks faced by the United Farm Workers in their work ecology activism.[39]

The Steelworkers were also strong advocates of environmental protections in collective bargaining, most aggressively in Canada. The USWA signed the 1970–72 agreement with the Cominco mining company, which included giving workers a voice on environmental policy. It was used as a model for other Steelworker locals. The union, still grappling with the memory of the 1948 steel zinc smelter disaster in Donora, Pennsylvania (which killed twenty and sickened seven thousand more), had held a U.S. legislative conference on air pollution in 1969, reportedly the first in the nation. Laurie Mercier's *Anaconda* details an equally important priority for the postwar USWA, aggressive red-baiting against unions purged from the Congress of Industrial Organizations in 1950.[40] A campaign against the Mine, Mill and Smelter Workers, most organized in Montana, ran from 1950 to 1967 despite strong local community resistance. This distracted from health and safety advocacy and efforts to attain stronger collective agreements. Both unions advocated environmental health and safety in smelter work through major grievances and contract negotiations. This included the control of sulfur dioxide and arsenic discharges into the surrounding environment. These discharges bleached chlorophyll in tree needles and leaves, leaving little vegetation between Anaconda and Butte, and left Anaconda with a lung cancer rate above the national average. The struggle for environmental health and safety remained a priority despite debilitating labor politics.

Labor's efforts were not restricted to old mill towns, however. The Communications Workers encouraged AT&T to pressure automakers to invest in low-emission transport for its nationwide fleet of 128,000 vehicles; the Glass Bottle Blowers union organized recycling campaigns; the American Federation of Teachers commissioned lesson plans on environmental problems for use in the classroom; Newspaper Guild leaders urged the printing industry "to adopt a policy of using recycled paper in its operations in order to prevent the depletion of our ever-diminishing forest reserves"; the Air Line Pilots Association organized against "the dumping of kerosene from the pressurization and drain cans of jet aircraft," which amounted to "millions of pounds of jet fuel each year" dumped into the skies; the Pulp, Sulphite and Paper Mill Workers had a "detailed environmental program for its local unions" including joint environmental control committees to "consider, investigate and make proposals to the company with respect to the environmental problems arising from the operation of the plant." The aim was collective bargaining that would make the phrase "unfair environmental practice" roll off a worker's tongue as frequently and easily as "unfair labor practice."[41]

Labor consciousness of health and safety formed a unique constitutional insurgency. These were moral actions in the individual and the collective interests of society. North American labor history illustrates that the right to refuse unsafe work has been a struggle to decide who is empowered to define it. This debate would soon become a global concern, and Anglo-American countries would play a significant role on the global stage. The right to refuse would come to be defined by ILO Convention No. 155 on occupational safety and health in the working environment. But North American political and economic hegemony would leave a heavy footprint upon international worker health and safety policy.

Refusal Rights as Fundamental Human Rights

The right to refuse unsafe work is a critical global policy debate today because occupational safety and health is a fundamental human right under international law. Because human rights embody a different understanding than traditional legal rights, seeing worker health and safety—and refusal rights—through the human rights lens requires understanding what it means when one says something is a basic human right. The question is intertwined with the issue of labor as a commodity; both value systems recognize the inherent moral worth of each human being. Human rights are also inherently linked with environmental protection, as environmental degradation often restricts the ability to exercise human rights and enjoy a fully human life. What a human rights view adds is a detailed framework for respecting human beings in law and everyday society.

The Universal Declaration of Human Rights of 1948 states that "everyone has the right to work, to free choice of employment, to just and favorable conditions of work and to protection against unemployment."[42] Likewise, the International Covenant on Economic, Social and Cultural Rights, adopted in 1966 and ratified widely, protects "safe and healthy working conditions" and "rest, leisure and reasonable limitations of working hours."[43] Together, these documents form part of the International Bill of Human Rights and establish the basic principles from which the fundamental human right to a healthy and safe working environment is to be derived.

The international body that defines economic and social human rights under the International Covenant on Economic, Social and Cultural Rights (ICESCR) is the Committee on Economic, Social and Cultural Rights (CESCR). The CESCR was established by a 1985 resolution of the UN Economic and Social Council (ECOSOC) as the treaty had enabled ECOSOC to report to the UN General Assembly on the "progress made in achieving general observance of the rights recognized" in the Covenant. The CESCR therefore reports on an array of economic and social rights under the Covenant, from education and health to food, clothing, and housing, to the right to form a trade union.

The CESCR has noted repeatedly that implementing ILO Convention No. 155 is a part of the human right to occupational safety and health. Since the right to refuse unsafe work is a part of Convention No. 155, the protection of the basic right to refuse is thus a human rights obligation under international human rights law. How the right to refuse is to be protected, however, remains undefined. For workers' refusing work due to safety and health concerns, the means by which the right to refuse is protected is the difference between exercising and enjoying the human right versus suffering from retaliatory discharge and victimization as a result of acting on one's concerns.

The UN international human rights system and its treaty bodies are a different legal system than the ILO system of labor conventions. This means that although the ILO supervises workplace health and safety under, for example, Convention No. 155, human rights treaty bodies may differ with the ILO's interpretation. The CESCR has one interpretation of ILO conventions and the ILO makes its own legal interpretation. Some legal scholars have even suggested the CESCR expects the ILO to conform to the CESCR's interpretation of ILO Conventions as the CESCR evaluates laws and policies based on fundamental human rights principles.[44] ILO supervision is based on no more than the text of a convention as agreed on through tripartite negotiation.

When the CESCR cites Convention No. 155, therefore, it does not signify that it is in agreement with all ILO supervisory decisions on the topic. For example, the CESCR views safe and health working conditions as a universal protection, where the ILO's interpretation of Convention No. 155 allows for excluding specific branches of economic activity.[45] The CESCR has agreed, however, that a coherent national policy on occupational safety and health must be established, as Convention No. 155 states.

On the right to refuse unsafe work, the CESCR has yet to articulate its specific interpretation of the human right. Despite recognizing the basic right to refuse unsafe work, the definition of the right remains undefined by the international human rights system. The ILO definition, on the other hand, is very clear and is a focus of critique throughout this book. To help the CESCR and other human rights bodies deduce the right to refuse unsafe work as a human right, there are elementary road signs of basic values found throughout human rights norms. Deducing what the human right would look like requires more than a focus on the law. As Tony Evans notes, human rights entails a discourse of law, a philosophical discourse as well as a political analysis.[46] Throughout this book, as evidence is presented about how the right to refuse unsafe work is exercised in practice, a model emerges that defines the specific boundary lines that would logically demarcate protecting the right to refuse as a basic human right.

Although the CESCR jurisprudence is silent on the specific constitution of the right to refuse unsafe work as a human right, reviewing some of the committee's key observations over the last two decades can begin to clarify what principles might be used to determine the constitution of the right to refuse as a basic human right. One relevant topic that the CESCR has elaborated in detail is the human right to health.

The CESCR has noted how the human right to health is "closely related to and dependent upon the realization of other human rights."[47] Among these connected human rights is the right to work, the right to nondiscrimination, and "the freedoms of association, assembly, and movement." All are defined as "integral components of the right to health."[48] Recognizing how the human right to health is dependent on other human rights means rethinking whether limitations on these other human rights are legitimate in light of their exceptional importance in protecting the right to health, apart from their own value as fundamental human rights protections.

The human right to health as defined under the International Covenant on Economic, Social and Cultural Rights encompasses the right to control one's health and body, and a right to be free from interference in the protection of your health. The CESCR has considered safe and healthy working conditions and a healthy environment as two factors important to the human right to health. This explicit right to control one's health and body and freedom from interference in the safeguarding of one's health is of direct relevance to the right to refuse.[49] Workers exercising rights to protect their health should not meet with interference such as employer retaliation. Were the CESCR to elaborate on its specific legal scope, these are among the human rights principles that should shape and define the human right to refuse unsafe work.

The CESCR has also noted the principle of meaningful participation. The right to health encompasses a right to participation "in all health-related decision-making." The CESCR places a clear priority on the participation of the human rights holder in the governance of his or her own human rights. On the topic of employment injury benefits, for example, the CESCR finds that employment injury benefit systems must include participation mechanisms not only in the design phase of these systems but also in the ongoing administration and governance of employment injury benefits.[50] Here, the right to refuse could be interpreted as an important form of the right to participation in the protection of occupational safety and health as a human right.

The baseline used to protect the human right to health under the International Covenant on Economic, Social and Cultural Rights is "the highest attainable standard of health." Altogether, the principles and standards defining the human right to health form a strong basis for protecting the right to refuse unsafe work. Given the "highest attainable standard of health" as the benchmark, the Committee must recognize that a variety of enforcement and participation mechanisms are needed to secure this human right. There is no reason why going to work should limit this fundamental protection.

There are challenges within this jurisprudence, however. Despite the strong and expansive language defining these economic and social human rights, the CESCR has suggested—in contrast to the viewpoint of some worker advocates and labor scholars—that hazards are "inherent in the working environment" and should be minimized only "so far as is reasonably practicable."[51] These words come directly from Convention No. 155, as the CESCR itself has indicated. This seemingly random limitation on workers' rights, however, is the product of a heated negotiation at the

ILO. It would behoove the CESCR and other human rights treaty bodies to recognize how this language has emerged from the ILO in clear contravention of fundamental human rights principles. Here, human rights principles that lay a clear foundation for the right to refuse unsafe work as a human right encounter opposition from tripartite negotiation at the ILO where formal participation by employers and corporations has shaped labor standards.

Another foundation for protecting the right to refuse as a human right is protection as a component of labor rights such as workers' freedom of association. As with the right to occupational safety and health, however, the CESCR has not elaborated on the right to refuse unsafe work as a component of the basic freedom of association of workers. In sum, the right to refuse unsafe work has been recognized as a human right through Convention No. 155, but its basic legal scope and definition as labor policy remains undefined in the international human rights system. This oversight leaves workers facing precarity and neoliberal employment relations without a human rights–based conceptual foundation from which to directly challenge hazardous work.

Considering the best foundation for elaborating the right to refuse unsafe work as a human right, another important tenet is the question of effectiveness. Article 8 of the Universal Declaration of Human Rights defines "the right to an effective remedy by the competent national tribunals for acts violating the fundamental rights granted him by the constitution or by law."[52] *Effective* human rights protections require the comparison of alternative laws and policies; questioning the ways "human rights are understood, valued, and embedded within society" and the "modalities and scope of the proposed procedure" used to protect human rights.[53] How labor rights policies make workers represent their claims is an important concern as "silencing of the victim may occur" where "the victim is forced to represent their claim in a language that either distorts or denies the substance of their claim"—if they can represent their claim at all.[54] On this point, the debates between individual and collective rights are important, and evaluating different forms of workers' protection and representation is needed based simply on the principle of effectiveness.

One debate that cuts across all economic and social human rights is the issue of progressive realization. The underlying assumption is that violations of economic and social rights are not the direct result of state conduct as are civil and political rights. Economic and social human rights form an *obligation of result* versus an *obligation of conduct* on governments. States must, in this view, protect social and economic human rights based on available resources, a lower standard than taking actions that have an "immediate effect" as with civil and political rights. The problem with applying this debate to the right to refuse is that labor and employment systems can be considered direct government conduct. States can change their labor policies with an immediate effect. As the "first responsibility" of government, human rights thus place an immediate, direct burden on the nation-state in labor and employment relations.[55] Such rights are not a "mere offshoot of the eighteenth-century tree of rights."[56] In the words of Simone Weil, they are not the rights pronounced by "the men of 1789" but are moral norms that form a new logic for the governance of economics and society.[57] Nation-states hold an obligation of conduct when it comes to conforming labor and employment relations according to basic human rights principles.

Even so, why does the right to refuse unsafe work remain in such a zone of fog under the international labor and human rights system? Why is the right to refuse not clarified so that it is among the strongest of human rights under international law? Although the right to refuse unsafe work has been recognized as a human right through recognition of Convention No. 155, the international human rights system has not yet prioritized and defined a strong and effective right to refuse unsafe work. Is there not space for the recognition of this human right as a critical component of participatory governance across the working environment? Can refusal rights be made effective protections? What is it about the right to refuse that makes the issue so different?

"Bargaining over certain matters," observed labor law scholar James Atleson, "is qualitatively different from dealing with customary matters such as wages and hours."[58] Working conditions strike at the heart of managerial control, illuminating underlying power inequalities. The right to refuse remains a moral dilemma faced by all nations. Be it through labor inspection, collective bargaining, works councils, or via individual employment rights, each offers differing protection in its effectiveness and serves different interests. Around the world societies decide how they will allow workers to protect their health and safety. These decisions determine whether or not people can "influence their own environment themselves."[59]

Where workers have no effective means to influence their working environment, it is imperative that people ask why.

As current global worker health and safety policy took shape in the 1970s, the ILO had entered a period of intellectual contraction. The ILO faced the overlapping challenges of declining industrial unionism, globalization, the rise of precarious work, the neoliberal resurgence, and the rise of the individual employment rights era. Despite this turbulent history, the right to refuse was not eclipsed from the human rights arena. Amid popular unrest and calls for a more humane economy, workers' movements advance autonomous definitions of hazardous work and struggle to control the right to refuse. In time, however, other values would confront these worker movements and transform global labor rights. A new values system emerged to promote managerial prerogatives and corporate decision making unhindered by the popular social controls of regulation and collective bargaining. Employers could not altogether eliminate the idea of "rights" due to their widespread acceptance. Instead, they advocated a value system that *made rights safe* for unilateral management control. The right to refuse unsafe work was at the center of these international labor politics as they reshaped the international norms protecting the human right to safe and healthy working conditions.

2

Theoretical Perspectives on Individual Employment Rights

With the decollectivization of rights at work over the previous generation, the notion of an "individual" employment rights era emerged as the alternative to national labor policies based on collective or association-based worker protections. The right to refuse unsafe work has been swept up in this trend. Global worker health and safety policy has likewise undergone a shift since the 1970s. Once viewed as a component of workers' freedom of association, the right to refuse unsafe work is now considered a matter of individual employment policy, with specific—and debilitating—controls. In this chapter I discuss some of the major theoretical perspectives in labor scholarship explaining the rise of the individual employment rights era. I also present a basic conceptual framework for this book, the idea of mobilization bias in labor policy.

Numerous individual employment rights laws have been enacted around the world in recent decades. These labor policies typically protect against different forms of discrimination, such as discrimination based on race, gender, or age. Worker health and safety is also addressed through individual employment rights. These laws range from protection against retaliation for calling a workplace health and safety inspector to protection against discrimination for seeking workers' injury compensation. These systems typically function through individual-level enforcement, in contrast to classic national labor policies based on association and collective workplace governance. The greater burden is thus placed on the individual to enforce specific legal rights.

North America has greatly influenced the rise of the individual employment rights era. In the United States and Canada in particular, collective labor protection has had an uneasy, even violent, history in an employment system that is rooted in the common law tradition. In that tradition, the judiciary has reinforced the traditional master-servant notions in labor relations, "giving a legal basis for the power employers desired."[1] Certain legal assumptions about the employment relationship were read as implicit in the employment relationship, even after protective labor law statutes clearly outlined stronger collective or associational protections for workers. James Atleson's study of U.S. national labor policy, for example, found that the common law was used repeatedly to maintain the status of workers in an employment relationship as disposable, even as new legal statutes were passed to protect workers from dismissal. "The servant's deference or respect need not be earned but, rather, was implicit in the employment relationship" as employer freedom was not "circumscribed on the theory that the 'common-enterprise' notion involves corresponding obligations of employer to their employees."[2]

Three key characteristics of individual employment rights distinguish them from collective and associational forms of workplace governance. The first is an absence of a negotiation with workers regarding what is to be protected. The second critical difference is that an obligation is placed on individual workers to seek enforcement, in contrast to enforcement through representation by a workers' collective institution such as a union. Third, as in the Anglo-American common law systems, individual employment rights afford no prescribed role for workers in direct day-to-day workplace governance. As the statutory obligations are established by politicians and elaborated in regulations for individual workers to enforce, the standards themselves are not subject to worker negotiation, are not tailored to a locality, come with no mechanism to be strengthened beyond the basics of the law where needed, and altogether leave workers with a more passive role in creating and governing the standards that are to be enforced.

Criticizing individual employment rights can be misinterpreted by those who advocate antidiscrimination protections as such rights attempt to prohibit basic human indignities in work and employment. It is important to note, however, that questioning the nature of the individual employment right is not the same thing as questioning the affronts to dignity they purport to protect against. The question is one of efficacy as a model for workplace regulation. Paul Frymer's study of racism and labor law gives an example of how advocating against discrimination at work has taken different forms. Some civil rights groups fought to have racial discrimination protections amended to the "duty of fair representation" provisions of basic U.S. national labor relations law. These protections would have created a collective avenue for protection against what is today only an individual employment rights protection. The question is one of efficacy in enforcement rather than of the social value of the protection.[3]

With the rise of the Washington Consensus in international relations and the growth of antiregulatory business ideologies in the 1970s, the practice of creating individual employment rights detached from collective and associational workplace governance expanded over time beyond North America's borders. These politics would shape not only national labor policies on occupational safety and health; they would also shape our definition and understanding of international labor and human rights norms. Understanding the origins of the individual employment rights era is, therefore, important to help understand the global model for the right to refuse.

The Origins of the Individual Employment Rights Era

The nature of the individual employment rights era is a contested topic across a labor scholarship that encompasses history, economics, law, sociology, and political science. At the center of this debate is the question of the nature of individual employment rights, their origins, and why they have come to now replace collective and associational workplace governance. Critiquing a collection of these theories, we gain a better understanding of this debate and lay the groundwork for a more accurate analysis of the current model protecting the right to refuse unsafe work as advocated globally under international labor and human rights standards.

Nelson Lichtenstein reinvigorated this debate by arguing that the rise of individual employment rights has resulted from the rise of individual rights discourse.[4] This created what he called a "rights consciousness" that has led to the decline of the organized labor movement in the United States.[5] American liberals implicitly endorsed the idea of a rights discourse, but took the view "long associated with anti-union conservatism, that the labor movement could not be trusted to protect the individual rights of its members or of workers in general."[6] This consciousness advocated "state protection as opposed to collective action," making this style of human rights rhetoric, in Lichtenstein's analysis, a great paradox in the rapid decline of trade unions:

> All this may well be contrasted, even causally related, to the remarkable growth that has taken place during the last quarter century in the moral authority and sheer political potency of the movement for international human rights. This worldwide endorsement of the human rights idea has become the charter for a new kind of statecraft, even a new kind of globalized civil society.
>
> As deployed in American law and political culture, a discourse of rights has also subverted the very idea and the institutional expression of union solidarity. This is because solidarity is not just a song or a sentiment, but requires a measure of coercion which can enforce the social bond when not all members of the organization—or the picket line—are in full agreement. Unions are combat organizations, and solidarity is not just another word for majority rule, especially when their existence is at stake.[7]

According to Lichtenstein, rights discourse and rights-based organizing strategies have resulted in a series of problems for workers: ineffective legal enforcement removed from the shop-floor concerns of workers, a dependency on legal and technical experts, an incapacity to respond to and deal with broad structural economic and social crises, and a failure to challenge or temper managerial prerogatives and supervisory authority at work.[8]

According to Lichtenstein, individual employment rights have arisen from this political history, a politics that persisted despite their ineffectiveness. Thus, the origin of the individual employment rights era rests on the shoulders of workers themselves, a tragic political miscalculation made from an unwise political consciousness that was followed regardless of how ineffective it was to protecting workers.

Richard McIntyre has concurred on this point. His book *Are Workers' Rights Human Rights?* argues that the human rights approach applied to labor policy has given rise to individual employment rights.[9] The connection of rights talk and human rights with individualism has discredited the idea of collective regulation to protect workers' rights. McIntyre likewise argues that rights claims exist in opposition to notions of collective solidarity and are thus a tragic and strategic weakness for labor unions. One case cited as an exception to this rule is the U.S. public employees' movements from the 1960s and 1970s, which successfully used rights discourse in their organizing.

A debate published in the *New Labor Forum* illustrated the influence these ideas have within the American trade union movement. Jay Youngdahl, debating Lance Compa, author of a Human Rights Watch report[10] on workers' freedom of association in the United States, argued against a rights-conscious labor strategy. Pointing to "right to work" laws as an example of rights talk run amok, Youngdahl argued that "unions are all about obligations to our fellow workers" and "the replacement of solidarity as the anchor for labour justice with 'individual human rights' will mean the end of the union movement as we know it." Social atomism is the basic charge:

> Philosophically, the human rights approach is part of a move to 'atomism,' which the Canadian philosopher Charles Taylor describes as the theory of advocating 'a vision of society as in some sense constituted by individuals for the fulfillment of ends which were primarily individual.' Atomism implies 'the priority of the individual and his rights over society,' which is the fundamental flaw of current human rights ideology and practice.[11]

The overall argument as described by scholars and activists alike has acknowledged explicitly the inefficacy of individual employment rights, yet has pinned the origins of these employment law and policy frameworks squarely on the human rights worldview and advocacy.

Kevin Kolben follows this thinking and characterizes the emergence of human rights as a strategic trap for unions and labor rights. Human rights offers a "radically different approach to freedom of association" compared to labor rights, he argues, and the human rights idea weakens the "commitment to economic justice and workplace democracy principles that have long underpinned labor rights thought and practice." Kolben finds failure on multiple levels. First, human rights regulate only the relations between states and individuals, not, he argues, the relationship between private actors. Second, labor rights are facilitative and procedural, not substantial and prescriptive rights that focus on standards "such as specified levels of health and safety." Third, human rights are grounded in notions of individual dignity, through which there is no reconciliation with the idea of collective interests. Fourth, Kolben argues that a series of differences between the labor and human rights movements amount to a culture clash. This includes a legalistic approach versus mobilization, top-down versus bottom-up worldviews, elite versus grassroots leadership, and charity and benevolence versus worker agency and voice.[12] Human rights scholars could take issue with each of Kolben's arguments, but this view attests to the conceptual challenges faced in the treatment of labor rights and worker freedom of association as a basic human rights concern.

Another explanation for the rise of the individual employment rights era is the shifting axes of social mobilization thesis. Michael Piore and Sean Safford explain the rise of the individual employment rights era and the eclipse of collective forms of workplace governance as a result of shifting identities.[13] Individual employment rights, according to this theory, were driven by shifts in the locus of social and political mobilization. Collective bargaining had emerged under political pressures generated by the mobilization of industrial workers, with unions organized around a set of identities rooted in craft, profession, industry, and enterprise. Employment laws (primarily those from the '60s and '70s) were conversely generated by political protest and mobilization around social identities linked to race, ethnicity, and personal characteristics associated with social stigmas.[14] The nature of society itself shifted, and the national policy simply followed, as one would expect in a democratic society, as Piore and Safford explain:

> We start from the accepted view that the New Deal collective bargaining system has collapsed. But our argument . . . departs from that view in three critical respects. First we argue that the regime that has replaced collective bargaining is not a market regime at all but rather a regime of substantive employment rights specified in law, judicial opinions, and administrative

rulings, supplemented by mechanisms at the enterprise level that are responsive to these rules and regulations but also susceptible to employee pressures. Second, we argue that the emergence of the new regime has been driven, not by neoliberal ideology, but rather by a shift in the axes of social mobilization from mobilization around economic identities associated with class, industry, occupation, and enterprise to mobilization around identities rooted outside the workplace: sex, race, ethnicity, age, disability, and sexual orientation. Third, the shift in the axes of social mobilization reflects the collapse of the underlying model of social and economic organization upon which the New Deal collective bargaining regime was based. Indeed, the collapse of the New Deal model reflects an even more fundamental shift in our understanding of the nature of industrial society and its direction of evolution in history.[15]

For Piore and Safford this shift in mobilization "reflects the collapse of the underlying model of social and economic organization upon which the collective bargaining regime was built." National labor policy is reflective of identity and consciousness as institutions are shaped by the popular will. As with other theories on the underlying nature of the rise of the individual employment rights era, the general regime change has occurred due to a changing individual identity and consciousness among workers.

Following these general sentiments, Nick Salvatore and Jefferson Cowie write in *The Long Exception: Rethinking the Place of the New Deal in American History*[16] about "a deep and abiding individualism" in U.S. culture. The conclusions they reach are similar to Piore and Safford's. They argue that the rise of collective bargaining was an anomaly in American society and history. With the individual employment rights era, the government has returned to reflect the natural disposition of a society untainted by collective hues:

> Despite the collective-sounding left rhetoric that often accompanied demands in the post-1965 civil rights and feminist movements, at the core of these and many other actions was a concern with expanding the rights and freedoms of individuals and social—but not economic—groups. The result would eventually be called "rights consciousness" or "identity politics," a political outlook that contrasted with the economic liberalism of the New Deal. . . . The draw of individual and group rights over collective material well-being actually speaks to more profound issues: the historical fragility of

class identity in American politics, the exceptional nature of the New Deal order, and the powerful allure of individual rights in American culture.[17]

Taken together, these theories of the rise of the individual employment rights era form a body of labor scholarship that shares an underlying political explanation. It was the changing society as reflected in workers' changing consciousness that gave rise to the individual employment rights era and the decline of collective workplace governance. The individual employment rights era is the result of a changing social consciousness that became manifested in specific labor and employment institutions of the nation-state. The nature of this era can therefore be explained as a shift in popular consciousness away from unions and collective or associational forms of workplace governance. Where individual employment rights are ineffective, it serves merely as an illustration of a strategically ignorant working class consciousness rooted in a failed system of values and beliefs.

Institutional Politics and Social Exclusion

Raising questions about these dominant theoretical perspectives on the rise of the individual employment rights era, David Montgomery offers a perceptive critique. Individual employment rights, he argues, are the consequence of exclusionary power dynamics and socially contested institutional politics. Depictions of the rise of the individual employment rights era as a reflection of free and open democratic politics "leaves unclear what is to be attributed to counter-mobilizations by business, what to the limited vision of liberal policymakers, and what to the aspirations and fears of workers."[18] This is in keeping with Montgomery's typology of the sources of employers' control: ownership of the means of production, company power over employees, the integration of the educational establishment with corporate power, and the coercive authority of government, which backs a variety of corporate rights.[19]

From this standpoint, determining which argument explains the rise of the individual employment rights era is no easy task. Where exclusionary dynamics and socially contested politics are evident, the dominant theories are called into question. Yet a problem remains on a methodological level when studying the dynamics of exclusionary power relations. If, as these dominant theories suggest, labor policy change is the result of an open and free democratic process, then the basic decision-making mechanisms should give evidence to support these views. If, however, social exclusion of one variety or another contributed to the rise of individual employment rights, then different tools are needed. Our methodological tools must be capable of studying exclusionary politics. If our analysis is derived from overt decision making and ignores social exclusion, we will likely never see any evidence of social exclusion. Social exclusion must be considered a factor.

Any conceptual model that analyzes labor policy and the rise of the individual employment rights era must capture contested politics. The dominant explanations of individual employment rights ignore great complexity in national labor policymaking. If society's labor rights institutions respond to social beliefs and values in a textbook democratic fashion, how do we explain socially contested institutional politics and any resulting social exclusion when we find evidence of these dynamics? The short answer is that we do not. Scholarship thus replicates these exclusionary political dynamics. What is required is a labor scholarship capable of capturing these exclusionary social dynamics and the full range of contested institutional politics at play.

Labor and industrial relations scholarship has been challenged by the problem of studying institutional politics over the last century. How social actors struggle to influence labor policy falls broadly under the category of nonmarket political forces. Employer influence-seeking strategies in the shaping of labor institutions have not been a focus in a classic industrial relations scholarship that preferences the study of the rules of the game as they already exist. John Dunlop, a key figure in industrial relations scholarship, did not follow his own advice and study the real-world political influences he deemed necessary to understand how labor policy works. In his analysis of industrial relations systems, Dunlop[20] describes the power and status of the social actors in an industrial relations system as "the product of public policy" and "within the explicit decision of the larger society by political processes."[21] Workers' organizations "are formulated in terms of the rights of management," he noted, but the actual status of management, in contrast to workers, can take a variety of forms, depending on the relationship that exists between business corporations and the government.[22] Dunlop argued "the status of managers and their enterprises in

the industrial relations system may depend upon their standing with bu-
reaucrats, ministers, legislators, or party leaders and their relative influence compared to leaders of workers' organizations."[23] Dunlop also noted,
moreover, that there may well be "a variety of very subtle relations among
the actors in a national industrial relations system and thus it is most significant for students of industrial relations systems to see through such veils of
government rulemaking" because "the actors in the system seldom confuse
form with reality."[24]

Although Dunlop's keen analysis on this point recognized these inter-
relationships and called for "sensitivity to the complex status of the actors and their interrelations" in an industrial relations system, his focus of
attention turned to the study of market rules. (Industrial relations is not
the only field to have ignored institutional politics. Chris Carter, Stewart
Clegg, and Martin Kornberger describe how business strategy has been
ideologically driven by free-market values and a jaundiced view of the role
of the state.[25])

Classic industrial relations theorists, despite their exclusive focus on
market efficiency frameworks and the related rules of the game, can be
commended for focusing on power relations within the employment relationship. The study of power is a core element in industrial relations. John
Kelly in *Rethinking Industrial Relations*[26] explains that how workers "come
to define their interests in collective or individual terms" is an enduring
problem across employment relations. "Since workers," Kelly writes, "oc-
cupy a subordinate position in the employment relationship, their collective definitions of interest are subject to repeated challenges by employers
as they try to redefine and realign worker interests with corporate goals."[27]
To study contested institutional power, however, one must be capable of
understanding the many *nonmarket* forces that shape workers' rights, including the full range of exclusionary political dynamics.

In a varieties of capitalism framework, liberal market economies are
those that rely "heavily on the market relationship between individual
worker and employer to organize relations with the labor force."[28] It is
important to note the role of policy institutions in constructing the landscape of employment relations, however, even where work is said to follow
laissez-faire principles. Many nonmarket institutions of the state and state
labor policy maintain market relations.[29] Analyzing the relationship between a worker and an employer could even be more accurately described

as being a largely *nonmarket* relationship rather than being any kind of "market" relationship. The study of contested political dynamics is thus all the more important.

A better power analysis is needed to understand the dynamics of labor policymaking, including the dynamics of employer countermobilization. My aim is in part to ascertain the origins of the individual employment rights era as it applies to occupational safety and health. This task requires a study of the full range of employer influence-seeking mechanisms in labor policymaking, from overt metrics such as policy demands and political contributions to the more insidious and covert advocacy of value systems, beliefs, and cultural assumptions that, when followed, create obstacles to effectuating workers' rights. One solution is to take the advice of certain labor and employment relations scholars who encourage the field to examine institutional politics from the "broad, economy and society perspective."[30]

Power and the Mobilization of Bias

An institutional environments approach recognizes how labor rights policies are embedded in an institutional environment, and how labor policies are "produced and reproduced through processes of social action" and often in self-reinforcing ways:

> Rules are embedded not just in behavior, but also in the economic, social and political institutions or arrangements that constitute this behavior, including market and financial structures, state agencies, legal structures, education and training systems, and others. These institutions, and the rules undergirding them, may be seen to comprise the institutional environment within which workers, their unions, and their employers act. They are produced and reproduced through processes of social action and in fact are what make such action possible. . . . Institutional environments shape (and are shaped by) the orientations and identities of the actors and the relationships between them.[31]

Studying the relationships between actors and institutions affords a more complex view of the social world beyond a pluralist decontextualized view of market rules. This approach broadens the study of labor and employment relations and complements the human rights approach to labor policy as it requires examining first principles and the basic effectiveness of rights frameworks.

In this approach, "nation state paradigms play an important role in shaping institutional environments and the rules that underpin them."[32] Historical analyses are likewise just as important. Policy templates are created through history and "give rise to deeply embedded 'institutional norms,' or beliefs, values, and principles as to the role, rationale for, and legitimacy of established institutions." These norms, beliefs, values, principles, or templates create a *mobilization of bias* that privileges some groups, practices, or social actors over others. These social biases can be strengthened if one group "effectively controls the agenda and achieves an ideological hegemony" that serves its interests. Likewise, it can be weakened if the ideological hegemony is challenged.[33] This approach, unlike that of traditional pluralist scholarship, moves industrial relations beyond rules-based pluralism toward the mobilization of bias and the impact that values and beliefs can have in industrial relations and human rights policy.

The mobilization of bias itself cannot be analyzed with any one-dimensional understanding of power. This problem was central to the scholarship of John Gaventa, a political sociologist and student of Stephen Lukes.[34] Like Lukes, Gaventa recognized three "dimensions" or "faces" of power that affect how society makes decisions. Decision making is a power process affected not just by competing social actors in a free market of democracy but also, at times, by both a second and third dimension of power. Gaventa articulated a method to study each face of power and as interrelated phenomena, at times reinforcing each other and at others playing off one another.

Gaventa built on the work of the early critics of simple pluralism, including the work of E. E. Schattschneider, who coined the phrase "the mobilization of bias" with his book *The Semi-Sovereign People: A Realist's View of Democracy in America*.[35] Schattschneider noted how the democratic pluralist accounts of political exclusion were ungrounded. He introduced the concept of suppression to a rigid political science field when he argued that "it is not necessarily true that people with the greatest needs participate in politics most actively—whoever decides what the game is about also decides who gets in the game."[36] Thus was born the mobilization of bias. This critique became known as the second dimension of the exercise of power:

Schattschneider introduced a concept later to be developed by Bachrach and Baratz[37] as power's "second face," by which power is exercised not just upon participants within the decision-making process but also towards the exclusion of certain participants and issues altogether.[38] Political organizations, like all organizations, develop a "mobilization of bias . . . in favour of the exploitation of certain kinds of conflict and the suppression of others. . . . Some issues are organized into politics while others are organized out."[39] And, if issues are prevented from arising, so too may actors be prevented from acting. The study of politics must focus "both on who gets what, when and how and who gets left out and how"—and how the two are interrelated.[40]

Peter Bachrach and Morton Baratz extended this critique and contrasted the second face of power with the simple pluralist view of power using the concept of "non-decision-making."

> [They] mistakenly assumed that power and its correlatives are activated and can be observed only in decision-making situations. They have overlooked the equally, if not more important area of what might be called "non-decision-making," i.e., the practice of limiting the scope of actual decision-making to "safe" issues by manipulating the dominant community values, myths, and political institutions and procedures. To pass over this is to neglect one whole "face" of power.[41]

Through the mobilization of bias, some issues are protected and made "safe" through "non-decision-making" while other issues, ideas, or political actors that may serve to threaten elite power and privilege are marginalized and/or are otherwise excluded.[42]

Lukes first documented the weakness of the two-dimension model of power, and Gaventa built on this work.[43] The two-dimension model did not recognize power where conflict *had been avoided altogether*. It recognized how people and issues are excluded, but this non-decision-making was said to exist only where the individuals and communities so marginalized hold an awareness of their exclusion:

> For the purpose of analysis, a power struggle exists, overtly or covertly, either when both sets of contestants are aware of its existence *or when only the less powerful party is aware* of it. The latter case is relevant where the domination of status quo defenders is so secure and pervasive that they are oblivious of any persons or groups desirous of challenging their preeminence.[44]

The second face of power focuses on cognizant exclusion, no matter how difficult that exclusion may be to observe and document. Gaventa and Lukes argued this focus may essentially "lead it to neglect what may be the 'crucial point': 'the most effective and insidious use of power is to prevent such conflict from arising in the first place.' "[45]

Silence and submerged conflict required recognizing a third dimension of power. In such a third dimension of power, influence shapes values and beliefs to "pre-empt manifest conflict" and shape "patterns or conceptions of non-conflict" overall. The aim for the social researcher in studying labor and employment systems is to uncover "latent conflict" to "allow 'for consideration of the many ways in which potential issues are kept out of politics, whether through social forces and institutional practices or through individuals' decisions'."[46] These three faces of power each focus on distinct elements of power yet they interact, be it through the functional representation of the first dimension, the cognizant social exclusion of the second face of power, or the preempting of manifest social conflict entirely within the third dimension of power.

The result is an approach capable of analyzing the range of influence-seeking strategies in labor rights policymaking. Studying the mobilization of bias allows for the examination of all forms of contested politics, something the pluralist approach fails to do. Understanding the full range of influence-seeking mechanisms means one can thus understand the full range of employer political activity and countermobilization affecting labor policies and worker protections.

Management scholars immediately grasped the usefulness of this mobilization of bias idea. Writing in the *Journal of Management Studies*, Cynthia Hardy described how social actors use power.[47] Describing the third face of power as "unobtrusive power," Hardy observed it being "used by actors to ensure that potential opposition groups do not challenge them . . . to prevent resistance" and to defeat "declared and identified opponents." Power includes the "ability to shape values, preferences, cognitions, perceptions so that grievances and issues do not arise or, if they do, they are never articulated or transformed into demands and challenges."[48] The "ideological hegemony of a wider society" serves as one source of power. The "ability to institutionalize existing power in structures and cultures to protect it from change" is another, as are the symbols, languages, myths, rituals, ceremonies, and settings "engineered by the political strategies of others."[49]

We can see an example of the value of analyzing the mobilization of bias in one long-standing concern in labor policy: the antiunion strategy of human resource management. Bruce Kaufman documented the early years of human resource management strategy in America in his book *Managing the Human Factor.*[50] Kaufman cites Sumner Slichter's account of these management strategies, which demonstrates how business activism moved from coerced issue exclusion to making conflict latent:

> [Human resource management] is nothing less than an attempt to control the effect of modern industrial development upon men's minds. . . . [It] has the ambition, the objective of preventing a class struggle, building up a very difficult kind of psychology, creating content with one's situation and faith and loyalty, faith in employers, a particular employer, and loyalty to a particular employer. It tries to inculcate a faith just as much as a religion tries to inculcate a faith.[51]

Buttressing coercion with psychological manipulation suppressed manifest conflict. Matters that were once the subject of heated conflict became non-issues. This approach opens new lines of inquiry into the range of obstacles that barricade labor-policy and worker protection alternatives.

Gaventa's contribution to the study of the mobilization of bias and the study of these "unobtrusive" power dynamics was his methodology. Lukes was challenged to show how latent social conflict could be studied without the researcher's assumptions about the "real interests" of the dispossessed or powerless group being projected on them within a study. Gaventa argued that the study of "interests" in the power process does not require their identification and attribution to any group. The researcher's task was to demonstrate how powerless people and groups "are prevented from acting upon or conceiving certain posited interests" that would logically appear to be closer to their own interests. This alone, he argued, "is sufficient to show that the interests that are expressed . . . are probably not the real ones."[52] Where negative impacts for a group are deduced from the dominant, expressed interests, this is evidence that the interests expressed are likely not the real ones manifest for that group. Where adverse social or human impact and the prevention of action or the prevention of conceiving certain alternative interests coincide, this was strong evidence in favor of the mobilization of bias and what Gaventa called a *false consensus.*

Studying the mobilization of bias is difficult within an exclusively variable-centered research design. Such an approach rejects "methodological individualism in favor of a more nuanced, historically informed analysis."[53] A qualitative and in-depth case study or a comparative analysis is preferred. Studying power within this analysis involves (1) defining the actual policy choices made in decision making, (2) studying the real-world impact on workers, communities, or any other dispossessed group, and (3) identifying obstacles in decision making, structural or cultural, that have prevented people or groups from acting on or conceiving other decisions more in their interest. By relating this methodology to a study of the right to refuse unsafe work in international labor law, we can, in this context, understand the origins and nature of the individual employment rights era. The remainder of this book accomplishes these specific tasks.

If policy bias is mobilized to a constitution of rights that is "safe" to power and privilege, a grounded, extended case study approach is best.[54] This requires "going outside the decision-making arenas and carrying on extensive, time consuming research" to document how those issues and actors are dispossessed by the politics in question. Here "non-actors and non-leaders become important, not as objects of scrutiny in themselves but to discover through their experiences, lives, conditions, and attitudes, whether and by what means power processes may serve to maintain non-conflict" through various mechanisms.[55] Examining bias mobilization in historical perspective makes it possible, as Gaventa did in studying power and quiescence in Appalachia, to document the disappearance of rights from a given political discourse; from outright exclusion to, in time, disappearance of manifest conflict and the removal of certain rights, however critical, from a political discourse entirely.

Despite claims of a new era of business social responsibility, union avoidance has grown into a multibillion dollar industry.[56] A de facto system of worker-based occupational health and safety enforcement centered on trade union collective bargaining over working conditions was dismantled over the last generation. The individual employment rights era claims to fill this void as workers face the prospect of pursuing rights via individual employment protections, not via collective means. The right to refuse unsafe work as a global human right has been made a "safe" right—a right of limited social protection but "safe" for business, management control, and laissez-faire economics. Business leaders often oppose labor protections, but at times the prospect of denying stronger rights makes supporting "safe" rights more palatable. A new values system had emerged to co-opt competing policy alternatives with a system of logic that said worker health and safety was a topic too important to be left to "adversarial labor-management relations" through collective bargaining. As this values system took hold at the global level, the realm of the possible shifted. Workers left the notion of strengthening the freedom of association and focused on bargaining the contours of a new ineffective rights regime. This is the story of the globalized model of the right to refuse unsafe work; it is the foundation of the failure of global workplace health and safety policy.

The last generation has witnessed the rise of an aggressive, take-no-prisoners antiregulatory political agenda. This agenda has been spear-headed by businesses and employer countermobilization. As Robert Reich described in *Supercapitalism*, this period saw "investors turn active" as both businesses and financiers "pressured the commissions, lobbied Congress and state legislatures, hired professors to do studies showing the benefits of deregulation. . . ." In time, "the regulatory dams broke," which "sucked relative equality and stability, as well as other social values, out of the system."[57] As Alex Carey and Andrew Lohrey described in *Taking the Risk Out of Democracy*,[58] three key developments unfolded in the industrialized democracies by the end of the twentieth century: The growth of democratic participation, including universal suffrage and the rights of workers to organize and collectively bargain; the power of corporations and their growing influence on the political process; and the growth of the use of "corporate propaganda as a means of protecting corporate power against democracy."[59] Businesses pushed an antiregulatory agenda and strategized "with the single-minded purpose of bringing some target audience to adopt attitudes and beliefs chosen in advance by the sponsors of the communications."[60] Workers' health and safety, however, was accepted by the general public as a good and worthy objective of government policy. The strategy in this case would become what economist Albert Hirschman called "the thesis of perverse effect" whereby corporations endorsed the social and economic policy change "sincerely or otherwise, but then attempted to demonstrate that the action proposed or undertaken [by the activists] is ill conceived," leaving "a chain of unintended consequences" that would result in "the exact contrary of the objective being proclaimed and pursued."[61] These strategies were used when sheer political force had failed. Corporate leaders throughout this period organized new political associations such as the Business Roundtable to do their political bidding. Their goals included both defeating new labor laws and moving beyond traditional concerns about collective bargaining to the "lack of public support and understanding for business."[62] As Harold Wilensky noted, over time business political associations would grow to exert significant power. One decade after the 1972 founding of the Business Roundtable there were over thirty-two hundred business associations lobbying Washington, D.C.[63] These dynamics extended to the international arena.

Whereas the private business corporation once was described as having no more than a "superficial familiarity" with environmental health and safety debates, now they were becoming active shapers of both the domestic and the international policy agendas.[64]

Studying the mobilization of bias can help us understand the true nature of the rise of the individual employment rights era. As a worker protection that was swept up in this trend around the world, the right to refuse unsafe work serves as an important case study for examining this question. It is a question that lies at the heart of industrial relations and global labor rights, namely, when can a human being refuse to perform work they deem as unsafe or hazardous? How does global society define the fundamental boundaries of employee dissent? It is to these questions we now turn. The findings indicate that the rise of the individual employment rights era was not a mere reflection of popular consciousness into new occupational health and safety laws but rather the manipulation of social values toward managerialism and employer control.

3

The Right to Refuse in International Labor Law

That human rights are individual rights at the expense of collective rights has been an argument against human rights frameworks in both national labor policy and workers' rights advocacy. The right to refuse unsafe work, however, introduces more complexity to this debate. As workers' freedom of association rights are often viewed as only those rights dealing with the establishment of trade unions, it is often forgotten that the freedom of association also entails certain individual rights. One example is a worker reserving the individual prerogative to support a union without discrimination or retaliation. There is a history of the right to refuse as an individual right embedded in the broader status protection of workers' freedom of association. A basic employee right to dissent and to act against inhumane working conditions has at times been an element of workers' freedom of association. This basic right is different than trying to enforce a particular health and safety standard; it is a protection based on the worker's status as a rights holder in another's employ, not based on a hazard threshold. Under this model of protection, workers have the right to act to improve their working conditions not in order to enforce predetermined health or safety regulations but through their status as workers. Because such models are not based on a hazard threshold, workers have latitude to decide what working conditions to contest; protection is afforded to allow for the pursuit of a satisfactory resolution of the dispute, which the workers themselves have defined. Again, the underlying logic of this type of right in employment is not contingent on a particular hazard threshold or a particular working environment. This logic is rooted in the basic status protection of workers as a class of people in an employment relationship deserving unique protections on account of unequal power relations.

When the freedom of association is removed as the philosophic foundation for the right to refuse, other rationales are needed to justify the legal protection. This is the case under global labor standards on worker health and safety. The primary alternative is to use an objectified definition of a hazard to define unacceptable work hazards. Workers under this policy model must demonstrate that a hazard at work meets such a predetermined legal standard. This second model is also clearly an individual rights framework as such a right is not a status- or association-based protection at its foundation. It does not create class-based assumptions but instead depends on an "objective" hazard as defined through a particular legislative, judicial, or administrative authority. This form of labor protection is a *safer* constitution of rights at work for employers because it dramatically limits the worker's class-based power.

Global labor standards on refusal rights follow this restricted model. Refusal rights are constrained in this way under ILO occupational safety and health standards. In turn, refusal rights are also limited under the freedom of association standards. The result is a global policy that eliminates preorganizational activity as a freedom of association protection. (Preorganizational activity is workers' collective action outside of formal union organization.) Furthermore, although health and safety norms and freedom of association norms appear to be independent of each other, they are not. On the right to refuse, each regulates the same single act at the workplace. The laws act on each other in the real world and can create contradictions in an employment system. Because the right to refuse is a freedom of association issue, any legal restriction of its exercise under health and safety laws implicitly restricts freedom of association rights, granting particular powers to employers even where stronger rights exist elsewhere in a country' legal framework. This may be difficult to grasp for lawyers who develop their expertise under various statutory regimes independent of one another, but for the worker the social reality is likely not difficult to understand. The single act of a dissenting employee faced with termination and hardship requires immediate legal protection. Conflicting statutory regimes cause confusion and confound effective and timely safeguards for workers.

The underlying logic of a restricted right to refuse requires the policy architect to construct and make a series of important decisions. A typology of the "refusable" hazards must be created and then justified; the basic threshold of risk must be clearly defined. A worker's psychology or "belief" may be judged when a concern is not deemed to be a hazard so as to determine whether the dissenting act is worthy of legal protection. There must also be a resolution of the legal boundary dispute that creates policy dissonance in national policy with the freedom of association so as to eliminate the perception and real existence of any conflicting and stronger refusal rights protections for workers.

Richard Brown described these required labor policymaking tasks shortly after Canada moved toward what has been called the internal responsibility system:

> A legal architect who sets out to design a model right to refuse law must perform several tasks. The first is to determine what type of hazard justifies a refusal to work. Second, a mechanism should be established for investigating the level of risk when a refusal occurs. Next, the architect must adopt a standard for reviewing an employee's perception of a danger which is not real. The fourth concern is an employer's response to a refusal, which could include disciplining an employee, withholding pay and assuming a second worker as a replacement. Finally, the blueprint must sketch the legal boundaries of concerted refusals to work.[1]

Key distinctions are highlighted in these tasks. The most important is a basic judgment of the merit of a hazard. With no judgment of the merit of a hazard, as is the case in the protection of the right to refuse as organization activity under a freedom of association framework, the worker has much more latitude in exercising the individual right. There is also much less of a focus on the worker's psychology as the worker's "belief" is not open to judicial review since the merit of the hazard itself is immaterial.

Thus, the "good faith belief" held by a worker regarding the danger of a hazard is never judged. The only grounds on which to judge a worker would be a simple "good faith" standard and not both simple "good faith" and the more complex "good faith belief" that a hazard meets a previously legislated objectified threshold.

Drawing out these divergent policy models on protecting the right to refuse is not simply an abstract debate. They are each based in sharp philosophical differences on the role of workers as human beings, the dominance of markets in society, and the state's legal support for the prerogatives of private enterprise. They also raise critical moral questions about business, workers' control, and each person's life and death. These issues complicate the scholarly debate about workers' rights as human rights being largely the promotion of individualism to the detriment of collective protections. One model of protection is associational based on participatory principles, yet it is a stronger protection of individual rights. The other provides no organizational or collective protection and restricts the exercise of the individual right. Both are individual rights, but each is markedly different for workers. The more restricted individual right has come to dominate in the so-called era of individual employment rights. A new vocabulary is therefore needed if we are to move beyond the totalizing and misleading characterizations of rights individualism in conflict with human rights and understand the inherently dual individual-collective nature of these worker rights.

International labor and human rights jurisprudence fails to give adequate protection to the right to refuse unsafe work. A comparative policy history of the right to refuse within one period of North American labor policy provides a contrast to the more restrictive international standard. I use the U.S. case because it illustrates clearly the logic of this associational model of legal protection. It also ironically illustrates how a belief in an "individual rights era" has not been the governing principle across U.S. labor and employment relations as a number of labor scholars have suggested. This stronger labor jurisprudence is no longer U.S. law. Recounting this history for its comparative value illuminates a chapter in U.S. labor policy that conflicts with the current standard adopted in the global norms under ILO Convention No. 155 on occupational safety, health, and the working environment. Alternative labor rights models did exist and were advocated and made into national labor policy in North America, an irony in the labor policy history of a region that remains a strong global advocate for market-based policy solutions.

Restricting the right to refuse, especially amid the ongoing problem of health and safety globally, means that the ILO approach falls short in protecting the human right to workplace safety and health. As an agency that predated the Universal Declaration of Human Rights by a generation, the ILO has struggled to develop a cohesive human rights policy. The ILO's approach to social justice, including its articulation of a set of core labor rights, has been critiqued from a human rights perspective.[2] The right to refuse is not adequately protected through either the freedom of association standards or the occupational safety and health standards. Workers' protest and activism against hazardous work receives limited protection in the global model for national labor policies. The right to refuse faces a very high threshold for securing protection under global occupational safety and health standards. As a result, international labor standards, as a body of worker protection, reinforce the market contours of the modern employment relationship. Unquestioned is a world of employee subservience, undignified but mandatory employer loyalty obligations, and the logic of arbitrary management charges of insubordination and disloyalty.

In the world of labor and employment relations where employers exercise the right to hire and fire employees, it is often said that any legal protection is better than none; that some rights, however weak and limited, are better than nothing at all. The problem with this view in the context of employment relations is that labor relations do not come before the law upon an untouched *tabula rasa*. Labor and employment is a relationship shaped by the law from the beginning; it is not an organic life system. Rights frameworks lay down boundary lines between management rights and workers' rights, shaping the degree of power to terminate employment. Any limited labor rights framework for workers, therefore, draws a broader scope of protection for managerial prerogatives. On the right to refuse unsafe work, this is the history of the jurisprudence that has become dominant over the last generation. What has unfolded is not the establishment of a limited but basic set of legal rights for employees from which they can leapfrog to stronger protections. What has happened is the limiting and restriction of a worker's right to the freedom of association and by consequence a worker's freedom in society.

Workers' Freedom of Association Standards

The ILO Constitution, including the Declaration of Philadelphia of 1944, reads, "all human beings, irrespective of race, creed or sex, have the right to pursue both their material well-being and their spiritual development in conditions of freedom and dignity." This goal of freedom was the "central aim of national and international policy" and achieving freedom and dignity was the ILO's constitutional goal: "It is a responsibility of the ILO to examine and consider all relevant economic and financial policies and measures in light of this fundamental objective." The vision of freedom and dignity in the ILO's Declaration of Philadelphia included the explicit view that "labor is not a commodity" and that to achieve social justice in society "the freedom of expression and of association are essential to sustained progress."[3]

The ILO Constitution is a treaty between nations under international law. Member states have an obligation to respect freedom of association, regardless of whether they have ratified the freedom of association conventions. This obligation includes having domestic labor policies supervised by the ILO. A special supervisory body created by the ILO Governing Body, the Committee on Freedom of Association, receives complaints from employers' and workers' groups made against governments irrespective of whether a country has ratified conventions on freedom of association. If a particular convention is ratified, supervision also occurs by the ILO Committee of Experts on the Application of Conventions and Recommendations (CEACR).

Together, the CFA and the CEACR have developed a detailed jurisprudence on workers' freedom of association under international law. Although the freedom of association is a subject matter in other human rights treaties, such as the International Covenant on Civil and Political Rights and the International Covenant on Economic, Social and Cultural Rights, no similar specificity anywhere else defines workers' freedom of association under international law. Taken together, the ILO Committee of Experts and the ILO Governing Body's Committee on Freedom of Association have formed an important body of global jurisprudence regarding workers' freedom of association.

Outside the context of a collective bargaining agreement, labor law scholars consider the right to refuse unsafe work to be a form of preorganizational worker activity. The term preorganizational comes from the view that even though workers have not yet organized for collective bargaining, they still are undertaking actions that are an important component of basic organizing and thus of workers' freedom of association. This is a broader legal classification than formal union membership and organizing activity.[4] Preorganizational activity is an important element of national labor policy protecting workers' freedom of association. Under these labor policy standards, any discrimination or retaliation against workers who have engaged in this form of preorganizational freedom of association activity is illegal and considered an unfair labor practice. Workers cannot be terminated for engaging in this protected activity.

Discrimination against workers for exercising the freedom of association is evaluated by the ILO according to a standard of "full freedom." This full freedom jurisprudence is the right "to establish and join organizations of their own choosing" free from discrimination in a manner "fully established and respected in law and in fact."[5] This form of discrimination "is one of the most serious violations of freedom of association" as it risks jeopardizing "the very existence of trade unions."[6] The ILO maintains a consistent voice against this form of discrimination at work.

How the ILO supervisory bodies constitute discrimination under the freedom of association conventions is important to the right to refuse unsafe work.[7] Because the right to refuse unsafe work has generally been viewed as organizational activity, national labor policies have a track record of affording protection of the right to refuse unsafe work in a workers' freedom of association framework through domestic labor laws. An important caveat for workers exists in the ILO's definition of retaliation and discrimination, however. ILO freedom of association rights extend only to employees "dismissed or prejudiced in employment *by reason of trade union membership or legitimate trade union activities.*"[8] Through its supervisory decisions, the ILO argues that "anti-union discrimination is one of the most serious violations of freedom of association,"[9] but the caveat is found in what constitutes a protected act under the freedom of association conventions. The rub for workers under these ILO standards is that the freedom of association jurisprudence fails to protect preorganizational activity by individual workers. The right to refuse unsafe work as preorganizational activity undertaken by unorganized workers in their own defense is not protected under the ILO freedom of association jurisprudence.

This nuanced distinction is important as more workers become vulnerable in the face of declining union density and the rise of precarious work arrangements and disguised employment relations.

The ILO is forthright in its legal definitions, stating that the ILO Governing Body's Committee on Freedom of Association "is not called upon to pronounce upon the question of the breaking of a contract of employment by dismissal except in cases in which the provisions on dismissal imply anti-union discrimination."[10] Although antiunion discrimination and interference covers a range of employer actions such as discriminatory hiring practices, retaliatory dismissals, and "transfers, downgrading and other acts that are prejudicial to the worker,"[11] this coverage applies only to discrimination against workers for "union membership" or "union activities" and not for preorganizational activity that exists before and extends beyond formal union membership activity and official unionization efforts. Workers that question their working environment and dare refuse to perform work that they see as unsafe receive no recognition for engaging in freedom of association. In this regard, ILO association rights are oriented toward institutional affiliation rather than to protecting preorganizational freedoms that more often encompass the exercise of the right to refuse today.

ILO standards on dismissal protection also fail to protect preorganizational freedom of association rights. The Termination of Employment Convention, No. 158, says "a worker shall not be terminated" for "union membership or participation in union activities," for "seeking office, or having acted in the capacity of a workers' representative," for "filing a complaint" for alleged violation of laws, or for "race, colour, sex, marital status, family responsibilities, pregnancy, religion, political opinion, national extraction or social origin." Convention No. 158 does not extend the definition of freedom of association beyond its definition under the core freedom of association conventions. The convention permits termination where "there is a valid reason for such termination connected with the capacity or conduct of the worker or based on the operational requirements of the undertaking, establishment or service."[12]

The right to strike under ILO norms on workers' freedom of association could be an alternative way of protecting the right to refuse unsafe work. Here, too, however, the ILO jurisprudence falls far short of affording workers adequate protection. The right to strike is not set out in the text of any ILO convention or recommendation. It is derived from ILO jurisprudence and the decisions of the supervisory bodies. While the right to strike is a right that workers are entitled to under the freedom of association standards, the supervisory bodies have accepted making the exercise of the right to strike subject to the agreement of a certain percentage of workers, regardless of any union membership.[13] Thus while the ILO has determined that "any work stoppage, however brief and limited, may generally be considered a strike" and that "restrictions as to the forms of strike action can only be justified if the action ceases to be peaceful," a national government remains in compliance with international standards by regulating strike actions through industrial relations procedures.[14] Requiring a certain percentage of workers to vote to strike is acceptable, meaning the right to refuse by an individual worker or a small group of two or more workers would rarely qualify as a legitimate labor strike, even if peaceful. National governments are allowed under the freedom of association standards to regulate labor strikes by requiring a larger workplace vote, raising an obstacle to the small group of workers that elects to protect themselves by striking to improve their conditions.

The question this ILO jurisprudence leaves unanswered is whether the right to strike or any other work stoppage for workplace health and safety is to be afforded to a small group of workers, or even a single individual refusing work, regardless of the particular merit of the hazard. Is the right to strike purely an institution-based right or is it an individual right under international labor and human rights standards? Laws requiring a quorum and a majority are acceptable under ILO labor rights standards, so long as they are fixed at a reasonable level as defined by the ILO supervisory bodies. Under the international standards on workers' freedom of association, therefore, states are not obligated to protect the right to strike as an individual right to strike, even in situations where common sense might dictate otherwise, as in a refusal to work.[15]

Another issue that arises from the protection of the right to refuse unsafe work as a component of the right to strike is the view that the right to strike is "a basic right," argue the supervisory bodies, "but it is not an end in itself."[16] The right is therefore considered a means to an end, an enforcement corollary to the industrial and labor relations system of a nation. Consequently, a strike action "cannot be seen in isolation from industrial relations as a whole," and thus exhaustion of the conciliation or the mediation process within an industrial relations system may be required:[17]

> In a large number of countries, legislation stipulates that the conciliation and mediation procedures must be exhausted before a strike may be called. The spirit of these provisions is compatible with Article 4 of Convention 98, which encourages the full development and utilization of machinery for the voluntary negotiation of collective agreements.[18]

In the context of the right to strike, the protection of the right to refuse is conditioned on exhausting mediation and conciliation procedures. This makes the stop-work protection meaningless for workers concerned about safety and health. Even if an individual worker was granted the protection, this poses an obstacle in the context of the right to refuse, especially in common-law countries where refusals are job abandonment, which is grounds for the termination of employment. Thus, the right to strike jurisprudence also fails, as do ILO standards protecting against preorganizational discrimination that might protect the right to refuse as a component of the freedom of association. Under this jurisprudence, the argument could be made that the current U.S. labor law protections for worker health and safety wildcat strikes, the *Washington Aluminum* decision, extend well beyond these minimum ILO labor standards.[19]

For the ILO supervisory bodies, protection of the right to refuse unsafe work as a component of workers' freedom of association commits the sin of omission. It is not recognized as preorganizational activity under discrimination protections on the right to organize, nor is it viewed as an extension of the right to strike under the freedom of association jurisprudence. Given the ILO conception of collective bargaining through voluntary negotiation principles, the collective bargaining jurisprudence as a component of the freedom of association also falls silent on protecting the right to refuse in collective agreements, leaving the question one of power relations versus fundamental principles. Overall, the ILO supervisory bodies have found that the right to refuse unsafe work is not a sufficiently worthwhile element of national labor policy to warrant protection as an element of the freedom of association under these international labor conventions. The right to refuse unsafe work as defined by ILO standards on workers' freedom of association would not follow what labor law scholars have considered to be logical labor jurisprudence, namely protecting refusal rights as basic freedom of association rights.

Occupational Health and Safety Standards

The right to refuse unsafe work was not a sui generis topic under international labor standards until the adoption of ILO Convention No. 155 in 1981. For more than sixty years worker health and safety focused on adopting labor conventions identifying specific hazards or working conditions of global concern significant enough to warrant an international treaty. This practice changed in 1981, when the ILO adopted a "policy-oriented approach" to worker safety and health that focused on developing more generic and unified national policy frameworks. This represented a new form of ILO standard-setting on occupational safety and health, beyond the basic agreement on hazards. This new approach meant a foray into the traditional domain of labor rights, addressing issues such as discrimination protection, worker participation, and union representation on safety and health. In response, it becomes necessary to recognize these aspects of occupational health and safety laws as components of traditional labor and industrial relations policy, in addition to being a unique and dedicated subject of a country's regulatory framework for labor and employment relations.

Under ILO Convention No. 155 of 1981, the right of workers to refuse unsafe work faces a high legal bar in affording protection under international labor standards. The International Labour Office (the headquarters staff of the ILO) is quick to explain how the right to refuse unsafe work is not an absolute right.[20] To dissect these limitations, I will begin with Convention No. 155 and also review a small group of other ILO instruments that followed this trend. According to a recent ILO General Survey on safety and health, there are very clear conditions that have to be established to govern the exercise of the right to refuse:

[Under Convention No. 155] no disciplinary action can be taken against workers who remove themselves from work if the following conditions are met: (a) the workers concerned have a reasonable justification to believe that there is an imminent and serious danger to their life or health;

(b) they comply with the workplace arrangements contemplated in Article 19(f); and (c) the actions by the workers have been properly taken in conformity with the national policy.[21]

Each of these obstacles—the adjudication of the merit of a hazard, the compliance with certain workplace arrangements, and the taking of actions in conformity with national policy—pose unique obstacles for workers. Before we visit each of these obstacles and the implications of these points as critical labor policy questions, a brief review of the language protecting the right to refuse within these standards is required.

Four provisions of the text of Convention No. 155 are relevant to the study of employee dissent and the right to refuse. The first is Article 4, which outlines in broad terms what is meant by a national safety and health policy. The definition of national policy laid down in this convention is important because the right to refuse unsafe work is protected only where it is "in conformity with the national policy." Article 4 reads:

> Article 4. (1) Each Member shall, in the light of national conditions and practice, and in consultation with the most representative organisations of employers and workers, formulate, implement and periodically review a coherent national policy on occupational safety, occupational health and the working environment. (2) The aim of the policy shall be to prevent accidents and injury to health arising out of, linked with or occurring in the course of work, by minimising, so far as is reasonably practicable, the causes of hazards inherent in the working environment.[22]

Article 5 continues to reference this national policy requirement. It requires national policies on occupational safety and health to take into account a basic list of "spheres of action" that affect occupational safety and health and the working environment. The right to refuse is therefore listed in Article 5 under the letter "e" subsection:

> Article 5 (e) the protection of workers and their representatives from disciplinary measures as a result of actions properly taken by them in conformity with the policy referred to in Article 4 of this Convention.[23]

Although vague, Article 5(e) is an employee protection against employer retaliation.

The right to refuse is detailed in Article 13. Under Article 13, a worker must be protected where there is a reasonable justification of imminent and serious danger to life or health. It further limits this protection in accordance with national policies:

> Article 13. A worker who has removed himself from a work situation which he has reasonable justification to believe presents an imminent and serious danger to his life or health shall be protected from undue consequences in accordance with national conditions and practice.[24]

The final article to discuss refusal rights in Convention No. 155 is Article 19, which gives more detail about what shape national labor policy should take on the right to refuse unsafe work. It describes how the right must be exercised "at the level of the undertaking" and what a worker has to do to receive the protection, as well as stating that *when properly exercised* a supervisor cannot make workers continue working:

> Article 19. There shall be arrangements at the level of the undertaking . . . (f). a worker reports forthwith to his immediate supervisor any situation which he has reasonable justification to believe presents an imminent and serious danger to his life or health; until the employer has taken remedial action, if necessary, the employer cannot require workers to return to a work situation where there is continuing imminent and serious danger to life or health.[25]

This collection of articles, Article 4, 5(e), 13, and 19(f), jointly define the right to refuse unsafe work under Convention No. 155. Despite the identification of workers' health and safety in the Universal Declaration of Human Rights and the International Covenant on Economic, Social and Cultural Rights, no international treaty defines in as much detail the precise boundaries and definition of the right to refuse unsafe work.

Subsequent health and safety treaties have followed the model first established by the ILO's Convention No. 155 after its adoption in 1981. An important example is Convention No. 176 concerning the Safety and Health of Mines. Article 13.1(e) of the convention grants workers the right to "remove themselves from any location at the mine when circumstances arise which appear, with reasonable justification, to pose a serious danger to their safety or health." Again, the protection is encased within the hazard threshold alongside a standard of judgment on the worker's underlying belief, a similar legal model as Convention No. 155.[26]

International labor standards include both conventions and recommendations. Two nonbinding recommendations adopted by the ILO also identify refusal rights. Recommendation No. 172, the Asbestos Recommendation, and Recommendation No. 177, the Chemicals Recommendation, address the right to refuse unsafe work. These standards also follow the general logic of Convention No. 155. The protection of the right to refuse unsafe work here covers situations of "serious danger to his [*sic*] life or health" and "imminent and serious risk to their safety or health," respectively. The following is the text of each relevant section.

Recommendation 172 (Asbestos)

Article 9 (1) A worker who has removed himself from a work situation which he has reasonable justification to believe presents serious danger to his life or health should—(a) alert his immediate supervisor; (b) be protected from retaliatory or disciplinary measures, in accordance with national conditions and practice.[27]

Recommendation 177 (Chemicals)

Article 25 (1) Workers should have the right: . . . (b) to remove themselves from danger resulting from the use of chemicals when they have reasonable justification to believe there is an imminent and serious risk to their safety or health, and should inform their supervisor immediately; . . .

(2) Workers who remove themselves from danger in accordance with the provisions of subparagraph (1) (b) or who exercise any of their rights under this Recommendation should be protected against undue consequences.

(3) Where workers have removed themselves from danger in accordance with subparagraph (1) (b), the employer, in co-operation with workers and their representatives, should immediately investigate the risk and take any corrective steps necessary.[28]

The recommendation on chemicals affords workers a slightly wider degree of latitude by the phrase "imminent and serious risk to their safety and health" versus "life or health" as is found in the asbestos recommendation. Nonetheless, the logic behind each is similar and creates a high bar to the exercise of the right to refuse unsafe work. ILO recommendations are also not considered binding under international law in contrast to ILO conventions, which are treaties to be ratified and implemented in national law and practice by governments.

Three policy obstacles in particular underlie these standards. Dissecting each legal obstacle one by one is an important task if we are to contrast this model of the protection of the right to refuse with other models, including the exercise of the right to refuse as freedom of association activity. First is the case-by-case adjudication of a hazard. Second is the requirement that managerial or supervisory procedures be followed. Third is the qualification of the exercise of the right to refuse by any number of wide-ranging national policies and national practices. Critiquing each of these provisions reveals inherent weaknesses.

Adjudicating Hazards

The individual merit of the hazard in question is considered before extending protection to workers who refuse to perform work they consider unsafe. Thresholds are defined in Convention No. 155 as hazards that pose an "imminent and serious danger" to workers' "life and health." Workers may refuse unsafe work only when they believe it poses an "imminent and serious danger" or a "serious danger to life or health" or an "imminent and serious risk" to themselves, depending on the global labor standard. Workers cannot refuse work and be protected against retaliation if they reasonably believe a hazard falls one degree below the "imminent and serious" mark. Refusing a working condition that is unhealthy but not an "imminent and serious danger" to life and health for a worker means insubordination and termination. The labor standard language and policy thus protects employer termination rights outside this narrow language.

Global labor rights require a case-by-case hazard assessment, which also means a case-by-case assessment of the merit of a workers' reasonableness in refusing a hazard. Under these standards some authority must adjudicate an employee's belief claims about each workplace hazard where employees assert the right to refuse. This places the legal protection on unstable ground. The labor protection rests only within a narrow scope of hazards, assuming other conditions do not first derail protection of these workers' rights. Workers who protest hazards one degree below this objectivist threshold are unprotected under these global norms and are subject to having the nature of their psychological belief in the decision-making process evaluated.

ILO standards on occupational health and safety charge the state with the responsibility for adjudicating complex belief claims even when no evidence may exist anywhere about the impact of the hazard at issue. Simply put, humanity does not know the danger of some hazards given the growing magnitude of hazards faced by workers. Asking the government to ascertain what is imminent and serious may be easy in some cases, but in other cases it is an impossible task that is often socially rather than scientifically determined. The standard affords no protection to workers who refuse new or emerging workplace hazards or hazards of an as yet unknown danger. The global norm is thus based on an objectivist view of science and makes no provision for cases in which this model of knowledge breaks down.

Illustrating the complex task behind making rights contingent on identifying the degree of danger of any particular workplace hazard threshold, the ILO acknowledges the challenge:

> Precise and reliable data on the number of existing natural or synthetic chemical substances, the quantities used and produced and hazard assessment data is difficult to find, often outdated and contradictory. Thirty-two million organic and inorganic, natural and synthetic substances have been identified and registered worldwide. Out of the 110,000 synthetic chemicals that are produced in industrial quantities, adequate hazard assessment data is available only for about 6,000 substances, and occupational exposure limits (OELs) have been set for only 500–600 single hazardous chemicals. Very little assessment data is available for mixtures of chemicals.[29]

Workers need only a "reasonable" justification for their concern, but there is no available evidence about most hazards. Reasonableness here becomes a subjective concept.

Introducing hazard thresholds into the formula for protecting workers' rights to refuse unsafe work sets the legal protection on unstable ground. The standard can in no way be objectively enforced. There are simply too many unknowns. Thus, global labor standards default to protecting only the most severe traumatic injury risks or similar known chemical or radiation hazards, leaving unprotected those workers faced with emerging or undocumented hazards, or workers otherwise unable to provide the scientific evidence to justify their actions. The logic of the sui generis employment right removes any hope that global labor rights will protect workers in a way capable of guarding against emerging hazards before environmental harm is done or in a way that recognizes the social limits of scientific evidence.

Evaluations of thresholds also generally marginalize people exposed to hazards with longer latency periods and leave off the radar socially based hazards such as violence at work or psychosocial hazards that can be just as debilitating and damaging to a worker's health.

The case-by-case qualification of hazards restricts the merit of worker's claims and places on workers an almost unattainably high burden of proof for protection of their refusal to perform unsafe or hazardous work. These rights amount to what can only be described as a restrictive limit placed on workers' rights. These same rights from another perspective serve to protect the prerogatives of employers to terminate workers.

Mandating Managerial Procedures

Presuming a worker successfully jumps the hurdle of establishing a legal claim with merit for a particular hazard, the Convention No. 155 model of worker protection requires that workers follow a prescribed process in their work refusal. Individual workers are obligated under the convention's norm to "report 'forthwith' to their 'immediate supervisor' any such situations representing imminent and serious dangers"[30] for evaluation of the refusal by a company's management.

Most troubling is the labor standard's failure to recognize the great social inequalities at play in workplaces worldwide. Establishing managerial-based procedures as a step in the exercise of human rights ignores the power dynamics in the employment context and assumes that managers and supervisors are somehow neutral adjudicating agents. This is far from the case, especially on occupational safety and health issues. The legal rights that are protected by the convention are the rights of corporate managers to have a say in the exercise of the right to refuse before a worker pursues any legal claim that may result in an adverse decision for employers.

Qualification by National Policies and Practices

The shift to "policy-based approaches" by the ILO in worker health and safety standards allows the ILO to accept a very wide range of labor policies under the rubric of national practice: "national policy connotes a cyclical process with different stages to be implemented at recurring levels." National health and safety policy under global norms may be established "in light of national conditions and practice." "National conditions and practice," the ILO explains, "indicates, first of all, that there is no 'one-size-fits-all' model and that national policy has to be developed based on an assessment of particular national needs and conditions."[31] Worker health and safety, according to the supervisory bodies, is pursued "so far as is reasonably practicable."[32]

Permitting a wide range of "national conditions and practice" and focusing on what is "reasonably practicable" for each country, with no assertion of any universal protections, was for the ILO a major paradigm shift in worker health and safety under international labor standards. Convention No. 155 on occupational safety and health, adopted in 1981, started this trend. The ILO recognized no fixed standard, marking a significant trend in ILO health and safety standard setting. This shift away from more concrete norms, while implicit in Convention No. 155, would eventually become an ongoing practice in future health and safety labor standards. The best example of this is Convention No. 187, which explicitly states that the aim of the convention is to be a "Promotional Framework" for occupational health and safety. The ILO deprioritized developing international labor standards on specific workplace hazards, standards that before this trend made up roughly half of all global labor standards adopted by the ILO.[33]

The consequences of this paradigm shift were enormous for employee health and safety protests. The failure of the ILO to establish concrete legal obligations meant that employee protections could fall through the cracks of international labor and human rights standards. This shift is demonstrated in Article 5 of Convention No. 155, which outlines general "spheres of action" that "must be taken into account" by states in their national occupational safety and health policies.[34] These include areas such as training, communication, and control of material elements at work. Only the broad areas of policy are identified, with few protective details. This list includes protecting workers from discrimination, yet there is no explicit definition of what constitutes discrimination against workers by employers.[35] This is a matter left to "national policy," to be defined by individual governments. The ILO has clarified the broad scope of the convention's "national policy" blanket on discrimination:

Article 5(e) does not itself seek to prescribe protection of workers and their representatives from disciplinary measures. It prescribes only that a national policy must provide for such protection. In other words, it is for the [ILO] Member to determine the extent and conditions of the protection."[36]

The underlying objective of the ILO in moving toward this new paradigm of "policy-based" versus "fixed rule" global labor standards is best summarized by the ILO itself:

Article 5(e) provides considerable flexibility in the manner in which this protection is to be applied and represents a careful balance between the interest of employers to manage the enterprise, on the one hand, and the protection of life and health at work, on the other hand.[37]

This fixation on balancing the interests of employers with workers' human rights is an open acceptance of a stringent market discipline in these global norms. Here, the preferred method of communication is discourse about the need to maintain labor market efficiency, improve the "functioning" of the labor market, and otherwise abide by the rules of the market metaphor in labor policy, regardless of their impact on human rights.

Leaving health and safety standards subject to vague national policy norms means that discrimination against employee work refusals does not follow human rights principles but is rather subject to "flexibility" in implementation. This "flexibility" in policy development means that countries can apply "any other method consistent with national conditions and practice" to implement their policy. Given these nebulous discrimination boundaries within ILO standards on employee health and safety, the ILO has accepted even the most highly restrictive and limited protections of the right to refuse unsafe work:

The nature of the work at issue may also have an influence on the exercise of the right to cease work. In New Zealand (as in Canada and Poland) this right cannot be exercised if the danger is a normal condition of employment (as, for example, for firefighters); in such cases, workers may only refuse such work if the understood risk of serious harm has materially increased in a given situation, that is, the risk of harm has become significantly more likely.[38]

What is missing under global labor standards is a strong definition of discrimination that outlines the legal obligations of the state to protect the right to refuse unsafe work in accordance with basic human rights principles. Workers are left with global norms that give wide latitude to employer discrimination while at the same time place restrictions on their own effective exercise of both the right to protest unsafe or hazardous work and the right to refuse.

The Right to Refuse as Organizational Activity

Considering the limited protection of the right to refuse as a labor protection under international labor and human rights standards, it is instructive to outline how the right to refuse would be protected under a broad workers' freedom of association protection. Despite the claim that U.S. labor policy has ushered in an era of individual employment rights over the last generation, the strongest protection of the individual refusal right was eliminated early in the so-called individual employment rights era. This history gives us a clear understanding of what the right to refuse unsafe work would look like as an element of preorganizational freedom of association activity. It also shows the fallacy of the individual employment rights era narrative as the idea applies to the development of national occupational safety and health policies.

The jurisprudence of the National Labor Relations Board has at times protected the right to refuse as a workers' freedom of association right. This was based on doctrines of protected concerted activity under Section 7 of the basic law on labor relations, the National Labor Relations Act. Section 7 outlines the rights of workers to self-organization and concerted activities for mutual aid and protection:

> Employees shall have the right to self-organization, to form, join, or assist labor organizations, to bargain collectively through representatives of their own choosing, and to engage in other concerted activities for the purpose of collective bargaining or other mutual aid or protection.[39]

How the right to refuse was protected by the NLRB is one example of how the refusal rights of workers are protected in a workers' freedom of association rights framework.

Jack Henley was a maintenance man for the Alleluia Cushion Company in the cities of Carson and Commerce, California. Shortly after starting his new job in 1974, Henley observed a pattern of neglect of workplace health and safety. There were no protective guards on the machines, no safety instructions for the chemicals used in production, and the factory lacked eyewash stations, much less a safety program. Unlike Henley, the majority of employees in the Carson factory did not speak English, and safety instructions were not communicated to the workers in their native Spanish.

Henley complained to management and was subsequently transferred to the company's facility in Commerce. Once there, he encountered similar conditions of work. Without speaking a word to co-workers, Henley drafted and sent a letter to the California OSHA office. The company, shortly after learning that he had drafted a letter complaining about working conditions, terminated Henley's employment.

Seeking protection against his discharge, Henley contacted the NLRB, which held a hearing on his termination. The administrative judge at the hearing found that Henley "was acting merely on the basis of his individual concern for safety" and cited "the total absence of any evidence that Henley was acting in conjunction with other employees" or that "other employees even shared Henley's concern for safety." The decision found that "if placed in the context of group action," Henley's complaint to OSHA "would be protected activity," but that his actions did not constitute concerted action. He was acting as an individual. Henley was not afforded Section 7 protection.

On review, a majority of the NLRB disagreed and overturned this decision. The majority argued that safe working conditions were "a matter of such obvious mutual concern" that "verbal communication or other outward manifestation of mutual interest was unnecessary." Further, Henley was advocating compliance with existing health and safety laws the company "was already under a legal obligation to comply." According to the reasoning adopted by the National Labor Relations Board, Henley's firing "would indicate to the other employees the danger of seeking assistance from Federal or state agencies in order to obtain their statutorily agreed working conditions, and would thus frustrate the purposes of such protective legislation."[40] The ruling continued:

> Safe working conditions are matters of great and continuing concern for all within the work force. Indeed, occupational safety is one of the most

important conditions of employment. Recent years have witnessed the recognition of this vital interest by Congress through enactment of the Occupational Safety and Health Act, 29 U.S.C. Sec. 651–678, and by state and local
governments through the passage of similar legislation. The National Labor
Relations Board cannot be administered in a vacuum. The Board must recognize the purposes and policies of other employment legislation, and con-
strue the Act in a manner supportive of the overall statutory scheme.[41]

The Board continued.

It would be incongruous with the public policy enunciated in such occupational safety legislation to presume that, absent an outward manifestation
of support, Henley's fellow employees did not agree with his efforts to secure compliance with the statutory obligations imposed on the Company for
their benefit. Rather, since minimum safe and healthful employment conditions for the protection and well-being of employees have been legislatively
declared to be in the overall public interest, the consent and concert of action emanates from the mere assertion of such statutory rights. Accordingly,
where an employee speaks up and seeks to enforce statutory provisions relating to occupational safety designed for the benefit of all employees, in
the absence of any evidence that fellow employees disavow such representation, we will find an implied consent thereto and deem such activity to be
concerted.[42]

The Board supported Jack Henley and ruled against the Alleluia Cushion
Company. The NLRB would protect workers invoking statutory rights
and would also grant individual Section 7 rights based on an "obvious mutual concern" legal standard.

The jurisprudence that followed the NLRB's decision in the *Alleluia
Cushion Company* case followed two lines of argument. First, legal protection was granted to individual employees seeking enforcement of the
law. In one case, the NLRB protected a lone female employee who refused
her reassignment to a job where all women in the positions were paid less
than men in violation of an equal pay for equal work statute.[43] In another
case, the NLRB protected an employee that tried to enforce state banking
regulations related to the late payment of wages that were due to employees.[44] The NLRB in these cases extended the definition of "obvious mutual
concern" to general law enforcement, leveraging the authority of Section 7
and the right of workers to protest to secure law enforcement.

A second group of post-*Alleluia* decisions dealt directly with the right of the lone individual employee to exercise refusal rights. In one case, the Board protected a single employee's walkout to protest terms and conditions of employment for all the employees, even where other employees refused to join the walkout.[45] This case was important because it recognized that individual workers need not rely exclusively on a preexisting statute to invoke the "obvious mutual concern" standard; the terms and conditions of employment at issue were alone enough to invoke Section 7 rights. In another case, the NLRB reinstated an employee after she individually walked off her job at an upstate New York knife manufacturing plant over a dispute about scheduling the night shift for the most dirty production work on a recurring basis.[46] In both these Section 7 cases, an individual employee walkout was protected activity as a workers' freedom of association right not because enforcement of some other statute or regulation was at issue but because the nature of the individual dispute was defined as being of obvious mutual concern.

In yet another *Alleluia* progeny case, an employee for a contract hauler of the U.S. Postal Service in Detroit had refused to drive a truck with defective brakes. The employee was found to be protected under Section 7 because "to drive a motor vehicle with malfunctioning brakes would clearly violate traffic regulations" and because the employee's "refusal to drive such an unsafe vehicle would inure to the benefit of all Respondent's drivers" and was thus of obvious mutual concern. In this case, all three justifications for protection were documented: the enforcement of a statute by an individual worker, action by an individual worker of obvious mutual concern, and that the employee had consulted with other drivers, providing a justification of united action.[47]

The policy debate post-*Alleluia* shows the basic nature of worker freedom of association as a status-based protection in employment relations and not based in some perceived severity of a danger or hazard at work. The Board jurisprudence from the *Alleluia* era recognized that the merit of a workers' health and safety grievance is otherwise irrelevant in determining a worker's protected status. In a case from Pittsburgh where retail workers refused to sell products in an unheated area of a shopping mall in cold weather, the Board unanimously agreed that the merits of such complaints "would not affect the employees' statutory right to seek what they regarded as a more desirable management response."[48] NLRB decisions followed this sentiment in judging the merits of the dispute. Among the decisions where Section 7 protections were extended was a case where the Board refused to judge the merit of worker complaints about working conditions, wages, as well as "racism, sexism and favoritism" when a worker wrote an individual protest letter.[49]

The Board also ruled that a grievance that qualifies as a workers' freedom of association right did not require a focus on the merit of a hazard so long as the general issue fell under the rubric of protected concerted activity. "We have recently held in *Alleluia Cushion Co., Inc.*," wrote a majority for the Board, that considering merit "is not necessary so long as there is evidence that fellow employees share the acting employee's concern and interest in common complaints."[50] That a safety statute existed was one element of common concern. The terms and conditions of work were also evidence of such "obvious mutual concern" and thus afforded workers protection.

The *Alleluia* Board also went a step further to protect the rights of workers under Section 7. The Board majority decided that in those cases where working conditions alone were cited as a basis for obvious mutual concern, direct evidence that the dispute pursued by the individual grievant was of mutual concern might be lacking because other employees were fearful to speak. The board developed a policy of an *assumption of mutual concern* on all health and safety questions. The majority wrote that "in the absence of any evidence that fellow employees disavow such representation, we will find an implied consent thereto and deem such activity to be concerted."[51] It was on this point that employer control was threatened the most. On all matters of health and safety, the NLRB had granted employees a great individual authority. They were to be protected in their employment as individual advocates for health and safety, deputized as rights-holding citizen-workers on questions of the working environment. This decision constituted refusal rights as altering the liberal market employee status assumptions and in turn effectively protecting a key individual component of workers' freedom of association, the right to refuse unsafe work as a fundamental human right.

The Harsh Consequences of Denying Individual Rights

Unlike the NLRB's *Alleluia* doctrine, Section 11(c) of the Occupational Safety and Health Act did not grant U.S. workers the right to refuse unsafe work. Instead, it afforded protection from discrimination because of the exercise "on behalf of himself or others of any right afforded by this Act." Although OSHA required that employers provide places of employment "free from recognized hazards" the vague language was looked upon as problematic from the start. As a result, federal rulemaking was used to establish a regulatory standard defining the statutory rights of employees under the Occupational Safety and Health Act. This regulatory standard—29 CFR 1977—became law on January 29, 1973.

The right to protest safety and health hazards in the working environment was set forth in federal rule Part 1977.12 (b). Two key paragraphs identified the right of employees to refuse unsafe work. The rule is listed here with emphasis added. It was a much more limiting right in employment than the NLRB's *Alleluia Cushion* doctrine:

1977.12(b)(1) On the other hand, review of the Act and examination of the legislative history discloses that, *as a general matter, there is no right afforded by the Act which would entitle employees to walk off the job because of potential unsafe conditions at the workplace.* Hazardous conditions which may be violative of the Act will ordinarily be corrected by the employer, once brought to his attention. If corrections are not accomplished, or if there is dispute about the existence of a hazard, the employee will normally have opportunity to request inspection of the workplace pursuant to section 8(f) of the Act, or to seek the assistance of other public agencies which have responsibility in the field of safety and health. Under such circumstances, therefore, *an employer would not ordinarily be in violation of section 11(c) by taking action to discipline an employee for refusing to perform normal job activities because of alleged safety or health hazards.*

1977.12(b)(2) However, occasions might arise when an employee is confronted with a choice between not performing assigned tasks or subjecting himself to serious injury or death arising from a hazardous condition at the workplace. If the employee, *with no reasonable alternative, refuses in good faith to expose himself to the dangerous condition*, he would be protected against subsequent discrimination. The condition causing the employee's apprehension of death or injury must be of such a nature that a reasonable person, under the circumstances then confronting the employee, would conclude that there is *a real danger of death or serious injury and that there is insufficient time, due to the urgency of the situation, to eliminate the danger through resort to regular statutory enforcement channels.* In addition, in such circumstances, the employee, where possible, *must also*

have sought from his employer, and been unable to obtain, a correction of the
dangerous condition.

The Supreme Court reviewed OSHA's authority to promulgate this key standard after conflicts developed across three appeals courts about the U.S. secretary of labor's authority to create the rule.[52] The Supreme Court in *Whirlpool Corp.*[53] upheld the regulation and the limited nature of the rule's protective language. The unanimous *Whirlpool* court cited the first paragraph of the rule, which proclaimed "as a general matter, there is no right afforded by the [OSH] Act which would entitle employees to walk off the job because of potential unsafe conditions at the workplace."[54]

Section 11(c) rights are afforded when workers meet a two-part test. First, the employee "is ordered by his employer to work under conditions that the employee reasonably believes pose an imminent risk of death or serious bodily injury." Second, the employee "has reason to believe that there is not sufficient time or opportunity either to seek effective redress from his employer or to apprise OSHA of the danger." Thus a great burden was established regarding what constituted a reasonable hazard under Section 11(c), in addition to the requirement to seek managerial redress first.

Contrast this labor policy with the right to refuse through workers' freedom of association and the NLRB's *Alleluia* doctrine. The health and safety law limited the rights of workers to refuse by accepting the proposition that the hazard threshold of a worker's complaint must be judged. *Alleluia*, in contrast, affords workers protection independent of an evaluation of the disputed hazard. Section 11(c), a limited standard, constructs what for many workers are insurmountable hurdles. Not only must workers speculate as to how a federal judge will interpret the hazard they face, they must also weigh the possibility that if the law finds no imminent danger, the courts may find that they had acted in an "unreasonable" way. "Moreover," explained the *Whirlpool* court, "any employee who acts in reliance on the regulation runs the risk of discharge or reprimand in the event a court subsequently finds that he acted unreasonably or in bad faith." The court can simply find that the employee did not have a reasonable belief and in turn subject the worker to discharge. The unanimous court knew exactly what kind of protection it was affording to workers. "The employees have no power under the regulation," Justice Stewart wrote in *Whirlpool,* "to order their employer to correct the hazardous condition or to clear the dangerous workplace of others."[55]

At this point, it is necessary to pause and consider the validity of the claim that the modern era of "individual rights" in employment relations has actually been an era of expanding "individual rights" at all. In the case of occupational safety and health and the right to refuse unsafe work, the so-called individual rights framework has been more a restriction on individual rights for workers. The right to refuse was extracted from the more expansive notion of the right to refuse within the doctrines and legal frameworks of workers' freedom of association. The end result was a restriction on workers' self-help protection by the legal machinery of the state.

Kenneth Smuckler noted the dreadful impact of *Whirlpool* once Reagan-era appointees assumed control of the NLRB and replaced the *Alleluia's* "obvious mutual concern" with a much more restrictive "united concert" standard.[56] This was accomplished in a series of decisions beginning with *Meyers Industries* in 1984. The results were "harsh consequences" for workers electing to protest their work hazards:

> The standards developed by the *Whirlpool* court for triggering section 11(c) protection restrict workers' self-help in safety disputes in a manner not found in the NLRA cases before *Meyers Industries.* The trilogy of cases culminating in *Alleluia Cushion* had accepted the proposition that the merit of an employee safety complaint had no bearing upon the determination of an existing unfair labor practice. The court also considered the degree of danger perceived by the employee to be irrelevant. The sole prerequisites for the establishment of a prima facie section 8(a)(1) violation were that the worker make a safety protest in good faith and that the complaint caused the employer's retaliatory action; thus, section 8(a)(1) could protect safety protests in which the danger was neither immediate nor grievous.
>
> By contrast, the Court in *Whirlpool* narrowed section 11(c) to encompass only those safety protests which were "reasonable" in light of the totality of circumstances. *Whirlpool* further distinguished section 11(c) protection from that afforded by section 8(a)(1) by requiring that the perceived danger pose "an imminent risk of death or serious bodily injury." Although the Court did not expand upon these two criteria, a few lower court decisions in this area have hammered out their meaning. . . . These cases show harsh

consequences which the *Whirlpool* limitations have upon the protection of individual safety protests. . . . The courts have demonstrated tight rein on the concept of "reasonableness" and "imminent danger of serious injury or death."[57]

On inspection, the era of so-called individual employment rights in labor policy resembles nothing of the sort. What was more accurately unfolding was that critical individual rights were being restricted and eliminated by ideologues forcing particular cultural values and beliefs about pseudo-individuality and the market on labor policy. All this was unfolding as the international human rights jurisprudence on economic, social, and cultural rights, including avenues for supervision, was still taking shape. Market ideology was the real culprit in this history.

Whether it was the rejection of the NLRB's *Alleluia* doctrine by courts of appeals, restrictions on workers' protected concerted activity under the conservative Reagan appointees to the National Labor Relations Board, or the unanimous U.S. Supreme Court justices in *Whirlpool* and the "tight rein" of its judicial progeny, the rights of individual employees to protest health and safety conditions through this era were harshly restricted. On the right to refuse unsafe work, if there was a period of individual rights in employment and labor relations, the state through this national labor policy quickly dispelled workers of the notion that any status protection of the right to refuse would ever be allowed to infringe upon the state-backed "laissez-faire" labor market.

The dissent in the Board's original *Meyers Industries* decision, the first attack by the new NLRB on the *Alleluia Cushion* doctrine, rejected the majority's turn to the protection of rational *homo economicus* from broad individual protection of different forms of concerted activity. The dissent as expressed by board member Donald Zimmerman argued for the *Alleluia* doctrine:

My colleagues report today that the Board is not God. If only their expectations of employees covered by the Act were equally humble. Protection for such employees, they now announce, will be withheld entirely if in trying to ensure reasonably safe working conditions they happen not to be so omniscient as to rally other employees to their aid in advance. No matter that the conditions complained of are a potential peril to other employees, or that they are the subject of Government safety regulation. This is a distortion of the rights guaranteed employees by the Act. The historical roots of "concerted activity" lie in the movement to shield organized labor from the criminal conspiracy laws and the injunctive power of the courts. It goes against the history and spirit of Federal labor laws to use the concept of concerted activity to cut off protection for the individual employee who asserts collective rights.[58]

Employees were left with the narrow employment protection of OSHA Section 11(c) regulating the right to refuse with a case-by-case assessment of contested hazards and a psychological assessment of an employee's "reasonable" belief in their refusal.

The dissent also articulated problems in the logic of this path:

> A perplexing problem is presented when no legal standard exists and the severity or likelihood of harm cannot be ascertained, but danger clearly exists. How should society respond to this known but immeasurable hazard? The law ought to err on the side of caution: but to what degree?
>
> Legal protection against reprisals for refusing to perform unsafe work should be provided regardless of the identity of the person at risk and source of danger. An employee may stop work in self-defense or to safeguard either a fellow worker or someone else. A person may be threatened by an unguarded machine, a repeated arm motion, a contaminated work environment or a co-worker who drives recklessly. The right to refuse may be properly invoked in all these settings.[59]

That employees would have their individual rights restricted was a question of little concern to the new majority on the NLRB. Labor policy here was not a matter of the state stepping back and allowing individuals to flourish under natural market forces. Instead, a state-led labor policy of repressing individual freedoms made employment rights safe for business, promoted unilateral management rights, and assured that these prerogatives would not be unencumbered by social control. This was a more invasive and intrusive state activism on behalf of business. Workers were no longer protected in their work refusals on the basis of their status of being employees in an employment relationship. Instead, the nature of the hazard, once deemed immaterial by the state, would be examined, objectified and held to a restricted standard, regardless of any concern for the genuine protection of individual rights at work.

Individual Employment Rights or Disciplinary Neoliberalism?

The critical distinction for vulnerable workers, which includes most work-ers around the world, is *how* each approach protects workers' rights. Pro-tections like the *Alleluia* doctrine recognize an underlying power inequality in employment relations. The NLRB had therefore originally held it to be immaterial whether a company is in compliance with the health and safety standards at issue as workers by their status alone hold "a protected right to seek more than compliance." Workers have, in this view, "a protected right to seek more than compliance with minimum standards or to seek redress of conditions which they believed or considered to be violations . . . whether or not their contentions were correct."[60]

The power granted to workers by this principle means that they should hold the latitude to define the merit of their claim. A market-based model, in contrast, is predicated on establishing, in an adversarial process rife with social inequalities, an objective work hazard that no single party, nor any-one for that matter, may be able to determine. The individual faces chal-lenges in overcoming an inequality in power relations: for example, they may lack legal representation; have scarce material resources; little access to information; face bleak emotional support by co-workers, family mem-bers, and community leaders; possess feelings of the need to get on with one's life; fear the consequences of being labeled a troublemaker; or seek to avoid disrupting career trajectories. Added to these unequal social bar-riers workers must now defend the merit of their own claim as it relates to a particular occupational safety or health hazard, something even an epidemiologist might find a challenge to do, plus do so following manage-rial or supervisory procedures that can be further conditioned on various national practices.

These changes came at a time of increasingly complex occupational hazards and during a period of direct attacks on collective bargaining across North America.[61] Challenging corporate control with a weakened labor relations regime would prove ultimately too much for the organized labor movement as employer opposition became increasingly aggressive. Because the two distinct models of protection of the right to refuse advance two opposing philosophies and policy logics, the argument that the lim-ited refusal rights protection acts as a basic "floor" of labor rights is incor-rect. Although in theory the two divergent policies could remain law in a national employment system simultaneously, their different policy logics are in conflict and create a legal and institutional incoherence, confusion, and contradiction. The restrictive refusal rights in practice inherently limit effective workers' freedom of association, especially for vulnerable workers seeking quick protection against hazards at work where every competing legal claim, every additional evidentiary burden, and every additional administrative process threatens their access to real world social justice. To many workers, institutional fragmentation in labor and employment relations is more a basic fracturing of rights at work, not a new layer of socio-legal protection.

Workers' freedom of association, although a collective protection, also holds a strong individual dimension. It is for many their only guard against "insubordination" and the loss of basic livelihood within a market society. It is the first fragile flower of unionism. It is also a necessity for the achievement of social justice in the struggle for healthy working conditions. As the jurisprudence of the right to refuse demonstrates, governments have placed barriers on individual rights. Certain freedoms are granted to employers while workers are provided rights that do not violate this managerialist market discipline. Individual actions that do not conform to market discipline are not protected. The process of protecting employer power can at times afford certain rights to workers. Such rights, however, are rights that do not interfere with business management prerogatives and the set

TABLE 3.1. Two general models for protecting the right to refuse

	Hazard threshold-based norm	Worker association-based norm
Adjudicating work hazards	Based on a predetermined standard such as "serious danger to life/health"	Adjudicating the merit of a hazard is not relevant to the exercise of the right
Behavior litmus tests for workers	Worker must demonstrate a good faith belief the work meets hazard threshold	No assessment of belief as protection is not contingent on a hazard threshold
Preconditions in exercising rights	Must comply with management's procedures, go through supervisors	Workers may exercise the right independent of management control
Other types of conditionalities	Administered according to national practices and as reasonably practicable	Generally considered a basic universal and fundamental human rights issue
Example	ILO Convention No. 155 of 1981 U.S. OSHA Section 11(c)	NLRB Alleluia Cushion Co. doctrine

authorities of private enterprise. This basic social process has been used in transforming labor and employment policy as a tool to placate various social challenges in the employment relationship and to maintain private power and privilege.

The global labor jurisprudence on the right to refuse unsafe work does not recognize the right to refuse as a fundamental human right. Contemporary global worker health and safety policy emerged at the same time as a broader political movement across the spectrum of global political affairs.[62] This movement, however, was not radical individualism. It was conformance to market principles and ideologies, which at times meant enacting harsh restrictions on individual rights. In the closing decades of the twentieth century, as economic globalization was altering communities and societies, the practice of restricted, marketized individual employment rights would move from provincial and national labor policy in the United States and Canada into ILO global labor standards. On refusal rights, this would become the global export of a neoliberal-disciplined employment right, both in ILO global standards that would be ratified and implemented by dozens of developing nations and in regional agreements on occupational safety and health such as in the European Framework Directive on Occupational Safety and Health.[63]

The turn to global "policy-oriented instruments" on worker health and safety with ILO Convention No. 155 has confounded workers self-help rights in occupational safety and health. These new policy-oriented instruments incorporated many elements of worker protection that had been considered within the traditional domain of labor rights institutions. The vague or restrictive standards of worker protection, however, have confounded efforts to "elaborate on the substance of the policy. Instead they turn straight to the measures to be taken for the application of the Convention."[64] Yet developing any measures to be taken in the application of these global norms is challenged both by their vagueness and their restrictiveness where specificity exists.

A secondary consequence to pursuing vague national policy instruments on occupational safety and health is that critical global treaties on environmental hazards, many also addressing occupational hazards, have been adopted *outside* the ILO. Examples are the Stockholm Convention on Persistent Organic Pollutants,[65] the Rotterdam Convention on the Prior Informed Consent Procedure for Certain Hazardous Chemicals and Pesticides in International Trade,[66] and the Basel Convention on the Control of Transboundary Movements of Hazardous Wastes and Their Disposal.[67] The need for concrete global norms on specific hazards has thus remained even after the ILO would preference more vague national policy notions versus fixed standards on occupational and environmental safety and health, a trend that can be marked as beginning with Convention No. 155 in 1981 and continued in subsequent decades.

There exist two divergent labor rights policy models for protecting the right to refuse unsafe work. The dominant policy as defined by ILO labor standards has failed to recognize refusal rights as a freedom of association, opting instead for the weak and restrictive model of protection within an occupational safety and health policy framework. The right to refuse in ILO global norms on occupational safety and health was noteworthy because it accompanied the more sweeping trend toward a managerialist focus in the global standards on worker health and safety:

> In 1975, the ILC [International Labour Conference] adopted a resolution that called for national policies as well as policies at the enterprise level. This was the first step in a shift toward a management approach to occupational safety and health, and is noticeable in Conventions adopted since in the emphasis placed on the responsibilities of the employer and the rights and duties of the workers.[68]

This "new departure" for the ILO was evident in Convention No. 155 on Occupational Safety, Health and the Working Environment of 1981. It was designed to be "a policy instrument rather than an instrument laying down precise legal obligations."[69] Worker's self-help and the protection of the right to refuse would suffer as a result. To study these dominant international norms in a way that illustrates the interests that are served by these legal frameworks, we must now evaluate how these policies work in practice and how they serve the basic interests of workers as human-rights-holding individuals. There are alternatives. Evaluating the impact of these dominant global policy choices, however, we see the complexity of the obstacles facing the pursuit of social justice.

4

How Effective Are Convention 155 Refusal Rights?

Convention No. 155 concerning Occupational Health and Safety in the Working Environment was adopted in Geneva by the International Labour Conference at its 67th session in 1981. Since adoption, the convention has been ratified at an increasing pace over thirty-one years. Fifty-nine member states were a party to the treaty as of August 2012. Among the notable characteristics of this group of countries is the large number of major developing and emerging market economies, including China, Brazil, South Korea, Turkey, Venezuela, Mexico, Vietnam, and South Africa. The population of these fifty-nine member states covers over 2.5 billion people, rivaling the freedom of association conventions in the number of people living within the countries that are a party to the convention. Each of these governments, with ratification of the convention, is obligated under international law to move their national policies into conformity with the convention. These countries also agree to participate in the ILO regular system of supervision, which includes the submission of periodic reports to the ILO Committee of Experts on the Application of Conventions and Recommendations. This ILO supervision is a high-level dialog that aims to ensure that each national policy conforms to the convention in law and in practice.

The ILO supervisory bodies describe the convention as "innovative" because it follows "a comprehensive approach" focused on "a cyclical process of development, implementation and review of a policy" versus a process that is "a linear one laying down precise legal obligations."[1] This "integrated approach" to national occupational health and safety policymaking is "the dominant feature of current global efforts to curb the incidents of accidents and disease at work," and has formed the basis for subsequent standards, including widely promoted norms such as the Promotional Framework for Occupational Safety and Health, Convention No. 187 of 2006.[2]

TABLE 4.1. States that have ratified Convention No. 155, with date of ratification

Norway (1982.06.22)	Hungary (1994.01.04)	Australia (2004.03.26)
Sweden (1982.08.11)	Nigeria (1994.05.03)	Albania (2004.09.02)
Cuba (1982.09.07)	Latvia (1994.08.25)	Turkey (2005.04.22)
Mexico (1984.02.01)	Viet Nam (1994.10.03)	Sao Tome & Principe (2005.05.04)
Venezuela (1984.06.25)	Ireland (1995.04.04)	Seychelles (2005.10.28)
Finland (1985.04.24)	Denmark (1995.07.10)	Montenegro (2006.06.03)
Portugal (1985.05.28)	Kazakhstan (1996.07.30)	Central African Rep. (2006.06.05)
Spain (1985.09.11)	Mongolia (1998.02.03)	Algeria (2006.06.06)
Uruguay (1988.09.05)	Russian Federation (1998.07.02)	China (2007.01.25)
Cyprus (1989.01.16)	Belize (1999.06.22)	New Zealand (2007.06.12)
Ethiopia (1991.01.28)	Belarus (2000.03.30)	Fiji (2008.05.28)
Netherlands (1991.05.22)	Moldova (2000.04.28)	Republic of Korea (2008.02.20)
Iceland (1991.06.21)	Cape Verde (2000.08.09)	Niger (2009.02.19)
Croatia (1991.10.08)	El Salvador (2000.10.12)	Syria (2009.05.19)
Macedonia (1991.11.17)	Serbia (2000.11.24)	Bahrain (2009.09.09)
Brazil (1992.05.18)	Luxembourg (2001.03.21)	Tajikistan (2009.10.21)
Slovenia (1992.05.29)	Lesotho (2001.11.01)	Belgium (2011.02.28)
Czech Republic (1993.01.01)	Antigua & Barbuda (2002.09.16)	Ukraine (2012.01.04)
Slovakia (1993.01.01)	South Africa (2003.02.18)	Grenada (2012.06.26)
Bosnia Herzegovina (1993.06.02)	Zimbabwe (2003.04.09)	

Source: International Labour Office, NORMLEX Database, as of August 2012

Taking a short walk through the text of Convention No. 155 reveals the nature of this policy-oriented approach versus a more fixed-standards approach. Although the scope and objectives are broad and focus on the development of policies seeking the prevention of accidents and illnesses, the labor convention permits such a range of actions that it illuminates the very character of ILO supervision of the convention. The "flexibility clause" language further implies that supervision could permit a sweeping variety of government policy actions, even irrespective of effectiveness:

> The Convention includes the following *flexibility clauses*. It allows for the exclusion, in part or in whole, of *particular branches of economic activity* (such as maritime shipping and fishing) in respect of which special problems of a substantial nature arise (Article 1(2)) and of *limited categories of workers concerned* in respect of which there are particular difficulties (Article 2(2)). It enables countries to: formulate national policy *in the light of national conditions and practices* (Article 4(1)); review the national policy at *appropriate* intervals either *overall or in respect of particular areas* (Article 7); implement the Convention through laws or regulations or *any other method consistent with national conditions and practice* (Article 8); carry out *progressively* certain specified functions (Article 11); ensure that designers, manufacturers, importers, etc., *satisfy themselves that, in so far as is reasonably practicable,* the machinery, equipment or substance does not entail dangers for the safety and health of those using it correctly (Article 12(1)); undertake certain measures or arrangements *in a manner appropriate to national conditions and practice* (Articles 13, 14 and 15); and undertake certain obligations *so far as is reasonably practicable or where necessary* (Articles 4(2), 6 and 18).[3] (emphasis added)

The stated goal of both the broad language and these flexibility clauses was to adopt a convention that all ILO member states, irrespective of their level of social or economic development, could ratify. Even though it appears that nearly any government policy action in the direction of safety and health could be made acceptable under the convention, the ILO supervisory bodies argue that the flexibility clauses should "be used for enabling provisions and should not be used as a means of derogation from effective occupational safety and health protections for workers."[4] The use of the flexibility clauses requires consultation with workers' and employers' groups, but it is unclear how any "derogation from effective occupational safety and health protection" could be evaluated as violating the convention when the *permitted* abrogation of the various requirements of the convention are themselves derogations from effective protection. The ILO's hands-off "integrated policy approach" would appear to have rendered the primary task of the ILO, namely the establishment of universal standards, obsolete.

Under the ILO Constitution, Article 19, Section 5(e), all ILO member states are obligated, even if they have not ratified a convention, to periodically report on the law and practice in their country on topics requested by the ILO Governing Body. In 2009, the ILO carried out a General Survey on Occupational Safety and Health to monitor the conformity of ILO member states with ILO Convention No. 155, the associated ILO Recommendation No. 164, and the Protocol of 2002 to Convention No. 155. The survey responses evidence the wide global dispersion of the national labor policy model on the right to refuse advocated in Convention No. 155.

TABLE 4.2. States reporting refusal laws with serious or imminent danger clauses

Algeria*	Finland	Poland
Australia	Ghana	Portugal
Azerbaijan	Greece*	Romania
Belarus	Ireland	Serbia
Belgium	Israel*	Slovenia
Brazil	Italy	Spain
Bulgaria	Latvia	Sri Lanka**
Burkina Faso	Lithuania	Suriname
Canada	Macedonia	Sweden
Cuba	Mauritius	Trinidad and Tobago
Cyprus	Mexico	Turkey
Czech Republic	Moldova	United Kingdom
Eritrea	Netherlands	United States
Estonia	New Zealand	Venezuela

Note: Table includes countries reporting either "imminent and serious risk," "imminent and serious danger," "imminent, urgent and life-threatening danger," "significant threat to life," "serious risk to life or health," "serious and unavoidable danger," "direct hazard to life or health," or "serious, imminent and inevitable hazard," This list does not include all of the countries implementing the European Framework Directive 89/391/EEC introducing measures to encourage improvements in the safety and health of workers at work, which includes a serious and imminent danger work refusal standard, nor does this list include information from countries that did not respond to the ILO 2009 General Survey, nor does it include information from countries whose survey response was unclear.

* Applicable to workplace safety representatives only.

** Included in draft legislation at the time of reporting.

A total of 123 member states responded to the 2009 General Survey. Although not all the countries responded to the question about how their national laws protect the right to refuse, nearly all of those that did respond indicated limiting the right to refuse to a standard of serious and imminent danger, in conformity with the minimum requirements of the convention. Table 4.2 lists the forty-two countries reporting serious and imminent danger standards on the right to refuse unsafe work. Half of these governments have not ratified the convention, but have elected to follow its model. Combining these nations with the national parties to the convention leads to the conclusion that the restricted refusal rights model, advocated in Convention No. 155, is the dominant global model of protection of employee dissent through the right to refuse within the domain of workplace safety and health law and policy at the national level.

Evaluating the effectiveness of this model of the right to refuse, in practice, is an important human rights exercise. A qualitative approach is necessary to understand the dynamics of power that workers face in exercising the right to refuse. Such a study would benefit, ideally, from understanding a variety of health and safety regimes reporting limited refusal protections. Given the logistical and financial challenges this poses, however, this approach is beyond the scope of this book. Other strategies can help to grasp the nature of these protections on the ground.

In an earlier chapter, stories of activism from North American labor history demonstrated the contested nature of determining who gets to decide the definition of hazardous work. While documenting the international law, a specific jurisprudential history from North American labor law was introduced to illustrate that there exists an alternative model for protecting the right to refuse. Although the focus of this book is an international social concern, the North American context informs this discussion in a unique way as a critical reflection on North America, the global model for liberal market labor policies, offers particular insights.

On the topic of refusal rights, the U.S. and Canadian cases pose a challenge to international labor law. Both countries have historically followed the more restrictive approach to protecting the right to refuse, mirroring Convention No. 155. At the same time, however, Canada and the United States are reported by the OECD as the first- and second-most laissez-faire nations on job dismissal protection. Convention No. 155 does mandate a particular model of protection of the right to refuse. If the general landscape of employment relations in a society gives employers broad powers to terminate workers from the employment relationship, how is this reconciled with global norms that prescribe only a narrow framework of rights but are otherwise silent? Should not treaty supervision be responsive when the liberal context of an employment relations system impedes the exercise of rights at work? If refusal rights such as those specifically advocated in Convention No. 155 are not effective under liberal market labor regimes, a fundamental problem is not being addressed. As the world moves toward liberal market employment policies, the case of labor rights in the United States and Canada serves as a critical case for the application of global norms that advocate individual employment rights. Advocating any narrow constitutions of rights at work absent understanding how those rights are effectuated in the broader system of employment relations ultimately calls into question any attempt to advocate for particular global labor rights in such a socially decontextualized manner.

Understanding how the restrictive Convention No. 155 model of refusal rights works in practice is the objective of this chapter. Because of the similarities in their design, refusal rights protections in North America, as with other countries reporting the same laws, serve as proxies for the study of Convention 155 refusal rights. As two leading liberal market economies, Canada and the United States offer a strong litmus test for workers' rights under Convention No. 155. As a key stand-alone global standard on occupational health and safety in the working environment, the interaction between these refusal rights in two affluent democracies with functioning systems of administrative law only adds to the critical dimension of this case study. Unlike in other countries where governance challenges exist, the failure of the nation-state is less a factor in effectuating rights, giving further weight to this particular focus within the overall global study.

Limited refusal rights in national labor policy, modern judicial systems, and developed market economies make the evaluation of North American refusal rights a critical part of assessing the Convention No. 155 norm. Accomplishing this task still requires diving systematically into not only case law but the social context of refusal cases. This approach reveals how limited refusal rights function in liberal market capitalism. The result is a critique of both the limited protection for refusal rights found in Convention No. 155 and in national health and safety policy as well as the idea of restricted individual employment rights frameworks generally.

The government of Canada was quick to point out to the ILO's 2009 General Survey that Canada has been at the forefront of protecting the right to refuse:

> The Federal Labour Code and all the provincial occupational safety and health legislations reflect fully the relevant provisions of [Convention 155]. The right to refuse to work in case of imminent danger is one of the cornerstones of the Canadian occupational safety and health legislation. The Code provides a very detailed definition of the term "danger" and conditions under which the right of refusal to work may or may not be exercised by workers. For example, an employee may not refuse work if the refusal puts the life, health or safety of another person directly in danger, or if the danger is a normal condition of employment. Thus the master of a ship or the pilot of an aircraft is empowered, having regard to the overall safety of the ship or aircraft, to suspend this right while the ship or aircraft is in operation. This right is also limited for fire fighters, health care workers, or correctional service workers. Both federal and provincial legislators have established mechanisms ensuring that no prejudicial measures are taken by the employer against workers who have exercised in good faith their refusal to work or have complained of a dangerous work situation.[5]

The protection of refusal rights must be made viable in this liberal market employment relations context if the protection is to be a viable protection anywhere. In this approach, we evaluate North America as a critical vantage point on the employee protection provisions of Convention No. 155, the main ILO labor convention on occupational safety and health in the working environment.

The North American Experience

The Canadian policy on occupational health and safety, while administered differently across federal and provincial jurisdictions, largely follows a model of what Eric Tucker has described as a "mandated partial self-regulation" labor policy.[6] This system—informally the "internal responsibility system"—mandates a regime of weak worker participation rights in occupational safety and health management. This includes legal rules for the establishment of workplace health and safety committees, the protection of the right to know about certain hazards encountered by workers, and a limited protection of the right to refuse unsafe work. The right to refuse unsafe work continues to be protected through negotiated collective bargaining agreements and the related arbitral jurisprudence. Our concern here, however, is the refusal rights model that emerged in the 1970s and came to dominate in North America. It is the labor policy model incorporated in and diffused through Convention No. 155. This policy design, now globalized, is the model this chapter endeavors to analyze and evaluate.

In this limited refusal protection model, an antisocial rational individualism becomes the legal standard and is enforced. This style of individualism enforces individual frames even where individual actors constitute their action beyond the individual self, as the seeds of collective or associational action. In Canada, according to Jane Jenson and Susan Phillips's work on citizenship, this means moving the public policy "from a regime of equitable citizenship in which the values of social justice and equity provided the justification for an expansion of social rights towards a marketized regime." This enforcement of the market logic is characterized by "a reduction of the space in which citizens can act together."[7] This is the story of refusal rights in the Anglo-American experience.

TABLE 4.3. Canadian statutes protecting the right to refuse unsafe work

Jurisdiction	Statute and refusal to work protection provision
Alberta	Occupational Health and Safety Act, §35
British Columbia	Workers' Compensation Act, Occ. Health and Safety Reg. §3.12 and §3.13
Canada (Federal)	Canada Labor Code, Part II, §128
Manitoba	Workplace Safety and Health Act, §43
New Brunswick	Occupational Health and Safety Act, §§19-23
Newfoundland and Labrador	Act Respecting Occupational Safety and Health in the Province, §45
Northwest Territories and Nunavut	Safety Act, §13
Nova Scotia	Act Respecting Occupational Health and Safety, §43 and §44
Ontario	Occupational Health and Safety Act, Part V
Prince Edward Island	Occupational Health and Safety Act, §28 and §29
Quebec	Act Respecting Occupational Health and Safety, §2
Saskatchewan	Occupational Health and Safety Act of 1993, as amended, §35
Yukon	Occupational Health and Safety Act, §15

Three problems have been documented with the limited refusal rights model found in Convention No. 155 as observed in Canada. The first problem is the disparity between union and nonunion workers in the exercise of the right to refuse unsafe work. Second is the challenge of establishing the merit of a work refusal where risk must be adjudicated. The third difficulty is the fracturing of refusal rights through individuation, limiting individual rights where they veer toward an associational or collective style protection; in essence, decollectivizing individual rights. Canadian labor and industrial relations scholarship provides evidence for each of the problems.

Robert Hebdon examined refusal to work complaints by union and nonunion status in the Province of Ontario. His 1992 study examined all unsafe work refusals investigated in the 1987–88 year. During that period, 297 individual work refusals were investigated. Only 16.2 percent of the complaints came from the nonunion workforce. The remaining refusal investigations, 83.8 percent, were work refusals from union employees protected by a collective bargaining agreement.[8]

In a study of refusal to work complaints in the first decade of the new statutory regime in Ontario, Eric Tucker observed that "the right to refuse has not significantly altered the balance of power or given workers much leverage in the internal responsibility system." He found that "unless workers already possess a modicum of power independent of the statutory right to refuse, then the right will not even be exercised." Tucker cited 1983–84 complaint statistics investigated by the provincial authorities. As in Hebdon's study, the 139 work refusals he examined came largely from unionized worksites. Ninety-one percent of refusal complaints were from employees protected under a collective agreement, with only 9 percent of the work refusals investigated from nonunion employees. "Those whose lack of power was greatest," Tucker wrote, "and who stood to gain the most from a statutory right of refusal have, in reality, gained very little."[9] In both the Hebdon and the Tucker studies, power inequalities and liberal market social relations in employment trumped basic statutory rights protections.

Marc Renauld and Chantal St-Jacques examined the right to refuse in Québec after the 1979 passage of the new occupational safety and health regime. Examining some twelve hundred refusal cases running from 1981 to July 1985, Renaud and St-Jacques reported that only 2.9 percent of refusal complaints in Québec were exercised by nonunion employees. At the time, nonunion employees represented 72.2 percent of the working population.[10]

At the same time as ILO members adopted a limited right to refuse, Canadian labor scholars documented that "the right to refuse is inextricably linked to an enterprise's labor relations."[11] The Canadian sociologist Vivienne Walters argued "the legislation itself is problematic, for occupational health and safety cannot readily be separated from social relations in production" because "even the progressive decisions, which recognize the problems of compartmentalizing occupational health and safety, are limited in their ability to address the broader issues."[12] What was revolutionary in the new legal regimes were shifts in the role of the state in relationship to health and safety hazards and worker rights. The regimes created boundary lines whereby once "forbidden disciplinary actions" against protesting workers were made legal by objectifying and adjudicating the definition of a work hazard. By rationalizing, adjudicating and narrowing the legal realm of safety and health hazards, workers continuing to refuse to work could be terminated, reinforcing an employer's power where this was once forbidden. When the state makes forays into adjudicating hazards in the context of employee dissent and a refusal to work, it is conditioning traditional labor relations activity on a workplace hazard threshold. The role of the state is consequently enlarged as worker protection and refusal rights are, at the same time, limited.

Garry C. Gray studied the right to refuse dangerous work through a grounded in-depth, five-month participant observation ethnography of a large industrial factory in Canada with a unionized workforce and a full-time health and safety representative on staff. Given the progressive disposition of the company (a unionized workforce and a stated company position that safety was a top priority), Gray's observations on the limitations of the right to refuse in this context illustrate the limitations found with the hazard-contingent right to refuse unsafe work. His ethnography found significant subjectivity in the workers' perceptions of what constituted dangerous work as the definition of risky work was constantly negotiated and shifting. Varying perceptions of danger were observed, for instance, when Gray was asked to climb a stack of pipes on the back of a truck trailer fifteen feet high. To him, the job was dangerous. To Gray's coworker, a former mine worker from Poland, the work hazards were "not that bad." Workers in Gray's ethnographic case study ultimately avoided refusing work due to safety concerns because of the inherently confrontational nature of the refusal.[13]

In Québec during the early years of the new statutory protection of the right to refuse, the province afforded a broader protection for workers refusing unsafe work due to personal concerns. Renaud and St-Jacques describe refusal cases upheld during this period, including an electrician with an allergic reaction to insulation, an office worker blind in one eye and impaired in another refusing to use a photocopier due to irritation from the light source, and a teacher of students with disabilities refusing to lift the students regularly, fearing the aggravation of an injured back. After a few years of protecting an array of personal conditions, this legal standard was overturned in the *Bootlegger, Inc. v. Couture* and *Hôtel-Dieu de Québec v. Lévesque* cases.[14]

In both the *Bootlegger* case and the *Hôtel-Dieu* case the court ruled that the right to refuse could not be exercised on grounds tied to a personal condition of the worker.[15] Health and safety inspectors from the provincial authority, the Commission de la santé et de la sécurité du travail (CSST), had been given latitude in deciding whether a specific danger existed for an individual worker refusing work. After these cases changed the reading of the law, CSST inspectors were much more restricted in their interpretation. Because personal conditions were restricted, another standard for evaluating hazards needed to be created that did not factor the worker (beyond basic job training) into the equation of measuring the degree of risk. One standard typically used in this situation is to construct the idea of an average worker and evaluate the hazard based on the risk that would be faced by that fictitious average worker. The practice adopted by the CSST inspectors in Québec was to evaluate whether the working conditions were "normal" or "abnormal" for a particular industry. Work refusals exercised in "abnormally dangerous conditions" were protected. Work refusals in "normally dangerous conditions" were not protected. Convention No. 155 offers a similar logic.

During the first two decades of the internal responsibility system in Canada, as these cases were working their way through the courts and this work refusal protection jurisprudence was being established, the response from some worker health and safety activists was to criticize the narrowing of the legal definition of risk.[16] Risk was being defined in reference to an abstract or theoretical standard or risk facing a typical worker, not based on a given worker. Other labor activists criticized the underlying idea of making the exercise of labor rights contingent on a hazard threshold, as will be described in the following chapter.

Although the risk to the individual worker in this new model of worker protection was not judged on an individual basis, each case still had to be investigated on an individual basis, with each employee's individual relationship to the hazard of concern evaluated separately from every other worker for the purpose of adjudicating the worker's claim:

> Workers may exercise a right to refuse together, but this is not considered as a collective exercise of the right because it is not exercised under the union's authority, as the unions wanted, and different decisions may be made for each separate case. Therefore, a worker who exercises a refusal, even within a group, is personally responsible for the consequences in the event that the refusal is judged undue.[17]

Arturo Brion described this individual construction of refusal rights another way:

> The individual character of the right of refusal is one factor that inhibits direct union involvement. A group of workers who claim that they are all at risk can legally refuse to work. However, their refusal will not be recognized as a refusal by a group but as refusals by individual workers belonging to a group. Their claim cannot also be the basis for work refusal by others, whether they belong to or are outside their group, who are not individually at risk. No other entity, whether a union or another worker, can refuse work for a worker: the worker who believes that he or she is at risk must exercise the right of refusal for himself or herself. In line with this basic characteristic the Labour Relations Act itself does not provide that health and safety concerns can be the basis for collective action.[18]

The statutory right to refuse thus required coordination with the industrial relations regime. Where an individual's right to protected concerted activity is already limited, this coordination is easy. No legal changes are necessary and the limited refusal protection clarifies (and solidifies) preexisting restrictions on the workers' freedoms of association. Richard Brown called this one of the "disturbing implications" in cases of concerted refusals to work.[19] This is perhaps the most significant issue to address, the sharp contradiction in institutional logics between the limited statutory "individual" protection of the right to refuse unsafe work in occupational safety and health policy on the one hand and, on the other hand, an industrial relation system's protected concerted activity rights for vulnerable workers to dissent and protest poor working conditions.

The limited right to refuse at a basic level requires that the workers possess a "sufficiently close relationship to a perceived hazard that they are themselves in peril of or that they will put another employee in peril by performing their work." So, for example, this policy model affords no protection of the rights of a group of employees to refuse to perform work "because of health and safety concerns over such factors as the location or design of a plant, the choice or design of tools and equipment, the kind of materials used and the overall method of production."[20] What is abandoned in this model of protection is the basic social process of negotiating working conditions.

Mark Harcourt studied the right to refuse in Canada and how these protections have been reconciled with the rights of management to control the private enterprise. He found "shortcomings as a method for combatting health and safety problems":

> The scope for refusing to work is limited, because workers must satisfy several rigid conditions to qualify for protection from discipline. . . . Boards [tribunals responsible for adjudicating refusal to work cases] do not, in contrast, require managers to justify their right to manage. . . . As a result, boards have, perhaps unwittingly, endorsed an approach to occupational health and safety that stresses the maintenance of managerial control over the workplace rather than the protection of workers from harm.[21]

Harcourt found that tribunals give undue examination to questions of insubordination, length of service, and work record issues versus finding ways to protect worker action under the rubric of concern for the health and safety of the working environment. This was the case even in situations where workers avoided what Vivienne Walters called "built-in deterrents" of the decollectivized rights model that dominates refusal rights.[22]

The Canadian experience demonstrates that the global model of protecting the right to refuse is on its own an ineffective means by which to protect the human right to refuse unsafe work. A more protective human-rights-based model would broaden the protection of individual rights to encompass principles of mutual concern to other workers and to the broader society, or to ensure the protection through union representation. This means strengthening individual rights and expanding the ability of workers to autonomously express themselves in their own independent way, irrespective of any threshold standard related to a particular risk or hazard at work. It also means exploring new ways of extending collective protections to those without representation.

Although the right to refuse unsafe work has been a cornerstone of Canadian health and safety policy, the United States has also vigorously adopted this model of worker protection through numerous federal refusal-to-work statutes. These are in addition to a mix of similar protections at the state level. As in Canadian history, each of these federal and state statutes has been enacted in the neoliberal post-1970s era. Under federal law in the United States, the first of these protections was Section 11(c) of the Occupational Safety and Health Act of 1970.[23] In a 1988 report the U.S. General Accounting Office summarized the scope of the protection afforded to workers under Section 11(c) of the OSH Act:

> Section 11(c) provides all such workers with protections against reprisal when they exercise their rights to file a safety or health complaint, testify about hazardous conditions on the job, and, under certain conditions, when they refuse to engage in work activities which they believe put them in danger of death or serious injury in violation of federal regulations. Any employee who believes that he or she has been discharged or otherwise discriminated against, for one or more of these reasons, may, within 30 days, file a complaint with the Secretary of Labor alleging such discrimination. Upon receipt of such complaint, an investigation is made as the Secretary deems appropriate, and the complainant is to be notified of the Secretary's determination within 90 days after receipt of the complaint. If the Secretary determines that an employee has been discriminated against in violation of Section 11(c), he or she shall bring action in any appropriate U.S. District Court against the employer. The District Court may order all appropriate relief including rehiring or reinstatement of the employee to his or her former position with back pay.[24]

Over the subsequent four decades, the U.S. Congress passed ten statutes protecting the right to refuse (see table 4.4). OSHA has become the agency responsible for the enforcement of the employee protection provisions of these statutes. Whereas these types of complaints once were considered under the rubric of general employee discrimination cases and investigations, over time these employee complaints in the United States became viewed as "blowing the whistle" and not as the basic exercise of some fundamental human right in the employment relationship.

What emerges with the rise of the "whistle-blower" idea is the idea of a public hero sacrificing themselves through the public identification of some kind of affront to the public good. Whistle-blowers illuminate anomalies from the norm and the norm is viewed as normally consistent with the public good. Whistle-blowing is not, therefore, a mechanism that has been conceptualized for structural governance beyond the identification of "a few bad apples" with substandard practices in a given context. Risa Lieberwitz has criticized whistle-blowing as a form of corporate governance in the employment context. She views whistle-blowing as a "shift from labor protections" in U.S. labor and employment policy as whistle-blowing laws inherently limit the full articulation of collective labor interests on health and safety topics by predefining protected employees and predefining the protected harmful acts while developing complex procedures for protection. "Whistleblowing laws have limited potential for advancing the potential actions promoting collective labor interests," even though these protections "often overlap with the health and safety interests as members of the public."[25] Today, the Occupational Safety and Health Administration is the default U.S. whistle-blower protection agency. Workers individually enforce these protections under this detailed enforcement framework. Many of these statutes meld public and environmental health and safety issues with specific occupational health and safety provisions, causing further confusion.

A nationwide audit of cases under OSHA 11(c) by the U.S. Department of Labor inspector general in 1997 found that 67 percent of complainants had been terminated from their job, and many of the complainant case files were incomplete. This included the incomplete documentation of back wages lost after termination and the incomplete documentation of complainant statements. Although employees with "merit" cases under this system are entitled to "all appropriate relief" under the statute, 81 percent of the cases referred to the solicitor of labor were not promptly acted upon. The management system for the 11(c) complaints was deemed ineffective and not consistently relied on by investigators. Settlements had been

TABLE 4.4. United States "whistleblower protection statutes" with employee refusal rights

Year	Statute	Scope
1970	Occupational Safety and Health Act, 29 U.S.C. §660, §11(c)	Employee with a reasonable belief of death or serious injury and there is no reasonable alternative
1978	Energy Reorganization Act, 42 U.S.C. §5851	Employee refusing to engage in practices made unlawful by this Act or the Atomic Energy Act of 1954
1980	Federal Railroad Safety Act, 49 U.S.C. §20109	Employee refusing to violate or assist in the violation of federal laws, rules, or regulations relating to railroad safety or security.
1982	Surface Transportation Assistance Act, 49 U.S.C. §31105	Employee refusing to operate a vehicle because operation violates a U.S. law on commercial motor vehicle safety, or has a reasonable apprehension of serious injury to themself or to the public because of the vehicle's hazardous condition
2002	Pipeline Safety Improvements Act, 49 U.S.C. §60129	Employee refusing to engage in any practice that violates federal law on pipeline safety, if they have notified employer of alleged illegality
2007	National Transit Systems Security Act, 6 U.S.C. §1142	Employee refusing to violate or assist in violating any federal law, rule, or regulation relating to public transportation safety or security
2008	Consumer Product Safety Improvement Act, 15 U.S.C. §2087	Employee refused any assigned task believed to be in violation of the laws enforced by the Consumer Products Safety Commission
2010	Affordable Care Act, P.L. 111-148, §1558	Employee refusing any assigned tasks believed to be in violation of the Affordable Care Act of 2010
2010	Consumer Financial Protection Act, 12 U.S.C.A. §5567, §1057	Employee refusing any assigned task believed to be in violation of the laws enforced by the Bureau of Consumer Financial Protection
2010	Seaman's Protection Act, as amended by the Coast Guard Authorization Act of 2010, P.L. 111-281, §611	Seaman refusing to perform duties ordered due to a reasonable apprehension or expectation that performing such duties would result in serious injury to the seaman, other seamen, or to the public

Note: As of January 1, 2011, the OSHA Office of the Whistleblower Protection Program is responsible for enforcing the employee protection provisions of twenty different federal statutes. This table includes laws where the right to refuse is explicitly protected in the statute or the regulation enforced by OSHA. Excluded, for example, is the right to refuse under the U.S. Federal Mine Safety and Health Act of 1977, a refusal protection enforced by the Mine Safety and Health Administration.

negotiated in 99 percent of cases where remedies were received under Section 11(c).[26]

Responding to the DOL inspector general's 1997 evaluation, OSHA officials defended the negotiation of settlements as a form of alternative dispute resolution:

The conclusion in the report stating that OSHA's actions to settle merit cases without referring them to the Secretary of Labor for litigation limits the participation of the courts in developing the discrimination provisions of the Act, clearly indicates a failure to discuss this issue with the Secretary of Labor or with the U.S. District Court Judges, whose dockets are filled with a range of federal litigation. The Attorney General of the United States chaired a briefing in June 1996, on the need for "Alternative Dispute Resolution." Two U.S. District Court Judges specifically identified whistleblower cases to get out of the Courts. The whole basis of Alternative Dispute Resolution (ADR) is compromise. The Department of Labor presently has a proposal for a DOL ADR Program with whistleblower cases being the primary focus of the program. This action by the department flies in the face of the report's recommendation for more litigation and seeking "all appropriate relief."[27]

OSHA Section 11(c), our concern here, provides for enforcement through the U.S. District Court system. There is no private right of action. The solicitor of the Department of Labor must bring the case to court. To prove merit in a Section 11(c) case, OSHA must show the presence of four essential elements in the complaint: (1) the complainant engaged in protected activities, (2) the employer knew about the protected activity, (3) the employer retaliated against the employee, and (4) that there is a connection, or nexus, between the protected activity and the retaliation. Of the cases examined by the inspector general in 1997, the settlements negotiated by OSHA investigators contained back-pay awards and, sometimes, employee reinstatement. No abatements of hazardous working conditions were reported as being included in any settlement.

The inspector general again investigated the OSHA 11(c) complaint system in September 2010. Again, the Office of the Inspector General (OIG) found incomplete case files and settlement procedures that "deprived complainants of full and appropriate relief." The DOL inspector general found that the on-the-ground investigators lacked the resources needed to make thorough investigations of refusal to work cases in accordance with stated policies, and that they lacked training and legal assistance required to understand the various statutes and perform investigations. Reinstatement of employees occurred in less than 3 percent of cases. The OIG also found a failure to follow one or more of the eight essential elements of a complaint investigation process under federal policy: conducting a formal complainant interview, the documenting of the interview via a signed statement or digital recording, obtaining suggested witnesses from the complainant, interviewing or attempting to interview all pertinent complainant witnesses, documenting complainant witness interviews via signed statements or digital recordings, conducting face-to-face interviews or on-site investigative work, allowing the complainant an adequate opportunity to refute the employer's defense or resolve other discrepancies, and holding a closing conference with the complainant.[28]

The U.S. Government Accountability Office evaluated the "whistle-blower protection" system at OSHA in January 2009 and August 2010. A total of 1,864 employee complaints were investigated and closed in 2007, of which 1,211 complaints (65.6 percent) were dismissed. Complainants withdrew 253 of the remaining cases (13.5 percent) and 390 (20.9 percent) were found by the investigators to have "merit." Of those cases found to have legal merit, 371 complaints (95.1 percent) entered into a negotiated settlement process and were settled. The settlements negotiated under OSHA Section 11(c) with monetary payments for Fiscal Year 2007 averaged $5,288. Settlements ranged from $65 to $94,500. The remaining nineteen cases that did not settle were forwarded for litigation to the solicitor of labor, with twelve of these dismissed.[29]

One-third of investigators reported that inadequate equipment hinders their whistle-blower investigation. In some regional offices, 80 percent of whistle-blower investigators reported inadequate equipment as a hindrance to their investigation work. Over one-half of investigators reported spending some out-of-pocket personal funds on work-related equipment, supplies, or transportation in 2007. The amount of these personal expenditures ranged from $75 to $2,000. The equipment purchased with personal funds included laptop computers, printers, and personal cell phone service. Recording devices were also reported by some investigators as not available. Other stories of the difficulties faced by investigators were also reported:[30]

> In one instance, an investigator who was preparing to attend a mandatory 2-week investigation training course learned that the course required participants to bring laptops with operating systems that were compatible with the software being used for the course. Lacking this, the investigator used his or her own money to buy a laptop with a compatible operating system.[31]

Although Section 11(c) covers all forms of health and safety discrimination and not only cases of retaliation against workers who refuse to perform unsafe work, these material resource challenges to occupational health and safety whistle-blower investigations handled by OSHA exacerbate the already complex nature of individual refusal to work cases.

According to government oversight reports, nearly all OSHA Section 11(c) health and safety investigation files contain a final investigation report (FIR). Each FIR documents the employee complaint, states the grievance of the worker, provides the employer's defense, gives the investigator's analysis, and lists the final agency disposition of the case. Analyzing the refusal to work investigations documented by the final investigation reports under OSHA Section 11(c) is one way to evaluate the effectiveness of the protection of the right to refuse under this type of legal model.

According to the OSHA case management database, a total of 402 cases under OSHA 11(c) were investigated as "refusal to work" cases in the five years between 2004 and 2008. Another 473 refusal to work cases were opened under Section 405 of the Surface Transportation Assistance Act. These documents were released by the Department of Labor under a Freedom of Information Act request made for this book. Altogether, this collection of cases may be the largest collection of previously nonpublic refusal to work cases in private hands. Every regional OSHA office holding the reports with the exception of Region 2 complied with this public data request.

Final investigative reports open with a copy of the official letter mailed to the complainant indicating the investigator's final disposal of the case. These letters are typically one of three generic form letters: a letter acknowledging the settlement agreement, a letter dismissing the case outright, or a letter acknowledging that the complainant had withdrawn the case. Dismissal letters have similar language across the regions, as in this May 2006 letter from the Tampa Bay Area office in Region 4:

> Your complaint of discrimination in violation of Section 11(c) of the Occupational Safety and Health Act (the Act) has been investigated and the results thereof carefully considered. As a result of the investigation, the burden of establishing jurisdiction or a violation cannot be sustained. The evidence developed during the investigation was not sufficient to support the finding of statutory jurisdiction and a violation. Accordingly, further proceedings in this matter are deemed unwarranted and the complaint is hereby dismissed.[32]

TABLE 4.5. OSHA 11(c) refusal to work cases by region, 2004–2008

OSHA region	Jurisdiction	Cases in DOL system	FIRs released through FOIA
Atlanta (4)	Alabama, Florida, Georgia, Kentucky*, South Carolina*, North Carolina*, Mississippi, Tennessee*	151	120
Chicago (5)	Indiana*, Illinois**, Minnesota*, Michigan*, Ohio, Wisconsin	119	105
Dallas (6)	New Mexico*, Oklahoma, Texas, Louisiana, Arkansas	42	38
New York (2)	New Jersey**, New York**, Puerto Rico*, Virgin Islands**	23	0
Boston (1)	Vermont*, New Hampshire, Maine, Massachusetts, Connecticut**, Rhode Island	22	20
Denver (8)	Colorado, Montana, North Dakota, South Dakota, Wyoming*, Utah*	14	20
Philadelphia (3)	District of Columbia, Delaware, Maryland*, Pennsylvania, Virginia*, West Virginia	11	4
Kansas City (7)	Iowa*, Nebraska, Kansas, Missouri	9	9
Seattle (10)	Alaska*, Idaho, Oregon*, Washington*	7	6
San Francisco (9)	California*, Arizona*, Nevada*, Hawaii*	4	4
Total		402	326

* Indicates states with OSHA State Plan. **Indicates states with OSHA State Plans that cover only public sector employment. OSHA defers to state OSHA agencies to investigate Section 11(c) complaints. The variation in the number of cases collected across OSHA regions is due in part to cases being handled by state OSHA agencies. This chart only includes investigations by OSHA in locations under federal jurisdiction. It does not include cases investigated by state OSHA agencies.

Cases that conclude in settlement agreements are closed with slightly different letters. Settlement information, including the name of the complainant and the amount awarded, is not public information. Letters indicating withdrawal of a case are similarly brief. One of these form letters closes the investigation documented in the final investigative report.

Final investigative reports, including cover letters, range from two to thirteen pages, with an average of five or six pages. Regional offices elected to redact different portions of information from each FIR, but generally the documents included a standard format page listing the date the case was opened, the name of the regional investigator, the complainant's name, the complainant's representative, the respondent, and the respondent's representative. This first section also includes a brief statement of the complainant's allegation, the employer's defense, and a "coverage" line indicating how the employer falls under OSHA's jurisdiction. Each also included a redacted list of the witnesses, where there were witnesses. The most extensive section of the document is the "Investigative Findings" narrative. This is followed by the "Analysis" section, a "Closing Conference" section, and a "Recommendation" section.

An in-depth content analysis of the 402 OSHA Section 11(c) refusal cases was conducted for this book. The number of documents that arrived in the mail was less than the total number reported in the overall OSHA case management database. There were 326 cases under OSHA 11(c) analyzed and coded. The complainant information and the list of witnesses were redacted throughout every one of the 326 cases. The only other sections redacted across the regions was the "Analysis" section, which documents the investigator's thinking, and the "Recommendation" section, which can be deduced by the case closing cover letter despite this redaction. The "Investigative Findings" section is the investigator's narrative report of the complaint, the statement of the employee complainant, the investigator's conversations with witnesses, and the investigator's discussion with the respondent. Through these narrative sections, each case can be reconstructed, giving insight about the social experience of this legal recourse.

Among the information that was either not collected or not available across all investigation reports was union presence, industrial sector, number of employees at the worksite, and complainant occupation. Despite no systematic information on these topics, the following is a rough count of the top ten occupations pieced together from the Atlanta region office, which provided over one-third of the documents examined:

1. Equipment operators, from forklifts to cranes (14.4%)
2. Manufacturing and fabricating employees (13.5%)
3. Commercial drivers, all varieties (13.5%)
4. General laborers (12.5%)
5. Retail services, including food service (9.6%)
6. Other construction workers (8.6%)
7. Mechanics and maintenance workers (8.6%)

8. Cleaners, all varieties (7.7%)
9. Pipefitters and welders (6.7%)
10. Social service and health care employees (4.8%)

This list notably includes service and health occupations although the dominance of the traditionally dangerous occupations on this list may be indicative of the difficulty of pursuing the right to refuse unsafe work under a limited refusal protection model.

The number of work refusals remains extremely low relative to the number of work-related illnesses and injuries nationwide. The number of fatal workplace injuries in the United States (not including fatal workplace illnesses) over the same period (five years) is 28,209 people.[33] We can deduce that either the current legal recourse protecting the right to refuse is an ineffective framework for protection, or that recorded workplace fatalities have occurred so suddenly that no time exists to contemplate the refusal of unsafe work, something that seems unlikely given the nature of many of these cases. American workers are either dying for work without question or coerced to death by a failed industrial relations system where only 6.9 percent of all private sector workers nationwide are unionized and enjoy basic rights of freedom of association and collective bargaining.[34]

The 11(c) refusal to work complaints received by OSHA regions significantly exceed the number of cases opened for investigation. Many complaints are "screen-outs" and are not opened as cases by the regional offices. A count of the screened-out refusal complaints under Section 11(c) is unavailable. According to correspondence with the Office of the Whistleblower Protection Program, the number of refusal screen-outs to open investigations under Section 11(c) was estimated to be a 5:1 ratio. This would place screened 11(c) refusals closer to five hundred cases annually and at over two thousand cases for the five years covered by the FOIA release and period of study.

The majority of Section 11(c) work refusal investigations are closed by either a dismissal or by the complainant withdrawing the case. Complainants who withdraw the case are often told by OSHA investigators that their case is going to be dismissed, and the investigator extends a courtesy period to the complainant to withdraw the case to avoid a formal dismissal.

In a handful of cases withdrawn, the worker indicates to the investigator they are seeking remedies through the grievance procedure of a collective bargaining agreement. There is evidence that workers terminated for their refusal seek unemployment compensation; by withdrawing their case, they avoid jeopardizing their unemployment compensation claims with a negative investigation.

Where cases have "merit" the practice is negotiating settlement agreements versus the pursuit of broader enforcement remedies. In these cases, the complaint mechanism and its basic back pay remedy thus is little more than a supplemental unemployment compensation benefit, rather than a viable mechanism for the operational governance of occupational health and safety.

Altogether, 12.1% of cases were withdrawn by the complainant; the majority of the cases, 66.3%, were dismissed as being without merit under the statute; and 21.3% of cases had negotiated settlement agreements. These figures are consistent with past oversight reports of Section 11(c) investigations. The average time to disposition of the cases examined, from the date OSHA received the complaint, was 90.95 days. The longest disposition was 818 days and the shortest was one day. Over two-thirds (the standard deviation) were disposed between 34.8 days and 146.7 days after receipt of complaint.

As settlement agreements were the overwhelming method of choice to resolve merit cases, the negotiated process of alternative dispute resolution needs scrutiny. Settlement agreements, to the displeasure of labor scholars, are exempt from public release under the Freedom of Information Act. There are indications that the vast majority of negotiated settlements do not include reinstatement of the complainant.[35]

The antidiscrimination protections under OSHA Section 11(c) do not function as workers' rights protections. No evidence suggests that any settlement negotiations have entailed negotiating changes to the original health and safety hazard that was of concern.

The dominant remedy is a small lump sum payment to the individual complainant. Such remedies do not conform to the statutory requirement of providing workers with "all appropriate remedies." These remedies also keep the authority of 11(c) insulated from a litigation record that might be developed and pursued by the solicitor of labor. Developing a litigation strategy to push refusal to work cases could serve to broaden the protection of worker activism on health and safety concerns. Overall, the general disposition of cases by OSHA sacrifices workers' rights without a fight while failing to push the boundaries of an admittedly restrictive statute.

Refusal Rights Enforcement from the Worker's Perspective

Arguing the case before an occupational health and safety investigator, the OSHA 11(c) refusal protection grants employers a very strong defense. The legal standard is not adequate to overcome a given employer's privileges of terminating the employment relationship. As a result, the regulatory model that requires evaluating the degree of the hazard never effectively happens. Workers face a major hurdle overcoming the burden of proof required to secure their legal protection. Precarious, temporary, and contract workers face even greater obstacles.

Dismissal letters offer complainants a detailed explanation as to what is required to prove an allegation of discrimination for refusing unsafe work. One dismissal letter, sent to a Florida man employed as a temporary worker contracted to Consolidated Minerals in Orlando, Florida, included a clear and detailed description of the various requirements he failed to meet to prove his refusal case:

> Specifically, in order to have proven allegations under 29 C.F.R. 1977.12 (b) (2), the investigation needed to establish that the following conditions were met: 1) where possible, Complainant asked Respondent to eliminate the danger, and the Respondent failed to do so; **and** 2) Complainant refused to work in "good faith." Specifically, that Complainant genuinely believed that an imminent danger existed. Complainant's refusal could not be a disguised attempt to harass Respondent or disrupt business; **and** 3) a reasonable person would agree that there was a real danger or serious injury; **and** 4) there was not enough time, due to the urgency of the hazard, to get it corrected through regular enforcement channels, such as requesting an OSHA inspection.
>
> Further, when all of the above conditions are met, the investigation needed to establish that Complainant took the following steps: 1) he asked Respondent to correct the hazard; 2) he asked Respondent for other work; 3) he told Respondent that he would not perform the work unless and until the hazard was corrected; **and** 4) he remained at the work site until ordered

to leave by Respondent. By your own admission, you were not told by management you were being discharged and you did not remain at the worksite until ordered by Respondent to leave. Finally, there is no evidence that you attempted to contact OSHA to report the hazard prior to leaving the worksite.[36] (Emphasis in original letter)

These requirements shift the burden of proof onto the worker-complainant. This shift thus creates a major social inequality that most complainants are not able to overcome.

Because the burden of proof is on the complainant, and not on the employer, the employer is not obligated to demonstrate that the workplace will not harm a worker's health or safety. Employers simply fall back on their everyday privileges and powers to control their workforce. Table 4.6 ranks the primary employer defenses used in each case. The existence of a safe and healthy workplace was used as an employer defense in only 8.3 percent of cases. The other 91.7 percent of the time employers used arguments based in their liberal market, common-law assumptions regulating the employment relationship. These include allegations of worker insubordination, job abandonment, behavioral issues, voluntary quits, poor performance, and reduction or layoffs. These were the arguments employers used for terminating employees, thus shifting the focus from any debate on health and safety in the process. As the burden of proof is on the worker-complainant to show imminent and serious danger,

TABLE 4.6. Primary employer defenses in OSHA 11(c) work refusals (n=241)*

Defense	Percentage of cases
1. Insubordination	29.5
2. Job abandonment	22.4
3. Voluntarily quit	14.5
4. Poor performance	12.0
5. Behavioral issues	9.5
6. HEALTH / SAFETY	8.3
7. Reduction or layoff	3.3

*Cases where employer defenses were documented by the investigators.

employers rarely engaged in this debate on health and safety and instead fell back on their legal and traditional power base: employment termination rights.

Shifting this high burden of proof would, in this highly unequal framework, still, however, leave obstacles and afford employers advantages. The obligation that workers are to first ask the employer to eliminate a hazard *as a precondition* for exercising the right to refuse afforded some employers time to build a case against those workers unfortunate enough to voice their concerns. This included shifting or altering of the work site without safety or health hazard abatement. When workers voiced their complaints and refused a work assignment, the delay from the time of termination to the time an OSHA inspector arrived at the work site was critical. Sometimes the delay was two days or longer. This gave employers time to tamper with evidence. In one case, an employee complained about unsafe scaffolding. When the OSHA inspector arrived to investigate the refusal to work, the scaffolding structure had been removed entirely.[37] In another case, a worker made a complaint about inadequate cave-in protection while working in a trench. By the time the OSHA inspector arrived at the work site, the trench had been filled with earth and was no longer there, making any evaluation of serious or imminent danger impossible.[38] In some cases the labor inspector never conducted an on-site investigation of the work refusal. These cases show the social inequities built into the limited refusal protection, leaving unchallenged the employer's historic defensive posture of control of the worker, inequalities unchallenged and codified globally under Convention No. 155.

The employer defense of a reduction in work or a layoff takes on a special meaning when the complainant is a temporary or contract worker. Employers in these cases shaped their defense around the contract or temporary work relationship. In one case typical of the cases in this category, an employer argued that no termination had occurred: the temporary agency was still a client of the employer, but there was no work available at that moment to be contracted; they would be contracted when their services were needed.[39] Employers have extra degrees of leverage in shaping their legal defense under such precarious employment arrangements.

Because employers have no burden of proof to demonstrate the safety and health of their workplaces, the legal inquiry shifts and an employee's character is called into question repeatedly in the process of investigating employee dissent in refusal to work complaints. This buttresses an employer's standard and traditional defensive posture because investigators subsequently turn to collect evidence as to the worker's moral character and honor, respect and trustworthiness as an employee and as a human being. Some investigators in this position spend most of their fact-finding work collecting evidence of the worker's character and job history. This may include the number of days they are late to work, their attendance records, and their past disciplinary experience. In a handful of cases, a fixation on moral character was the entire focus.

The following case chronology from OSHA Region 4 is illustrative of this point:

Investigative Findings (chronology)

6-27-05   Complainant was hired as a **(redacted)** installing glass block at various construction sites in South Florida. The job required employees to work on a ladder installing the glass block masonry. Respondent said Complainant was unable to work on ladders and he would try to work solely on the ground. Respondent said Complainant took 7 personal days in 60 days of work.

8-1-05   Complainant took day off for personal reasons.

8-15-05   Complainant took day off for personal reasons.

8-17-05   Complainant left work early with shoulder pain.

8-18-05   Complainant had back pain and went on workers' compensation until 8-22-05.

8-24-05   Complainant was 20 minutes late for work.

8-25-05   Complainant took day off for personal reasons.

8-31-05   Complainant took day off because he broke his glasses.[40]

Other refusal to work investigators even compared the complainant's "insubordinate" behavior behind the work refusal to the policies outlined in management's employee handbook, something that has no legal basis being evaluated under the federal occupational safety and health law:

The records provided by the Respondent documented the events which led up to the Complainants termination. She was terminated for refusing to perform her assigned work which is considered insubordination per company policy 6-1-B. The Complainant signed the Review of Employee Handbook on May 6, 2003. Section Six "Personal Conduct" identifies causes for immediate discharge. Item B states "Refusal to perform assigned work" as one of the reasons for immediate discharge.[41]

In each of these cases, the fact-finding work of the refusal to work investigator was focused on the insubordination of the employee, from character flaws to violating company policy. Under the limited framework of Section 11(c) and Convention No. 155, a worker who has a poor work attendance record, or violates company policy, for instance, is thus less likely to be protected, even if some workplace hazard is observed as being evident. Workers with questionable moral character as interpreted by the employer and labor inspector would thus be in a more vulnerable position to exercise these rights compared to another employee faced with an equally hazardous assignment.

Section 11(c) work refusal investigations are qualitatively different than the standard health and safety inspection. The relationship between the investigator and the complainant is especially important given the aggregate social inequities that unorganized workers face in representing their legal claims. In the 326 refusal to work cases examined here, employees had no representation in 95.9 percent of cases. Only 3 percent of complainants listed lawyers as the address of their legal representatives. Conversely, employers responding to refusal to work complaints listed a variety of legal and business representatives: in-house company attorneys; corporate counsel; company owners, presidents, and executives; plant and worksite managers; senior human resource directors; and safety directors. All employers had some representation, with 22.9 percent reporting lawyers (in-house or otherwise), 26.1 percent reporting company executives, and 48.6 percent reporting managers or other representatives such as human resource managers. Health and safety directors were reported as the company representatives in 2.4 percent of 11(c) refusal to work cases where the employer representatives were identified in the investigation reports.

Adequate legal representation for unorganized, nonunion workers exercising individual employment rights is dealt with as a social justice issue in other settings. In Ontario, the provincial government funds the Office of the Worker Advisor as an independent agency of the Ministry of Labor. This agency provides free services to nonunionized injured workers regarding the pursuit of workers' compensation claims. Another example is the general counsel under the U.S. National Labor Relations Act where "Information Officers" receive charges made by workers and conduct preliminary fact-finding to determine whether there is sufficient evidence to warrant a formal charge. If a formal complaint is issued, the investigator becomes a legal advocate for the worker as the case moves before an administrative law judge for adjudication. Case investigators in OSHA 11(c) cases wear the dual hats of an investigator and adjudicator, never fully assuming the position of a worker advocate. Section 11(c) refusal to work investigators hold the role of investigator and adjudicator at the same time, with workers advocating for themselves absent representation through a highly complex maze of administrative requirements, each one capable of undercutting a worker's case if not successfully navigated.

Findings of legal merit under Section 11(c) are contingent in part on meeting an imminent danger standard. There appears to be evidence across these investigatory documents indicating that Section 11(c) investigators give more weight to hazards that directly violate current OSHA health and safety standards. This means new and emerging hazards that may pose an imminent and serious danger but may not violate current health and safety standards face a higher threshold to achieving any legal merit status. Investigators should be trained to know that OSHA Section 11(c) cases do not need to demonstrate a direct relationship to OSHA health and safety standards. Merit cases can exist with hazards that are not defined in the current body of OSHA standards.

The loss of contact with complainants is also a problem for investigators. One-third of work refusal cases ended with the OSHA investigator losing contact with the worker-complainant. This was the result of either a simple disconnected telephone line or from returned postal mail marked undeliverable, for example. Losing contact with individual worker-complainants is a further indication of the social inequity inherent when workers are forced to independently self-represent themselves in pursuing individual employment rights. When you are terminated from your employment and no longer have an income to pay the bills, keeping the telephone bill paid or even maintaining a home can be a challenge. Contrast this challenge to the representation listed on the employer's side, all of whom are professionals who would be responding to legal complaints as part of their on-going work duties, be they labor and employment lawyers, workplace health and safety managers, or human resource management specialists.

A more fundamental problem with the limited individual refusal rights model was also evident in OSHA Section 11(c) refusal to work case documents. This model, the dominant model in international labor law, decollectivizes individual employment rights. This was documented by the Canadian studies mentioned earlier, and the U.S. cases provide evidence of this phenomenon as well. The U.S. cases illustrate a sociolegal misfit between the dominant rights framework and the very basic social experience of the employment relationship itself. Section 11(c) forces workers to represent their legal claims in ways that do not fit their social experience in employment. In light of this finding, it is not, therefore, the rights-based framework per se that can be held responsible as the factor that has weakened worker's efforts to promote their interests; it is the restriction of the rights framework through an individualist market ideology that has challenged the development of labor advocacy and threatened health and safety in the working environment.

OSHA Section 11(c) protections, which are afforded to individuals, encounter an interesting problem in relationship to activity that once would have been afforded a broader organizational freedom of association protection under labor law. Evidence exists of refusals to work that were indeed *objective* concerted activity, in contrast to *constructive* concerted activity where there is no overt demonstrable joint act with other workers (even though the act itself might be clearly of obvious mutual concern). Objective concerted activity exists where two or more workers are jointly engaging in a refusal to work. Section 11(c) cases examined here are filled with specific instances of *objective* concerted activity. The legal process, through case investigations, slices up worker complaints, employee after employee, one by one. This phenomenon highlights a fundamental weakness in the refusal protection model under ILO international labor standards: the dominant legal framework atomizes workers by making individual employment rights an exclusively individualistic endeavor, even in situations where workers consider, seek to pursue, and overtly represent their individual complaint in broader social terms that include themselves but extend beyond themselves to encompass other workers. Thus the OSHA Section 11(c) legal model reconstitutes social or collective claims as being exclusively individualistic legal complaints. This is thus a fundamental problem with the dominant model of protecting employee dissent through the right to refuse unsafe work under global labor standards. This fundamental weakness only underscores the importance of protecting the right to refuse through labor rights and freedoms of association.

Table 4.7 breaks down the types of employee concerted activity observed in the OSHA Section 11(c) work refusals. Since each case is either a type of objective concerted activity or a constructive concerted activity, adding constructive concerted activity to this table brings this total to 100 percent. In many cases, as a caveat to this analysis, there simply was not enough information in the investigative report to assess the situation with any degree of certainty. These cases are coded as missing data and are not included in the total, reducing the total number of refusal to work cases examined on this question.

Where there is a case narrative documented with no evidence of any objective concerted action, the case was coded as constructive concerted activity. In these cases, at least according to the legal record, the complainant worker was acting alone; any interpretation of their action being of a concerted nature would be a legal construction. The number of objective concerted cases could, therefore, be much higher than the figure shown here, as this analysis requires that the documentary evidence indicate objective concerted action. Where objective concerted activity is noted, the cases have been categorized through a simple content analysis in order to give the reader a better explanation as to what is being observed. This method likely undercounts the extent of the objective concerted activity because

TABLE 4.7. Concerted activity in OSHA 11(c) work refusals by type (n = 190*)

Objective concerted activity	54.2%
Joint refusal to work or investigation indicated that other workers had previously refused the same or similar assigned task being refused	22.1%
Another worker hurt, hospitalized or nearly hurt/made ill by the hazard	15.8%
Investigator documented co-worker support for the complainant refusal	12.6%
Co-worker expressed hesitation or fear regarding the hazard at issue	3.7%
Constructive concerted activity	45.8%

* Full field investigations only

investigators are documenting individual cases and often ignore the social context, giving no further evidence about the position of co-workers in a case.

Over half of full field investigations of refusal to work cases showed evidence of objective concerted activity or, simply put, of two or more workers expressing their interests in favor of improving the working environment. Despite the high percentage, not a single investigation documents a referral to the National Labor Relations Board for protection as a freedom of association issue under Section 7 of the National Labor Relations Act. Four groups of objective concerted activity were documented in the course of this analysis. The first type observed was the classic collective work refusal where two or more complainants either refused the work task or another employee or employees were mentioned as refusing the same task previously. These joint refusals involved 22.1 percent of all refusal cases receiving a full OSHA field investigation.

A second form of objective concerted activity was documented when any co-workers expressed support for the lone refusing complainant. These represented 12.6 percent of cases. Other co-workers expressing a shared hesitation or fear about assuming the hazardous assignment was found in 3.7 percent of cases. In 15.8 percent of cases a co-worker was reported as being hurt, hospitalized, endangered, or the subject of a near-miss accident from the hazard or exposed to a hazard for which OSHA had issued the employer a citation. Each of these scenarios was identified through a basic content analysis of the individual case files and was coded into the one category that best described each situation, making the categories listed in table 4.7 mutually exclusive.

This analysis shows that occupational health and safety investigators charged with the enforcement of OSHA 11(c) refusal rights were therefore placed in the role of atomizing and individualizing what were otherwise genuine social concerns explicitly shared between two or more employees. This legal framework thus uses individual employment rights as a tool to decollectivize and desocialize advocacy for a healthy and safe working environment.

Given the available evidence from Canadian labor relations scholarship and the documentation of U.S. work refusal investigations, the limited legal protection of the right to refuse unsafe work as a stand-alone labor and employment policy represents nothing more than a failed approach and in turn a *false consensus* in global worker health and safety policy. It is ultimately neither in society's interest nor in a worker's interest. This model of worker protection instead serves employer interests. A new discussion is needed about the protection of workers' rights in the working environment. If society is to continue on its present course of atomizing worker advocacy in the working environment and enforcing labor rights models that buttress and protect the liberal market contours of the employment relationship, it is likely that occupational safety and health hazards will go on unabated as work-related illness and injury continue in a world of increasing precarity and poor working conditions.

Considering the complexity of workplace hazards and the convergence of occupational health and safety hazards with broader environmental protection issues in and outside of the working environment, the failure to establish real workplace or industrial representation systems where workers can ameliorate their environmental concerns bodes ill for the ecology of work and society. Ensuring effective rights for workers in the working environment is an endeavor too often ignored by market-based worker health and safety policy. Global worker health and safety policy under this paradigm of worker protection is ineffective and must be altered in response.

5

Ideological Origins of the Global Framework

The global norms on employee dissent and the right to refuse unsafe work were crafted under a strong Anglo-American influence. This history further informs our analysis of the mobilization of bias. The negotiation and adoption of Convention No. 155 involved intentional political activity that extended beyond a simple pressure tactic or influence-seeking mechanism commonly employed in labor policymaking. Cultural strategies played a formidable role. Culture in this context is defined not in the narrow sense used in everyday speech but as a general term used in social science to encompass all "symbolic and learned aspects of human society" including knowledge, beliefs, values, morals, ideas, and customs.[1] Through the reshaping and the negotiation of global worker health and safety policy, cultural strategies were used as effective influence-seeking strategies. These efforts created the current norms on refusal rights and the resulting false consensus within global health and safety policy.

New ideas emerged in the field of worker health and safety policy prior to the creation of Convention No. 155. These cultural ideas were spread and caused the ILO to undergo striking changes in its standards-setting policy on health and safety and the working environment. The right to refuse unsafe work played an important role in the construction of this narrative. The global influence of North America in the second half of the twentieth century made market-based policy models influential as the neoliberal "Washington Consensus" dominated international institutions from the 1970s onward. Today, Convention No. 155 is the ILO's primary global response to worker health and safety hazards. Adopted in 1981 after a period of social discontent with business and an increasing sentiment seeking social, economic and trade protection throughout the 1970s, Convention No. 155 was drafted and advocated as a strategy for more easily tying global labor standards to trade liberalization.[2] The self-regulatory logic underlying the labor convention made the demand for labor-standards-linked trade easier to digest for neoliberal advocates.

The United States pushed this debate by asking what the "truly minimum" international labor standards actually were. Health and safety was made subject to a managerialist set of values, beliefs, and cultural understandings. This worldview created a contested political negotiation for Convention No. 155. The right to refuse unsafe work was at key moments promoted by business to appease a suspicious global union leadership that was seeking stronger, more effective rights-based discrimination protections. Ultimately, refusal rights were used at key decision-making junctures to obtain tripartite support in lieu of stronger antidiscrimination protections. New values and beliefs emerged on health and safety and dictated a new range of acceptable policy choices. When worker representatives became suspicious and attempted to shift course in the negotiation, the accepted arena of values and beliefs that had been established made any change impossible. The result was a new chapter in the history of market consciousness and culture spread globally through a new era of managerialist thought on global health and safety policy.

When the United States returned to ILO membership in 1980, after a two-year absence, the first of two formal negotiations on Convention No. 155 had begun at the International Labour Conference.[3] The Employers' Group was among the strongest advocates globally for advancing what would become the new ILO values and cultural system in global labor rights policy. Canada, at the intersection of a British legacy of self-regulatory economic ideology, pro-market Fabian socialism in industrial relations, and a North American political culture of atomized market individualism, possessed the unique formula needed to blend the right to refuse unsafe work with this cultural political strategy. The recasting of the old-style values of British industrial relations voluntarism was the political response to an increasingly contentious debate on global trade and labor rights that had workers and environmental activists demanding government action to protect labor and worker rights.

These were cultural political strategies at work, designing a global labor rights policy that was not safe for workers, but instead was safe for private enterprise, managerial rights, and the liberalization of trade policy. An individual's right to be protected against employer discrimination for occupational health and safety activism was, in reality, of little to no importance.

The Antiworker Origins of the Convention No. 155 Values System

The first major postwar effort to reconceptualize the trajectory of labor policy on workers' health and safety developed in Great Britain. Alfred Robens, a member of the House of Commons since 1945, was considered the Labour Party's rising star. In 1960, however, Robens's career trajectory would change. He accepted the offer of Conservative prime minister Harold Macmillan to lead the National Coal Board, at the time "one of the most important nationalized industries" in Britain.[4]

The consummate politician, Robens enjoyed convening meetings "to discuss the big policy questions" with people in the industry. Raising the fears of many miners, a focus on productivity would run throughout his ten-year reign as NCB chairman.[5] In 1960 there were 602,000 workers "on colliery books." After ten years, 285,000 would remain.[6] Robens's primary focus was productivity, with occupational health and safety a distant secondary concern to the mechanization and automation of the coal industry.

This was the case until the black avalanche of October 21, 1966.

It began an otherwise normal morning as elementary students gathered to sing "All Things Bright and Beautiful" in an assembly at the Pantglas Junior School in the small Welsh mining village of Aberfan. Silence broke the song as the rumble of what some thought was a loud jet plane was heard approaching the building. In seconds, walls were collapsing and windows cracking as 140,000 cubic yards of dense liquefied coal mining byproduct called "tip complex" rushed down the nearby mountainside:

> Mr. Davis, our teacher, got the board out and wrote our maths class work and we were all working, and then it began. It was a tremendous rumbling sound and all the school went dead. You could hear a pin drop. Everyone was petrified, afraid to move. Everyone just froze in their seats. I just managed to get up and I reached the end of my desk when the sound got louder and nearer, 'til I could see the black out of the window. I can't remember any more but I woke up to find that a horrible nightmare had just begun in front of my eyes.
>
> I was there for about an hour and a half until the fire brigade found me. I heard cries and screams, but I couldn't move. The desk was jammed into my stomach and my leg was under the radiator. The little girl next to me was dead and her head was on my shoulder.[7]

The Aberfan disaster killed 116 children between the ages of seven and ten. Twenty-eight adults including five school teachers also perished. The disaster started a full-on political firestorm surrounding the leadership of Robens and the National Coal Board.

Robens would admit fault to a parliamentary tribunal, which placed the blame on the National Coal Board for failure to properly regulate health and safety and the working environment. This was not before a "devastating" report was released to the public as Robens explained in the weeks leading up to the final inquiry report about an "unknown hazard" in an "unknown spring" beneath the liquid byproduct. The village residents, however, informed the inquiry they "had known for years that the [National Coal Board] had been tipping on top of two streams." The inquiry pointed directly to the National Coal Board. Despite his apology, Robens was defiant with his "inconsistent answers" under cross-examination. He "hoped the Government would never again set up a tribunal of this nature" as it was "a conspiracy of silence" for not blaming the local NCB officers. The Aberfan disaster inquiry pointed to Robens's ineptitude:[8]

> As we shall hereafter seek to make clear, our strong and unanimous view is that the Aberfan disaster could and should have been prevented. We were not unmindful of the fact that strong words of calumny had been used before our Inquiry began. But the Report which follows tells not of wickedness but of ignorance, ineptitude and a failure in communications.[9]

The Aberfan inquiry cited "ignorance on the part of those charged at all levels with the siting, control and daily management of tips" and "bungling ineptitude on the part of those who had the duty of supervising and directing them." It found "failure on the part of those having knowledge of the factors which affect tip safety" and failure to in any meaningful way "communicate that knowledge and to see that it was applied."[10]

As the Aberfan disaster pushed Robens and the National Coal Board into full damage-control mode, Lord Robens became nasty. He initially offered fifty pounds compensation per bereaved family, holding fast at five hundred pounds after the public outcry. The NCB refused to remove the waste tips remaining above the village. Ministers were "advised against holding a memorial service at Westminster Abbey on the grounds that 'the Welsh Church was disestablished and had no claim on Westminster Abbey'." Buckingham Palace "discouraged the Lord-Lieutenant of Glamorgan from laying a wreath on the first anniversary of the disaster 'on the grounds that there will be an anniversary every year and no doubt there will be other disasters too'."[11]

The historic implications of the Aberfan disaster would provide one of the most ironic and odd political twists in modern labor policy. Robens would not only "survive a report condemning him in forthright and emotional terms"—an inquiry that concluded his actions were a part of the "ignorance, ineptitude" and "failure" that resulted in the gruesome deaths of 116 Welsh children. He "was able to bully and bluster out the remainder of his term of office until he was appointed to chair a committee reviewing the law on health and safety at work," a committee that concluded "that negligence of health and safety should not be a criminal offense."[12]

Robens would become chair of the major policy review ordered by the British Parliament to examine occupational safety and health. In a further twist of irony, the "Lord Robens Committee Report" outlined sweeping changes in the values, beliefs, and cultural approach to be taken by government to protect health and safety in the working environment. This cultural logic would not only be influential in Canada and the United States, it would over time form the basis for a sweeping and remarkable paradigm shift in global norms.[13] The importance of the Robens Committee's timing was acknowledged by industrial health experts. One professor noted that "although there have been a number of committees which have studied segments of the subject, there has never, until Robens, been a comprehensive review by a single body."[14]

The Robens Committee Report criticized the existence of nine health and safety statutes under separate legal authorities and recommended consolidating responsibility for worker health and safety under a single national authority.[15] The single national authority would assume the management of all statutory enforcement. The authority prescribed, however, was not to have strengthened enforcement powers or to empower trade unions. Instead, the value system constructed was a paradigm where worker health and safety was the responsibility of "day-to-day good management" and "a more effective self-regulating system."[16] Robens had repackaged the voluntarism of old for a new age:

> The first and perhaps the most fundamental defect of the statutory system is simply that there is too much law. . . .
> The primary responsibility for doing something about the present levels of occupational accidents and disease lies with those who create the risks and those who work with them. The point is quite crucial. Our present system encourages rather too much reliance on state regulation, and rather too little on personal responsibility and voluntary, self-generating effort. This imbalance must be redressed. A start should be made by reducing the sheer weight of the legislation. There is a role in the field for regulatory law and a role for government action. But these roles should be predominantly concerned not with detailed prescriptions for innumerable day-to-day circumstances but with influencing attitudes and with creating a framework for better safety and health organization and action by industry itself.[17]

The Robens Committee Report argued the best way to avoid the sluggishness of the regulatory state would be "to associate outside interests right from the start with the process of making regulations." Furthermore, the committee argued, "No further law should be made if the situation can be met by a voluntary code of practice."[18]

In responding to the parliamentary mandate to answer "What is wrong with the system?" the Robens Report wrote fondly of the Fabian industrial relations theorists: "None has put the matter more aptly than Sidney Webb," Robens exclaimed in the introduction of his final report. The Robens Report quoted Webb, who advocated market-based labor policy:

> This century of experiment in factory legislation affords a typical example of English practical empiricism. We began with no abstract theory of social

justice or the rights of man. We seem always to have been incapable even to taking a general view of the subject we were legislating upon. Each successive statute aimed at remedying a single ascertained evil. It was in vain that objectors urged that other evils, no more defensible, existed in other trades or amongst other classes, or with persons of ages other that those to which the particular Bill applied. Neither logic nor consistency, neither the over-nice consideration of even-handed justice nor the quixotic appeal of a general humanitarianism, was permitted to stand in the way of a practical remedy for a proved wrong.[19]

Robens and Webb were doppelgangers when it came to designing their labor policy solutions to unsafe working conditions. The solution, whatever it was to be, was not to interfere with business productivity and the idea of a self-regulating marketplace.

At a critical time in the history of policymaking on workers' health, safety, and the working environment, the Robens Report became an international sensation in the occupational health and safety field. The report was cited by the first OSHA leaders in the United States as they charted the new regulatory agency's enforcement strategy.[20] The inquiry also served as a model for a royal commission in Canada on workplace health and safety. Two years later, an employer-friendly model of labor policy on occupational safety and health had emerged and its underlying logic was one of classic managerialist self-regulation. Robens's prescriptions were cast as aiming to solve the problem of workplace accidents and injuries as the primary goal. They did not, however, address the rights of workers to refuse unsafe work. On the right to refuse unsafe work, Canada would be the country to offer its unique domestic experience as the model for the new international norm.

Reshaping the Right to Refuse Unsafe Work

Canada followed the Robens model closely, with key modifications. Within two years of the publication of the Robens Report, the Province of Ontario, as the most populous and industrialized province in Canada and holding jurisdiction over almost all private sector labor relations in that province, conducted an investigation seeking recommendations for worker health and safety policy. In 1974 James M. Ham was appointed to head the Ontario Royal Commission on the Health and Safety of Workers in the Mines (also known as the Ham Commission). Professor Ham was an MIT-trained engineer who had joined the Department of Electrical Engineering at the University of Toronto. At the time of his appointment to the Royal Commission he was dean of Applied Science and Engineering and would later be appointed president of the University of Toronto.[21]

Joining Ham on the commission was an industrial advisor, R. Peter Riggin. Riggin was vice president of corporate relations for Noranda Mines, Ltd., an established Canadian mining company incorporated in 1922. Edmund A. Perry was the commission's engineering advisor, a representative to the mining branch of the Council of the Association of Professional Engineers of Ontario. Jean Beaudry, a member of the staff of the United Steelworkers of America, was the labor advisor to the commission. Frederick Hume, a principal in the firm of Hume, Martin and Timmins, provided legal counsel. Cameron Gray, executive vice president of the Ontario Lung Disease Association and professor in the Department of Medicine at the University of Toronto, acted as medical consultant. Arthur L. Gladstone was the commission's executive secretary and did the heavy lifting for the group. Gladstone would play an important role as he was also the senior policy advisory to Bette M. Stephenson, a Progressive Conservative firebrand member of the Ontario Parliament and minister of labor from the York Mills riding.[22]

The nature of employer political influence in the Canadian polity made the role of the royal commission one of providing key political leadership. Michael Useem described this phenomenon in *The Inner Circle: Large Corporations and the Rise of Business Political Activity in the U.S. and U.K.* Useem observed how political action on matters important to business was the product of diffusely structured networks:

> These networks define a segment of the business community whose strategic location and internal organization propel it into a political leadership role on behalf of the entire corporate community. John Porter's description of Canada's system of power could equally well have been developed for the American and British counterparts. He closes his study of the Canadian "vertical mosaic" with the conclusion that the multiple directors linking the country's large corporations "are the ultimate decisionmakers and coordinators within the private sector of the economy. It is they who at the frontiers

of economic and political systems represent the interests of corporate power. They are the real planners of the economy."[23]

John Porter's sweeping study of Canadian society and decision making singled out the imperative role of the use of the royal commission as important shapers of discourse. The various royal commissions are "outstanding among the official bodies in which the economic elite are found." Royal commissions are "not composed exclusively of the corporate elite" because in most cases they are put together "to represent various institutional orders."[24] Porter noted that often the "economic elite" provide significant input and influence on royal commissions to assure that the various private sector interests are protected. The extension of power beyond the boardrooms occurs by the "creation of a cultural social product" able to extend power "beyond the economic system."[25]

These cultural strategies aim "to make their ideology pervade the entire society until it becomes identified with the common good." If, at times, they "accept changes like labour legislation or health insurance," wrote Porter on Canada's political culture, "it is not because of an opposing social movement based on class conflict, but because other elites, such as the political, are at work seeking to consolidate their power" as the ideology articulated by one sector of elite actors is adopted as the ideology for all:[26]

> In public debate words often undergo a strange metamorphosis. . . . From the point of view of social power it is not so much a question of whether these propositions are true or false, but rather the influence the corporate elite has far beyond their own board rooms. The ideology they articulate becomes that of all business large or small.[27]

In the Canadian context, the Ontario Royal Commission on the Health and Safety of Workers in the Mines, although focused on the extractive industries in one province alone, was a broad exercise of political debate that would shape labor policy across domestic jurisdictions. The importance of the extractive sector to the economy in Canada and the stature of private interests within Ontario only served to heighten the influence of the Ham Commission in establishing this future labor policy trajectory.

More important than the various technical findings discussed by the final report of the royal commission, known as the Ham Commission

Report, is the overall cultural system on workplace health and safety that set forth the terms of the debate on each page and in every chapter. Great Britain was first among the countries visited by the Ham commissioners in the course of fact-finding and the work of the Robens Report is discussed in the Ham Commission Report. Like Robens, Ham made sweeping recommendations for changing worker health and safety policy to move to a system of voluntarism and the self-regulation of private enterprise.[28]

The Ham Commission concerned itself with uncovering the "defects in the institutional arrangements" among "government, industry, and the workers for dealing with the hazards at work." The "overriding concern" was to "establish a more coherent basis for government, industry, and the workforce to deal with the problems of industrial disease and accidents according to their skills and in accordance with well-defined duties and responsibilities."[29] The commission, in keeping with the themes of the Robens Report and its focus on self-regulation, defined the need for what it called an "internal responsibility-system at the company level" and described this as "key to the quality of the over-all control of occupational hazards."[30] In turning to define an "internal responsibility-system" the commission advanced a razor-sharp tone against unions and collective bargaining.

"Questions of health and safety" said the commission, "are not suitable issues for collective bargaining." What was needed was "a carefully defined framework" of joint labor-management health and safety committees. Workers must "fulfill a proper responsibility to contribute to the resolution of problems of health and safety," said the commission, which hoped for a "new measure of labour-management co-operation." "The adamantly confrontational character of Canadian labour-management relations," it said, "has deterred the creation of sensible arrangements for worker participation":

> The Commission believes that a part of the wide variation in accident frequencies among different companies is related to the quality of human relations that exist within them, relations in which both management and the collective bargaining unit (where such exists) play crucial roles. A well-founded internal responsibility-system in which labour and management co-operate to control occupational hazards ought to exhibit a high measure of self-regulation for which mines inspection and openly reported environmental and epidemiological reviews can provide the necessary external evaluation.[31]

The Ham Commission advised that health and safety issues be divorced from workers' freedom of association and collective bargaining. This was the consolidation of an institutional framework on worker health and safety within the logic of voluntaristic self-regulation that had served for years as the ideological basis for Anglo-American labor relations.

Unlike the Robens Report, the Ham Commission embraced the right to refuse unsafe work. It argued that it was "the responsibility of the shift boss to assign work and to decide if the conditions for that work meet standards for its performance." Given the importance of the right to refuse to mineworkers, however, the Ham Commission found themselves in a corner with their anti-collective-bargaining stance. Any "substantive difference in judgment between a worker and his shift boss about a condition of work" would be "a relatively infrequent event." This assessment was asserted despite what the commission had called the "adamantly confrontational" nature of industrial and labor relations. Protecting some form of a very limited employee dissent through the right to refuse within this framework was devised as the solution.

The Ham Commission recommended legislating a restricted right to refuse and argued such a right could be adequately protected within the framework of an "internal responsibility-system." The state would act as the last resort to determine the merit of the hazard under protest. All work refusals must have the approval of management:

> That where a worker, after due consultation with his immediate supervisor, believes that the work then assigned cannot be performed by standard procedures without encountering personal risks deemed by him to be unreasonable, there be a statutory requirement that the work situation be examined and judged by a member of senior supervision in the presence of a worker-auditor acting as an observer and that a report of the circumstances be made by the mines inspectorate to the manager.[32]

Ham recognized that these situations "would by their nature be ones of great tension between the workman and his supervisor." Nonetheless, the report argued, "the worker has a right in natural justice" that "a well-considered disagreement in judgment between himself and his immediate supervisor about the risks of work" is "fairly examined" without "discrimination for having stood by his convictions."[33]

For the Ham Commission, the *internal* responsibility system shaped "external" state intervention. Management rights would be defined as "internal" rights, requiring the state to stay away, and the "natural right" to refuse would be subject to protection only after a "well-considered" disagreement and a "fair examination" of the risks was made. Supervisory and governmental authorities would determine whether a workers' action was well considered, subjecting refusal rights to both internal supervisory control and external state review via a new formulaic procedure.

Worker Opposition to the New Refusal Formula

The effort to consolidate occupational health and safety law and policy into a single self-regulatory framework was unfolding as Canadian labor advocates pushed for stronger, hard-law basic labor rights protections. As the demand for change continued, managing dissent would become an important political task. Workplace health and safety advocates challenged the elite political discourse of the Ham Commission in Ontario as well as in Saskatchewan.

Hard law on health and safety had been the Canadian tradition. Most Canadian jurisdictions at the time could prosecute employers for violating health and safety legislation.[34] Seven jurisdictions were empowered to levy fines and imprisonment of between three to twelve months for an offense of health and safety legislation. Between 1971 and 1973, Québec initiated 1,130 prosecutions and Ontario initiated 1,359 prosecutions under these health and safety laws.[35] Some provinces also permitted lawsuits by workers against some employers to seek compensation for workplace accident and injuries.[36]

The story of Saskatchewan begins the history of the political management of dissent surrounding the right to refuse. Saskatchewan was a unique case because the political history of populist agrarian socialism coupled with the lack of a politically aggressive private sector in a provincial economy dominated by farm cooperatives and crown corporations afforded policymakers a unique window of opportunity through which to craft and advocate significant creative labor policy changes throughout the 1970s without any well-organized and coordinated private business opposition.

The New Democratic Party of Saskatchewan held power from 1971 to 1982 and formed a government under party leader Allan Blakeney. He had served in the cabinet of the revered Thomas C. Douglas who helped establish the first public health-care system in North America. The NDP came to power on a campaign called New Deal for People and won forty-five of the sixty provincial assembly seats.[37] The Saskatchewan NDP introduced the Occupational Health and Safety Act modeled on the U.S. Occupational Safety and Health Act of 1970.[38] The 1972 act consolidated occupational health and safety into one administration and mandated that joint labor-management committees on occupational health be established in every workplace with more than ten employees.[39]

In time, the Saskatchewan Federation of Labor "complained to the Minister of Labour that they were dissatisfied with the administration of the Act, especially with regard to the role of workers on the joint committees." In response to the continuing complaints to the NDP government, the minister of labour advocated strengthening the laws. In 1973, the right to refuse was proposed as an amendment to the provincial Labour Standards Act as a way to strengthen these joint committees.[40] The new right to refuse clause prompted "outspoken employers in the province to criticize this amendment as unnecessary."[41] Organized labor generally supported the clause as a way to strengthen the rights of workers on the joint health and safety committees.

Strengthening the joint labor-management health and safety committees would be an important issue to the NDP in Saskatchewan between 1971 and 1982. This was to include a unique series of actions in support of the committees, including requiring the labor ministry to keep a central registry of all health and safety committees in the province, including the names of their members. Each joint health and safety committee was required to record the minutes of each meeting and supply the meeting minutes to the provincial labor ministry, which would in turn make the minutes public. By 1981 there were more than 2,800 joint health and safety committees covering 80 percent of the Saskatchewan nonfarm workforce. Government records had been collected on 29,723 committee meetings between 1972 and 1981.[42] When the NDP lost the 1982 election, among the first acts of the new Progressive Conservative government of Grant Devine was to destroy the computerized files and end the practice of a central government registration and monitoring of these joint health and safety committees.[43]

After a 1977 amendment, the language of the Saskatchewan statute robustly protected the right to refuse by including broad prohibitions on discrimination against health and safety activists with presumptions in favor of workers. The statute defined discrimination as "any action by an employer which adversely affects a worker with respect to any terms or conditions of employment or opportunity for promotion, and includes the action of dismissal, layoff, suspension, demotion, transfer of job or location, reduction in wages, change in hours of work or reprimand." The law had a presumption in favor of the worker where discrimination was alleged and empowered the health and safety committee to investigate workplaces. "The onus shall be upon the employer to establish that the worker was discriminated against for good and sufficient other reasons" it read.[44]

Although the right to refuse was codified in Saskatchewan under an "unusually dangerous" standard, this was "unusually dangerous" to a given worker's health and not "unusually dangerous" for a given industry. The protection extended to workers "by reason of the fact that he has exercised" the right to refuse, and not based on any hazard threshold. This was not the limited refusal model formulated by the Ham Commission. The Saskatchewan model protected the right to refuse unsafe work as a fundamental human right. Bob Sass, who worked in the Ministry of Labour at the time, described these basic refusal rights as based in an Aristotelian philosophy of knowledge and experience. The workers' experience was coequal to society's knowledge about what constituted a hazard worthy of affording the right to refuse.

Saskatchewan's occupational health and safety committees were empowered with the authority to investigate as government labor inspectors, including investigating work refusals. In a pilot project at the Potash Corporation a Work Environment Board was established to deal with "*all* matters pertaining to the work environment."[45] A worker chaired the committee, thus giving the workers a majority. This approach was started with an eye toward expanding the idea throughout the private sector. What was certain about how the Saskatchewan model was developing was that it was not a laissez-faire industrial relations enterprise. The state had a key role in establishing strong health and safety committees. This included mandates on the subjects that were to be discussed in the committees, as well as requirements to consult, cooperate, and to protect against discrimination.

The government considered this expansion of rights a policy it called "stretching" the current law:

> Such an expansion or "stretch" more directly confronts management prerogatives. Employers have demonstrated greater resistance to this expansion than to expenditures relating to lowering noise, better ventilation, machine guarding, chemical substitution, and provision of safety equipment of all sorts. This "stretch" . . . is seen as an unwarranted intrusion upon management's legitimate right to manage (for example, to pursue greater productivity and efficiency) through absolute control over the human factor of production. This resistance was evident in Saskatchewan, as elsewhere.[46]

An expansion or "stretch" was the case as Bob Sass and the Ministry of Labour offered blanket support to all work refusals. Between the 1973 work refusal law and the end of the government in 1982, over fifteen hundred individual work refusals were reported to the Ministry of Labour in Saskatchewan. All work refusals were protected as if there was a universal protection.[47]

As a political expedient, strong enforcement was an effort to keep the alliance between the NDP and organized labor intact in the wake of unpopular NDP support for wage and price controls. Strong protection of refusal rights kept the party-labor alliance together. This Saskatchewan model, however, was in conflict with the internal responsibility system proposed by the Ham Commission in Ontario. In Saskatchewan it was understood that there was an important role for the government, because the state was needed to enforce workers' rights. Trade unionists, nevertheless, expressed skepticism about protecting the right to refuse through an individualistic legal framework, even as they were supportive of strengthening the law. Sass would later reflect upon the countermobilization against these policies: "In 1977 and 1978, all provincial governments and industry began a counter-plot to the rights-based approach with the intent of reducing the legislation to a mere paper and returning to a pre-rights-based approach."[48] The Saskatchewan model was threatened by Ham's new internal responsibility ideology.

In Ontario, Bill 139, an Act Respecting Employees' Health and Safety, passed the Legislative Assembly in early 1977, the same time that the NDP in Saskatchewan was strengthening their refusal rights law. Bill 139 was interim legislation, a trial run at reform that would be replaced with permanent legislation after one year in Bill 70. Bill 139 established a formula for work refusals for a broad test of danger. This was a move, as in Saskatchewan, toward considering the right to refuse unsafe work as an absolute right. It contrasted with other provincial laws such as those in Manitoba where a worker could be disciplined for refusing to work for a "frivolous" reason.

In Canada, it was organized labor's position that collective bargaining was the best mechanism for dealing with safety and health hazards in the work environment:

> Labour's basic position is that it has often been impractical for a worker to refuse to undertake a hazardous job on an individual basis, either out of fear of victimization, or because the well-being of fellow workers may also be jeopardized. The fact that the degree of protection afforded workers through legislation, regulatory enforcement, and arbitration practice has often been viewed as inadequate, and has otherwise varied widely over the years, is cited as support for greater union involvement in such situations.[49]

Trade unions and labor leaders in Canada were not at first entirely opposed to the new laws on occupational safety and health. As the policy debate shifted to the use of health and safety committees, however, the right to refuse by an individual worker was prescribed as a way to strengthen joint committees. It was written in articles at the time that the right to refuse for a health and safety committee was akin to the right to strike for a trade union. In this context, although there was organized labor support for the right to refuse for individuals, collective bargaining was organized labor's preferred method of advocating for the rights of workers. This stance was perhaps in part the result of a self-interested institutional bias, but certainly there was also a broader and deeper understanding of the inherent lived inequalities in the employment relationship that realized that employee rights could not generally be effective as exclusively individual rights.

The Ontario legislature had been considering a new law on occupational health and safety well before the Ham Commission reported in 1976. Ham's recommendations, however, shaped the discourse of the final Bill 70. The Ontario Federation of Labour thought the progressive elements of Bill 139 would be brought forward into the omnibus Bill 70. The concerns of labor on occupational safety and health had been growing throughout the 1970s. The activism of Stephen Lewis as the leader of the left-of-center Ontario New Democratic Party and the NDP's "specific and persistent criticism" in part led to the push for reform. The Ham Commission served to consolidate the activists' discourse along safer, more palatable, political lines.[50] When the new Bill 70 was reported in the legislature, organized labor quickly realized how the notion of rights could be used against them. The right to refuse was made into a restricted, limited right. The draft permanent bill included what the sociologist Vivienne Walters called "built-in deterrents" advocated by management and corporate leaders to the minister of labour. It caused an uproar within the labor movement.[51]

Organized labor considered the new legislation "regressive" and challenged the constitution of the right to refuse. Business views were notably split on refusal rights between two camps, those corporations opposed to the protection of any employee rights on the one hand versus the more politically savvy companies and employer associations that viewed the Ham Commission's constitution of the right to refuse unsafe work as a way to remove worker health and safety from under trade unions and collective bargaining. Employer briefs submitted to the Ham Commission in response to a survey by the Ministry of Labour in Ontario requesting reaction to the interim Bill 139 and as part of the hearings of the Resources Development Committee of the Ontario Legislature, illustrate that many employers supported this new right to refuse.

The new draft law was applauded by the Canadian Manufacturers Association: "We concur with the approach taken by the government on many of the items in Bill 70, especially those pertaining to safety committees and the right of refusal to work." The Dominion Foundries and Steel Company was "pleased with the approach that the Bill takes in three areas; right of refusal to work; health and safety committees and/or representatives and toxic substances." Other employers opposed the inclusion of any new employment rights on the matter of occupational safety and health.[52]

When the new version of the proposed law was released, organized labor was "mortified" at the changes. One Ontario Federation of Labor delegate called it "a piece of garbage." Labor's opposition solidified around their "profound disappointment" with the work of the minister of labor and the failure to provide strong antidiscrimination protections for workers protesting working conditions. Workers were being treated as "guinea pigs" and the new bill was "infuriatingly indifferent" to the prevention of health hazards.[53]

Modifications would be made before passage, yet the labor movement had been bested by the business community. Employers had influenced the drafting process and effectively moved the bill toward overall weaker protections. In the words of one trade union leader, the employers refused to face the social calamity, instead opting for a sophisticated politicization of the worker health and safety issue:

> It is as though there has been, in the last five years, no deaths from cancer of sintering plant workers, no Gus Frobel to single-handedly wage an unforgivably difficult struggle to win compensation for lung cancer induced by radiation exposure, no Matachewan, no Johns-Manville deaths from asbestos-induced cancer, no deaths from vinyl chloride induced cancer, no liver damage from PCB ingestion and so on and so on.[54]

Organized labor remained disappointed with the reform. Three years after the law was passed, the Ontario NDP established a task force to study the new Occupational Health and Safety Act of 1978. Visiting ten cities across the province—Hamilton, Sudbury, Thunder Bay, Peterborough, St. Catherine's, Ottawa, Toronto, Kitchener, London, and Windsor—an advisory committee of twenty-eight leading union health and safety activists held hearings and collected over two hundred statements from individual workers and union members, university experts and environmental activists with experience with the new internal responsibility system. The task force report opened with a quote published by the ILO in 1963; the International Labour Organization had asserted clearly that the objective of occupational health is "the promotion and maintenance of the highest degree of physical, mental and social well-being of workers in all occupations."[55] Ironically, this history would in time help to change this strong policy of the ILO.

The report found "workers struggling to use the Act to improve health and safety conditions in their workplaces."[56] The law "left workers vulnerable to the economic decisions of their employers" and in a new dependency on "the willingness of management to institute suggested reforms." When workers faced "an uncooperative management, workers had far too little power to make their workplaces safe":[57]

The Task Force was told repeatedly that the Internal Responsibility System did not work. The imbalance of power between workers and management meant cooperation and information-sharing often broke down to the detriment of workers' health and safety. As long as management enjoys a monopoly over final decisions to clean up the workplace, health and safety conditions can never be improved to the satisfaction of workers.[58]

Joint health and safety committees were charged with being "management-orientated." Unions recounted fruitless correspondence to the Ministry of Labor trying to correct the inequality in committee assignments. Union representatives also complained of no central registry of the joint health and safety committees under the new Ontario law.

On the right to refuse unsafe work, the worker had no legal right to assistance by her fellow workers and had to engage in work refusals on their own. The task force dedicated a special section to the right to refuse dangerous work under the new law. The final report of the task force said in no uncertain terms that the right to refuse was a failure.

Recognizing that the right to refuse was one of the most important rights to be protected by the new legislative act, the task force reported that many workers found it not to their advantage to refuse hazardous work out of a fear of discharge and losing their livelihood. Labor inspectors treated work refusals as simple complaints to health and safety inspectors. By not recognizing refusals as protected rights, labor inspectors left workers more vulnerable to termination even as they cited employers for health and safety hazards identified by the worker as being the cause of their work refusal.[59]

The New Democratic Party task force report recommended specific changes to the statute protecting the right to refuse unsafe work. Among the changes sought was protection of group work refusals, extending protections beyond a narrow definition of hazards to include hazards such as causes of stress, assault, and attempted assault, extending the law to all workers, and providing wage and benefit protection.[60] "The needless loss of one human life due to preventable occupational illness or accident," they argued, "is too heavy a premium."[61] The final report recommended adopting the ILO's standard of "the promotion and maintenance of the highest degree of physical, mental and social well-being of workers in all occupations."[62]

Another task force was organized on similar lines on the impact of health and safety reforms in the federal jurisdiction. That inquiry visited twenty-five cities and offered similar recommendations, reporting there were "Too Few Laws, Too Little Order" in what was a clear rhetorical swipe at Lord Alfred Robens and his original conclusion that there was "too much law" in his influential final committee report.[63] A third investigation, a follow-up task force in Ontario three years later found that the lack of changes in the legal regime were objectionable. It reported that many workers were "still not healthy, still not safe."[64]

Sass would later comment on the triumph of the internal responsibility ideology as current public policy. Ontario "took the lead" with "the intent of containing the occupational health and safety 'movement' and the demand for strong worker rights challenging that sacred fortress: Management prerogatives."[65] The idea of internal responsibility was used as a tool for business countermobilization:

> The IRS [internal responsibility system] became a code word for both employers and public policy regulators to bring work environment matters back into line. And this strategy required a shift from worker rights to the pre-OSHA practices of ensuring the privileged status of the varied experts and professionals who shape occupational health and safety. These experts were to again be the ultimate arbiters in worker/union disputes with employers and government regulators.
>
> It has, in fact, "tightened the noose" about worker activation and gripped workers and unions in a neo-liberal corporate agenda. The role of naïve and not so naïve "experts" orchestrated by their government and employer masters succeeded in undermining the occupational health and safety "movement."[66]

The emergent "safe rights" from this period would become the model for the rest of the world through the passage of a new kind of global norm via a new ILO health and safety convention.

The international community, throughout the drafting and adoption of a new global strategy for occupation safety and health, failed to recognize the domestic dissent of the organized labor movement across North America when it crafted the new global norm on a worker's right to a healthy and safety working environment. Two years after these Canadian legal changes, the ILO Governing Body decided to begin the official negotiation of a new global labor standard on occupational safety and health and the working environment. The limited refusal rights model had emerged across North America as a dominant policy strategy, including within eight Canadian jurisdictions that had by that time adopted reforms incorporating this refusal rights model: Nova Scotia, Ontario, Manitoba, Saskatchewan, Alberta, British Columbia, Québec, and Newfoundland. Similar language spread across the continent from "dangerous" and "unusually dangerous" to "hazardous" and "imminent danger" while workers and the organized labor movement continued to argue that the right to refuse unsafe work was an absolute right.[67] The idea that emerged wedded the limited right to refuse to notions of voluntary, managerialist self-regulation as North America served as the experimental laboratory for what would become the global model for regulating employee dissent in the working environment.

Negotiating "Safe" Rights versus Seeking Social Justice

The Anglo-American experience with regulating worker activism for occupational health and safety would in time be modeled around the world. As the United States pushed the "Washington Consensus" internationally, Canada would use its domestic experience with refusal rights on the global stage. The International Labour Affairs department at Labour Canada recognized the value of the intellectual precepts of the internal responsibility ideology early on as the solution to the global health and safety question. John Mainwaring, representing Canada at the ILO in Geneva, gave a review of international labor conventions in a report issued shortly after the Robens Report was published. He proposed a new "Modern International Labour Code" and advocated modernization of the ILO. The goal was "to redefine the role that standards-setting should play in the context of the ILO's program of action." This was needed as "the very quantity of ILO Conventions seem to defeat the purpose of using them as a measure of social progress." On occupational safety and health, Mainwaring wrote "there may also be a need for a policy framework for standard setting on specific hazards, as an improvement on the present rather arbitrary approach to the selection of subjects for Conventions."[1]

Canada's view came at a time of a growing consensus among all ILO delegates that new action was needed to address hazards in the working environment. Francis Blanchard was for years involved with technical assistance to developing countries under the direction of David Morse, the long-serving Truman confidant and one-time acting U.S. secretary of labor. Blanchard as director-general gained broad support as "practical" and "a sound administrator, forward looking, of warm human qualities, dedicated to the ILO's human rights objectives and to its principles, not a spell-binding orator but a convincing speaker."[2] He set the tone for the work of the ILO:

> Our world is striving for greater justice, which must be brought about gradually within each nation and among nations. The ILO must play a larger role in working out measures adapted to meeting these expectations. That implies that [the ILO] will remain a special place for dialogue and for interchange, a centre of reflection and research. It implies that it will deal realistically and boldly with bringing international labour standards up to date, and with working out new standards which should inspire governments, employers and workers to meet demands for greater equality of opportunity, greater security and greater human dignity.[3]

The first meeting of the Governing Body under Blanchard's direction set the agenda for a long-term plan for the years 1976 to 1981. "In striving to improve working and social conditions" the plan set forth a list of areas where greater concentration of ILO efforts was required. Among the top three items for ILO action on the list after the standard postwar agenda items of "promoting employment" and "developing skills and aptitudes for work" was a new item that had emerged in response to what Blanchard would later call the need to avoid "disruptions and disorder in the social systems quite out of proportion with the economic costs of any lucid measure to improve conditions of work." The ILO under Blanchard's leadership would now pursue new strategies for "improving working conditions and humanizing work."[4]

Another stated goal of the ILO's work agenda was "helping trade liberalization" through "increased efforts to secure ratification and observance of international labour standards."[5] The director-general was asked by the ILO Governing Body to "appeal to all governments which have not yet done so to give the most serious consideration to ratifying and putting into practice International Labour Conventions bearing on fair labour standards."[6] Blanchard's 1975 report to the International Labour Conference *Making Work More Human: Working Conditions and the Environment*, cited "a complete lack of progress" on the frequency of accidents in countries such as India where rates had increased by 50 percent the previous decade. Emerging hazards were cause for alarm as "the first victims of toxic substances are the workers." Blanchard's report asked "how many new products appear on the market each year whose effects on the human being are not really known?"[7] He continued to detail the global problems of the working environment, citing specific hazards such as vinyl chloride, ergonomics, the role of working time, and the organization and content of work. He concluded with a call for opening a dialog on the role of a new international labor standard that could serve as a basis to improve the working environment and make the experience of work and employment for millions of workers worldwide "tolerable or even attractive."[8]

The November 1978 Governing Body meeting started the drafting process for Convention No. 155 by officially placing the item on the agenda of the International Labor Conference for standard-setting. Canada held one of ten seats reserved for countries of chief industrial importance. It was also recognized as the chair of the newly formed and authoritative Industrialized Market Economy Countries caucus, a forum used to maintain a U.S. connection to and presence at the ILO during its lapsed membership.[9]

Canada spoke in support of drafting a new convention on safety and health and the working environment. Canada joined the United Kingdom in urging that the new draft convention, however, encompass "the broader approach to the problems of the working environment generally now being taken in a number of countries."[10] At the Governing Body meeting in November 1978 it agreed to move forward on Francis Blanchard's vision, encouraging "a broader approach." The ILO Governing Body moved to include on the agenda of the 66th session of the International Labour Conference the consideration of a new standard on Occupational Safety and Health and the Working Environment.

The ILO prepared the law and practice report used as the basis for drafting Convention No. 155 that eventually led to inclusion of a right to refuse. Questions were framed in a way that asked about a voluntarist, self-regulating approach. The original question on the right to refuse was Question 28 and posed an inquiry to each ILO member government in two parts:

Question 28—

(1) Should the instrument(s) provide that a worker has the right to refuse to commence work, or to cease work, when, through his knowledge and experience, he has reason to believe that there would be a high risk to life or health if he carried out the assigned task, on condition that he makes an immediate report, as envisaged in question 27(d)?

(2) Should the instrument(s) provide further that no measures prejudicial to a worker should be taken by reference to the fact that, in good faith, he complained of what he considered to be a breach of statutory requirements or a serious gap in the measures taken by the undertaking in respect of safety and health and the working environment?

Sixty-three countries replied to the two part Question 28, forty-nine in the affirmative, including Canada. The United Kingdom joined the minority in dissent. No other question in the law and practice report was posed regarding any form of antidiscrimination measure.

Canada was *the only country* to report that their national practice included the protection of the right to refuse as an individual employment protection outside the domain of trade union protection and workers' freedom of association. Although a majority of governments responded to the original Law and Practice survey agreeing in principle to the protection against prejudice and discrimination faced by workers advocating occupational safety and health, the majority had expressed very serious reservations about protecting the right to refuse unsafe work, especially about how it would work within an exclusively individualistic framework.[11]

Question 28 described the dominant legal model practiced in North America: an obligation to report to management before exercising the right coupled with the need for an outside evaluation of the hazard to assess the legitimacy of the worker's claim to protection. In response to Question 28 (1), Canada answered, "Yes. Such a right is now widely recognized and is explicitly provided for in the safety and health legislation of most Canadian jurisdictions." On Question 28 (2), Canada responded, "Yes, this is essential for the protection of the worker against discriminatory action; without this provision, workers (especially unorganized ones) will be reluctant to refuse unsafe assignments or to report serious hazards to safety or health."[12] There was no mention or discussion in the documentary record of the domestic dissent across North America against this model of protection of the right to refuse.

Despite Canada's enthusiasm, however, the ILO excluded refusal rights from the draft convention's national policy section. Some governments argued "such a provision may lead to abuses or strained labour-management relations." The refusal rights provisions that would emerge in the first draft of the new labor convention on occupational safety and health were moved to a section dedicated to employer action entitled "Action at the Level of the Undertaking" and thus were associated with a self-regulatory legal framework approach.[13]

Negotiating Global Norms in a Culture of Disempowerment

After a two-year exile from ILO membership, the United States wasted no time projecting itself upon its return. "The ILO should identify the most appropriate means for providing protection to the workers and trainees *while at the same time satisfying other objectives*," said Ray Marshall, U.S. secretary of labor and U.S. delegate to the 1980 International Labour Conference in Geneva (emphasis added). This speech began an important new chapter in the larger effort to set the narrative for the negotiation of the new international health and safety labor convention within a much broader conceptual and philosophical orientation.[14]

Of primary concern to the United States was the growing social antagonism to economic globalization and world trade. The impact of trade policies on human rights was being questioned internationally, including by advocates of a new international economic order.[15] Linking global trade to global labor standards, whatever shape that idea might ultimately take, had emerged as a U.S. foreign policy objective.[16] The U.S. delegation was ready to help the ILO work toward "the development of a system of minimum international labor standards." It was as if the United States had just learned about the ILO's standard-setting efforts, despite its work setting minimum standards since 1919. For the United States it was a world made new and the ILO history should be rewritten. Marshall asked what were "the truly minimum standards" and how the ILO could be supported with technical assistance projects to help countries with "true" standards. In his opening statement on the United States rejoining the ILO, Marshall laid out his views on how to help the ILO discover what the truly minimum international labor standards were:[17]

> First, does there now exist a basic set of truly minimum international la-bour standards which are universally accepted—or with few exceptions—in every region of the world? Second, is it possible to develop a specific set of multilateral technical co-operation programs which would assist all coun-tries in meeting such minimum international labour standards? Third, what role might the ILO play in any future system of minimum interna-tional labour standards in ascertaining the extent to which these basic stan-dards are in fact being implemented in practice? An analysis based on these questions would provide an essential point of reference for subsequent con-sideration by the ILO or other organizations of the development of a system of minimum international labour standards.[18]

"In the field of occupational safety and health," Marshal explained, "the ILO can play a unique role in the family of international organizations." As the conference made its assignments to a committee on safety and health that would draft the convention, Marshall explained, "the U.S. Govern-ment representative in the Committee on Safety and Health will expand on this suggestion in the days ahead." He ultimately clarified the aim of the United States:

> Our aim is to ensure that international trade flourishes under conditions which permit workers in all countries to benefit up to their full potential. We do not seek to propose a specific across-the-board minimum wage. Nor do we consider that all of the ILO's standards represent minimum levels of protection. Some standards are clearly, deliberately and correctly "promo-tional" in nature; that is, they establish desirable goals rather than minimum requirements.[19]

"The ILO must not avoid controversial ideas," Marshall said, "nor should it rush blindly into them." What was needed was a "careful and objective review of the facts," which meant reviewing "the case of minimum inter-national labor standards" especially on safety and health at work.[20]

As the Committee on Safety and Health gaveled to order at the 66th conference in 1980, the U.S. government representative was elected to the post of reporter, a key responsibility for reporting the work of the committee to the full conference. The United States held this position at both the committee's 1980 and 1981 meetings, seeing the drafting of Convention No. 155 through the ILO's double discussion process, the practice of negotiating a new international labor standard at two meetings of the International Labour Conference before adoption. The committee elected as chair a government delegate from Poland, with an employers' representative from the U.K. and a workers' representative from the Netherlands as vice chairs. These officers, along with one additional member, a French government delegate, would lead the work of negotiating the new convention. The total membership of the Committee on Safety and Health numbered 140, including seventy government delegates, twenty-nine employer members, and forty-one from workers' organizations.[21]

That the leadership of the drafting committee itself was composed entirely of ILO members from Europe and the United States was not expressed as a concern. "All countries were developing countries from the point of view of safety and health and the working environment," said Danuta Koradecka, the committee chair from the Polish government. This would prove a handy mantra that would be repeated throughout the negotiations.[22]

The committee's leadership encouraged adoption of "a new and complementary mode of approaching the question" of health and safety versus what it called "the piecemeal approach of the existing standards," which numbered "some 50 instruments." The draft before the committee "covered the entire question of the prevention of occupational hazards and the improvement of the working environment." The task at hand was to draft a labor convention "to lay the foundations for a national policy to establish as far as possible a total and coherent system of prevention, taking into consideration the present-day realities of the working world." The convention was "not a text which necessarily called for immediate action," but would instead claim to "promote the progressive application of new and far-reaching measures at the national level."[23] This new approach was "complimentary" to the more traditional notion of creating global norms outlining specific and concrete legal obligations. The new approach was billed as being able to promote "far-reaching measures" without any call for any immediate action through specific labor law and policy changes.

The cultural landscape for the negotiations had been laid. Excluded were any fixed standards (they were characterized as piecemeal approaches). The "present-day realities" needed "far-reaching measures" to protect workers. This meant not following the ILO's traditional role of adopting specific and fixed legal norms against discrimination but rather vague principles that would be more flexible and made subject to various national practices, ensuring a greater chance more countries would ratify the new convention. The organized labor movement, acting on the international level through the ILO workers' delegation, offered no counter narrative to these ideas.

The ILO's Employers' Group articulated concise, well-planned goals. They would accept a convention that followed four principles as "suitable criteria." First, "the whole purpose of the instruments must be to influence what happened at the workplace. Legislation had limited effect unless supported by both the employer and the workers at the workplace and was seen by them to make sense." Second, "employers and workers had a common interest" and "favourable results at the workplace could best be achieved by co-operation rather than confrontation." Third, any "elaboration of legal requirements" must not "erode the clear line of responsibility" at the workplace, with "employers accepting that they must bear the primary responsibility" for protecting workers. Fourth, the convention "must aim at instruments which would be widely capable of ratification, bearing in mind national practices both as regards to legal systems and enforcement arrangements." The Workers' Group members proposed no such framework of principles but shared the employers' seemingly honest concern with health and safety. They stated in earnest that they hoped for a new global standard with a "full legal basis" and that all workers in all sectors, from civil servants to domestic workers, would be covered without exception.[24]

As negotiations for the new labor treaty continued through the first meeting of the Committee on Safety and Health, the draft convention discussed was promotional, held a flexible, self-regulatory logic, and afforded significant latitude to "national practices and conditions" on key provisions that narrowed the basis on which traditional ILO international legal supervision of domestic law could occur. This was a major paradigm shift in occupational health and safety labor standards at the ILO, a body with a rich history of specific and concrete norms.[25]

Discrimination protections were nowhere to be found in the draft text passed after the first negotiation. The Workers' Group had proposed a new clause to address the issue of discrimination against health and safety activists. "Real-world experience" made the Workers' Group advocate strong discrimination protection. The employers were adamantly against any amendments, arguing that the issue of discrimination "was out of place in an instrument concerning safety and health." Some governments supported antidiscrimination laws but only to protect against retaliation for contacting health and safety inspectors, not for worker self-help activity like the right to refuse unsafe work. Others sided with employers and opposed the idea. Still others argued that antidiscrimination protections be moved to the nonbinding recommendation being drafted simultaneously, and not be in the stronger mechanism of the legally binding international labor convention. Amendments on discrimination protection failed to pass in the 1980 negotiation and the workers vowed to raise the issue of discrimination at the second and final negotiation in June 1981.[26]

As the first negotiation for Convention No. 155 drew to a close, the Workers' Group had brought forth a new proposal for workers' protection, this time specifically on the right to cease work. The convention was taking shape to address action that countries should take at both the national policymaking level and, given its focus on managerial responsibility and voluntary self-regulation, actions "at the level of the undertaking." The language proposed by the workers, however, was the limited protection of the right to refuse taken from the language of the original ILO Law and Practice report, the same language heartily supported by the Canadian government:

(1) A worker should have the right to cease work if he judges the work to cause immediate and serious risk to his life or health, provided that the cessation of work is immediately reported to the employer or the safety delegate.

(2) A worker ceasing to work under such conditions is not to be victimized or held responsible for any damages or liabilities arising from the cessation of work, as measured from the time the work ceases until a decision is made to resume work.[27]

Why the more restricted right to refuse was proposed by the Workers' Group is not recorded in the official record. The politics created by both employers and Western governments clearly impeded raising the question of discrimination, however. Given the lack of a guiding counter narrative by the Workers' Group, one could deduce that the organized labor movement was simply improvising. The overall approach assumed in the draft text of Convention No. 155 was one of cooperation and sharing. The negotiations and the accompanying cultural narrative did not recognize inherent power inequalities in employment relations.

The Employers' Group argued that it was impossible for countries to give a legal definition to the imminent hazard standard connected to the right to refuse as proposed by the workers in their last-minute amendment proposal. Given the difficulty even the U.S. Supreme Court had with the legal concept of protecting workers from imminent hazards, the Employers' Group was in all likelihood correct in asserting that "the principle behind the law proposed could not be enforced." Instead of agreeing to stronger laws, however, the employers used this weakness to argue against adopting *any* antidiscrimination protection. They again relied on the master narrative: "The primary responsibility for safeguarding safety and health must be that of the employer. To give rights to others could only dilute that responsibility."[28]

Government delegates were split on supporting the right to refuse unsafe work. A bloc of northern industrialized countries including Belgium, France, Japan, and the United Kingdom opposed the idea. Canada, despite enthusiastically advocating protection of the right to refuse unsafe work and pointing to its domestic labor policy the year before through the preparatory work, joined this western bloc in opposition.[29] The United States supported adopting the amendment, likely not because of any commitment to antidiscrimination protection but rather keeping note of the pulse of the overall negotiations which required tripartite consensus to ensure any international legitimacy for the new convention once adopted The U.S. government delegate in the negotiation was also a regional director of OSHA. He surely understood that the limited refusal rights protection model was weak and non-threatening to managerial control. The draft language protecting the right to refuse was added to the convention text by a slim margin: 47.8 percent voted to adopt the limited right to refuse (31,552 votes), 47.2 percent were opposed (31,142 votes), with the rest abstaining (3,277 votes).[30]

The U.S. government delegate, Donald MacKenzie, the regional director in Boston of the Occupational Safety and Health Administration, took to the podium at the conference plenary and lauded the committee's work during the first of two negotiations. He noted what he considered to be a new era in global worker health and safety policy. The original goal of the negotiation was nothing short of a "total and coherent system of prevention of occupational accidents and occupational diseases," with each state to promote "the progressive application of new and far-reaching measures at the national level." "We are all developing nations when it comes to safety and health," MacKenzie repeated, "and it will take the co-operation of all nations, all employers and all employees to stop the insults placed upon men and women in our workplaces."[31] MacKenzie then reported to the assembly on the work of the 1980 negotiations, describing the nature of the convention's negotiation:

> Prevalent throughout our discussion was the fact that co-operation, not confrontation, between employer, employee and government was the fastest way to success in reduction of the insults to men, that employers have a responsibility to provide safe and healthy conditions. . . . This document is shaping the model for safety and health for all men for the 1980s and probably beyond, shaping a coherent nation-wide system in the true spirit of tripartism. We are looking forward to the second discussion next year.[32]

For the Employers' and Workers' groups, however, each acknowledged in diplomatic tones that a contentious negotiation had just concluded. "Our subsequent differences," said the leader of the Employers' Group from

TABLE 6.1. Strategic cultural frames used in the negotiation of Convention No. 155

Employers	Governments
The focus must be the "undertaking level" and be supported by both workers and employers	Fixed standards approach used by the ILO was a "piecemeal" approach to labor standards
Employers and workers share a "common interest" in protecting health and safety	New convention was "complimentary" to the fixed standards approach to labor standards
Favorable results at the workplace were best achieved by "cooperation not confrontation"	New approach was "far-reaching" versus the traditional narrow fixed-standards model
Legal requirements must not "erode the clear line of responsibility" assumed by employers	New approach responded to "present-day realities" but did not suggest immediate action
Giving rights to others would "dilute the responsibility assumed" by the employers	New convention advocated "a total and coherent system of protection" for workers
Convention must consider different "national practices and enforcement arrangements"	The new convention advocated "practical measures" not "abstract philosophical criteria"

the United Kingdom, "which I may say were strongly—but objectively—debated, were about means and measures rather than aims." The delegate of the Workers' Group, Mr. A. de Bruin from the Netherlands was more explicit: "The positive role of the trade unions must," he said, "be more clearly spelled out in the Convention."[33]

The Final Negotiation of Convention No. 155

As the committee convened for the final treaty negotiation the following year, organized labor would find itself further thrown off balance. The workers held to their promise to take up the cause of antidiscrimination protections for health and safety activism. Donald MacKenzie, the U.S. government representative on the committee, continued as reporter through the second discussion. Martin Cobb, the British employers' delegate, and A. de Bruin, the Dutch workers' delegate, were again the tripartite representatives in negotiations. The representative from Poland as chair rounded out the unchanged Eurocentric drafting committee.

The opening remarks of the final discussion were punctuated with a deluge of sweeping statements attesting to the importance of the work at hand. "At no time during the era of industrialization has there been so great an awareness of the need to protect the life and health of workers as during the last few years," the committee explained:[34]

> The draft international instrument submitted for the Committee's consideration was clearly the reflection, at the international level, of this new national awareness. The instruments dealt with the whole question of the prevention of occupational hazards and the improvement of the working environment, an area where national legislation was often still fragmentary.[35]

Echoing these sentiments, the Employers' Group stressed the importance of the work of the committee and the need to take action to protect worker safety and health. They held fast to their original four guiding principles and cited Alfred Robens's influential conceptual work on U.K. health and safety policy with a fresh call for the adoption of "practical measures" versus "a text attempting to satisfy abstract philosophical criteria."[36] There was, to be certain, no mention of the role of Robens in the other major safety and health event of his career, the catastrophic Aberfan disaster of 1966 that took the lives of 116 children under his tenure at the National Coal Board.

The Workers' Group opened their remarks with strikingly less diplomatic tones. They launched into a critique of the basic drafting of the convention, charging the ILO secretariat with altering the draft text of the convention. They noted "several points in their favor had not been retained in the new document prepared for the second discussion." They complained about the recording of votes taken during the previous negotiation, where close votes in the employers' favor were not detailed, but close votes in the workers' favor were outlined in detail. This gave the illusion of consensus and harmony surrounding the employers' main points while at the same time giving a sense of discord and disagreement on the points proposed by the Workers' Group. Then, the workers proposed to continue the discussion of the critical topics about which they "had expressed reservations" the prior year. These reservations, the workers argued, had been "deleted or modified" in the draft text by "several editorial changes" made after the first negotiation, including redrafting the right to refuse unsafe work. Someone had reworded language on consultations with unions, and "dropped without any explanation" important language on regulating subcontracting work that had been agreed to and voted on in the first round of negotiations the year before.

Removed was a clause about protecting workers from being victimized for the cessation of work and not holding employees responsible for any related liabilities. The altered draft convention placed additional barriers to the exercise of the right to refuse, including the creation of a new hazard threshold:

Article 17

There shall be arrangements at the level of the undertaking under which—. . .

(f) a worker reports forthwith to his immediate supervisor any situation which he has objective reason to believe presents and imminent and serious danger to his life or health, and is enabled to cease work in such cases if it has not proved possible to obtain in time a decision of management as to whether work should continue, it being understood that the worker shall not incur prejudice as a result of cessation of work in these circumstances where he has acted in good faith.[37]

Astonishingly, the right to refuse was moved back to a list of subjects to be arranged "at the level of the undertaking." This was the section that highlighted the enterprise-level action to be taken voluntarily by employers, versus the requirements to be made a part of national law and policy. The agreed-upon text from the previous year had protected the right to refuse as a stand-alone item of importance. There is no indication in the historical record explaining how these changes made between the two negotiating sessions had occurred. Given how all the changes went against the workers' stated positions, however, these were likely more than simple transcription errors. With the contentious nature of the negotiations, one can deduce with authority the role of political underhandedness at some level between the two formal negotiations of Convention No. 155.

The final negotiation of Convention No. 155 saw amendment after amendment proposed by the Workers' Group. The delegation had awakened too late to realize just what had transpired with their tacit approval. Most of their amendments were shot down by a bloc of governments and employers keen to see the convention adopted quickly. Workers' delegates proposed amendments to replace the self-regulatory and voluntarist language throughout the convention's text. They proposed removing words such as "so far as is reasonably practicable" and that action would be required "in accordance with national law and practice," as well as language proposing the convention be made national policy "progressively" and "insofar as reasonably practicable." New proposal after new proposal by the Workers' Group made the Employers' Group "astonished that these amendments had not been proposed after all the discussion which had taken place on this question the previous year with the compromise which had been so laboriously arrived at."[38] The workers had been dealt the lower hand not only culturally but structurally as well. The Workers' Group had failed to articulate any fundamental first principles that were guiding their actions on occupational safety and health. They subsequently left unchallenged the employers' and governments' master narrative supporting voluntaristic self-regulation versus hard law labor rights.

The altered draft text fiasco still was not enough to stop the Employers' Group from making self-serving statements about how shocked they were about the ill-preparedness of the Workers' Group in conceptualizing, articulating, and offering their delayed amendments. The workers' delegates again proposed the inclusion of strong antidiscrimination protections. The workers wanted the convention to include concrete language to protect workers from employer "victimization and dismissal" for their activism for workers' health and safety. The employers disagreed completely and suggested that it be referred to another committee at the ILO that handled the termination of employment. According to the Employers' Group, protection against discrimination, victimization and job dismissal for safety and health activism by workers "went far outside the scope of the instrument under discussion."[39]

In the face of worker insistence, a broad clause on discrimination was included in the convention. Several governments questioned the language, citing conflicts with their current laws on discrimination. Further amendments encountered a wall of opposition from the Employers' Group and a split government bloc. This doomed strengthening of the vague language on discrimination and victimization, leaving the protections ill-defined and contingent on a "national practice" and an "as reasonably practicable" standard. "Some potential hazards," argued the Employers' Group, "were inherent in the nature of the work" and "the worker was aware of these and was free to not accept a contract of employment." Such amendments would allow a worker to "break his contract suddenly." The final antidiscrimination protection language in Convention No. 155 was a watered-down statement on the protection of workers from victimization "in accordance with the national policy." No further clarity was given about the definition of discrimination or the protected acts of workers.[40]

The workers persisted through the final days of negotiations. They sought to strengthen the role of governments to allow states to "have appropriate rights of intervention, control and negotiation in the fields of occupational safety, hygiene and health." They failed on almost every amendment during the final negotiation session. The Employers' Group characterized the amendments as simply the "watering down [of] responsibilities" reserved for employers in the new system of work safety and health.[41]

Considering the right to refuse unsafe work one final time, the Workers' Group again protested the changed language. The U.K. government member stepped in to mediate and explained with paternalistic authority that his government's Robens-based model legislation "laid the responsibility for ensuring the health and safety of workers squarely upon the employer," thus mitigating the need for a strong state.[42] The workers had lost traction. As the negotiations drew to a close, the employers had the upper hand structurally, given the language on the table, and culturally, as the overall vision of a new voluntarism in health and safety policy had been carried forward into the new global labor norm. These moves eliminated any hope for strong antidiscrimination legal protections despite the workers' eleventh-hour protests. This new paradigm, so precisely constructed over a few short years, would become the model internationally. The result was a new global norm with a particular set of rights made safe not for worker safety and health activism but for managerial prerogatives and control of the employment relationship.

Adopting a "New International Awareness"

The contentious negotiations for Convention No. 155 were not simple matters of tripartite dialog and decision making. What had occurred was a more insidious use of power. Classic laissez-faire self-regulation, the very problem that gave rise to the ILO itself, was now in part advocated through global worker health and safety policy. Workers were sidelined in their representation and could not gain a conceptual or rhetorical footing once this political environment was established and the approach tacitly agreed on in the mandate to draft the new convention. The best strategy for the workers might have been to withhold their support by leaving the negotiation and allow the drafting to collapse.

The cultural strategy first reconstructed by Alfred Robens had been creatively borrowed from Sidney Webb's work and was now bearing fruit for employers as the negotiation of Convention No. 155 concluded. The Workers' Group proposed amendment after amendment until the end of the negotiations, but the arguments underlying their proposals were inconsistent with the "new" logic of Convention No. 155. The only option was to support the strongest rights framework available within this hegemonic market narrative, namely passing the limited right to refuse unsafe work. Anything else was simply "adamantly confrontational" collective bargaining and support for union rights, regardless of how effective that confrontational approach may have been to protecting the human right to a safe and healthy working environment.

As the negotiations drew to a close the workers were clearly taxed. The Committee on Safety and Health had put off discussing the section containing the right to refuse for the end of the final session. Were negotiations not to implode or collapse entirely, the issue of rights and the altered text would need to be addressed to demonstrate at least on the surface some basic level of commitment to protecting workers' rights. In response to the deleted language fiasco, the workers submitted a final new amendment on the right to refuse unsafe work to add to the language on refusal rights that was already inserted in the text. The issue was raised as the final negotiations were about to conclude, just as the issue of weak retaliation and discrimination protection could no longer be avoided by the other parties. It read:

> (i) a worker shall have the right to cease work judged by him to involve immediate and serious danger to the life or health of the worker on the condition that the danger cannot be immediately corrected by the employer or his representative;
>
> (ii) work may be halted only to the extent that the worker considers necessary to avoid danger;
>
> (iii) the halting of work and the reason for this shall be reported without delay to the employer or his representative;
>
> (iv) a worker ceasing to work under the above conditions shall not be dismissed or otherwise prejudiced nor shall he be held responsible for any damages or liability by reason of having ceased to work in accordance with the provision of this Article.[43]

Government delegates were split on the proposal. The Federal Republic of Germany asked for the amendment to be redrafted. Belgium argued that workers could not leave their posts when it might endanger the lives of others. The workers' amendment was rejected by the committee with 44.5 percent in favor (24,597 votes) and 45.9 percent against (25,363 votes) with another 9.5 percent abstaining (5,265 votes).[44] The employers were quick to point out that the right to refuse "was not a question of an absolute right" and that the employer's consent should be required for its exercise. This quote placed in the official record would be in subsequent years used by the ILO Committee of Experts to justify interpreting the right to refuse as "not a question of an absolute right."[45]

Ultimately, language was added to the convention, passed with the support of a bloc of ten Western governments, requiring parties to the convention to develop, in accordance with their national practice, some unspecified form of antidiscrimination policy. This antidiscrimination policy, however, would not be supervised by the ILO to strengthen protection of the right to refuse. The final language on refusal rights was detailed and limited to situations of "imminent and serious danger to his life or health" and then only so long as the worker "reports forthwith to his immediate supervisor." The Anglo-American formula of protecting the right to refuse was thus codified as a global labor right. Including the restricted right to refuse ensured that organized labor's international delegates stayed at the bargaining table through the eleventh hour, while employers and allied governments advanced their paradigm of managerial prerogatives within a new international self-regulatory framework on occupational safety and health.

As the Committee on Safety and Health submitted its work for adoption by the International Labor Conference the morning of June 19, 1981, the delegate from the U.S. government, Donald MacKenzie, acting as reporter of the Committee on Safety and Health, took to the assembly's podium. The work of the committee was finished. Their goal had been accomplished and "co-operation, not confrontation, between employer, employee and government was the fastest way to success in the reduction of injuries to man." Workers' safety and health, argued MacKenzie, "is a recognized human right. Safety and health have no political or economic boundaries and both industrialized and developing countries suffer from these conditions":[46]

> It is the foundation for a national policy to establish as far as possible a total and coherent system of prevention of occupational accidents and occupational diseases. The purpose of the instrument is to encourage member States to promote the progressive application of new and far-reaching measures at the national level. As stated last year, we are all developing nations when it comes to safety and health and the co-operation of all nations, all employers and all employees will be needed to reduce the carnage that has occurred in the past. Governments cannot do it alone; employers cannot do it alone; employees cannot do it alone. But in the true sense of tripartism, we can all work together with a common goal toward reducing

these disabilities. . . . This document is shaping the model for safety and health for all men for the 1980s and beyond; it is shaping a coherent world-wide system in the true spirit of tripartism.[47]

The employers' representative from the United Kingdom, Martin Cobb, took the podium and argued that it was the employers "that have the primary responsibility for the protection of workers" and "both sides can feel that they have got a good and fair bargain when the provisions of the instruments are taken as a whole." The committee was able to "concentrate our discussions on practical steps which will help to avoid workers being injured, rather than on a text which attempted to satisfy abstract philosophical criteria. You now have the results."[48] The Polish chair echoed the sentiments, proclaiming the new global legal texts "model and realistic documents."[49] The "abstract philosophical criteria" line had been drawn directly from market-based industrial relations theory, revitalized through the work of Robens.

The workers' delegate from the Netherlands in the Committee on Safety and Health placed a positive spin on what were contentious and unsettled negotiations: "The instruments now definitely spell out that workers, their representatives, the safety delegates and their trade unions have a progressive role to play and shall be recognized as effective and responsible partners at all levels of the workplace and the undertaking, up to and including the national level."[50] The final vote on the Convention concerning Occupational Safety and Health and the Working Environment was 408 of the tripartite delegates in favor, and one delegate opposed. The U.S. employers' delegate could not bring himself to vote in favor of the convention, citing several unacceptable elements. Despite its foundation in a self-regulating and even implicitly antiunion philosophy, U.S. employers still found the convention offensive to their broader utopian philosophy of laissez-faire economics.

CONCLUSION

The Future of Labor Rights in the Working Environment

A remarkable increase in both social consciousness and government policy on occupational safety and health has emerged in the past half century. Workplace health and safety has now become an area of labor and employment relations that is "extensively regulated" with "intense legislative activity worldwide" in recent years.[1] This action has encompassed more than just labor inspection and the creation of rules to regulate particular hazards. It also includes legal protections against discrimination for the advocates of better working conditions and for refusing unsafe work. These protections even extend to worker representation arrangements, workplace health and safety committees, and powers and privileges for labor unions. Given the overlap between these new regulatory approaches and traditional labor rights protections, it is helpful to think of workplace health and safety policy not as a separate subject of employment regulation but instead a key part of national systems that regulate labor and industrial relations.

This study critiques the international consensus on the protection of employee dissent in the working environment. The global norms appear to be a welcome commitment to preventing acts of retaliation and discipline against workers who voice concern about and act for occupational health and safety. Although the subject constitutes an important pillar for national occupational health and safety policies, the global norms on these topics are encased in and constrained by important caveats that protect an opposing set of values. The International Labour Office now explains that on job health and safety, retaliation or discrimination protections should not be seen as absolutes. Worker self-help norms are subject to layers of carefully crafted conditionality to be granted "as a result of actions properly taken" by a worker.[2] This is not a human rights approach to occupational safety and health. The resulting restrictions confound worker protection. Key caveats protect the competing values of management power and employer control and limit the protection of worker-activists seeking better working conditions. On the right to refuse unsafe work, unbridled production is the principal value that trumps granting authority to and protection for workers seeking to take action and organize around particular workplace concerns.

Refusal rights are contentious. Global policy as represented in the ILO international labor standards discussed here has, in turn, taken a hard line. These choices were not made, however, after contemplative and democratic deliberation focused on human rights. They are decisions made from a type of tripartite negotiation that pushed an agenda rooted in management values, reinforced by a cultural strategy that seemed sensible, but was designed to advance employer aims. The result is a global model for occupational health and safety policy made "safe" not for workers and communities, but for investors and private business enterprise. Unobtrusive power dynamics prevented workers and union representatives from conceiving and acting on global policy alternatives grounded in a real commitment to national policy action that would afford stronger and more effective health and safety rights for workers.

The United States and Canada served as the model for the development of the current global norm on refusal rights. This experience thus provides a real-world litmus test on the effectiveness of this style of rights at work. The evidence indicates that refusal rights are not effective within a restricted legal framework that ignores the inherent social inequalities in the employment relationship. These restricted models of worker protection do not recognize the connection between one exercising rights at work and strong collective protection at the workplace. Global standards cannot ignore liberal market employment dismissal powers and expect that principles of labor protection will somehow be protected in practice without addressing this underlying context.

The global norms on employee dissent and the right to refuse unsafe work serve to disempower workers by removing the identification of a hazard from the realm of worker liberty while atomizing individual workers by limiting the idea of obvious mutual concern and thus the associational, collective dimensions of individual employment protections. The result is the current silent crisis in international occupational health and safety policy: global norms that restrict employee dissent and reinforce employer power, forcing workers at risk to make the unthinkable choice between hazard and hardship. Global labor rights norms can and should afford much more protection to the worker advocate.

The international labor and human rights system is not perfect. It embodies aspirations of the highest order, yet in some ways entrenches economic inequalities that threaten both the working environment and the overall environment. Ignoring these global inequalities leaves unquestioned a default moral order that further entrenches corporate power and values within national labor and employment systems. As workers and unions continue to press for the recognition of labor rights as human rights, these inconsistencies in turn need to be identified and addressed. The environmental dimension of these labor rights highlights the important need to quickly understand the relationship between human rights, the freedom of association, and the ecology of human work.

One answer is critical engagement. An informed analysis must critique these global norms where they threaten basic human rights principles and environmental values. Doing so does not necessarily mean a rejection of the entire international labor and human rights standard-setting project. It means being a global citizen that engages with the idea of human rights and, where needed, highlighting the inconsistencies where principles contradict policies and on-the-ground practices. Raising questions and suggesting alternatives should be held in high regard both inside and outside these formal international bodies. In regard to the ILO's unique system of tripartite negotiation, the desire for widespread agreement must never be allowed to result in decisions that can ultimately threaten human rights principles or environmental protection at work. Human rights principles must limit the boundaries of choices available within the ILO system of tripartite negotiation. The ILO should not advocate norms inconsistent with human rights values.

As workplace hazards grow in complexity across an economy that is global, financialized, and hypercompetitive, connections between worker health and safety and environmental sustainability are becoming more and more evident. Global norms must be critiqued and discredited where needed to strengthen protection of the working environment. New strategies must be created to alter an out-of-control economy so that it might function in a way consistent with such simple human values as environmental sustainability and human rights. To this end, there is a reason that labor and employment law and policy are focused on worker association and collective rights. Regardless of the economic or industrial relations system, labor and employment is an inherently shared social experience. Individualist-style protections in employment relations are thus artificial and are a restrictive constitution of workers' rights. These protections do not represent accurately workers' complaints as they define them, evidenced throughout this study on occupational safety and health.

Critics of a human rights approach to labor and employment have argued that all rights frameworks serve only to weaken social solidarity, promote social atomism and individualism, create a dependency on legal and technical experts, and harm the necessary collective dimensions of labor activism. Refusals rights fall squarely into this category of being rights-based labor policy, making it a good case study to help answer this charge. This argument in essence locates the ineffectiveness of refusal rights on their very constitution within a rights-based framework.

Applying a more thorough view, however, shows that contested politics, and not rights-based labor policy applied to refusals to work, are responsible for weakening labor protections. The stronger constitution of refusal rights is both an individual and an associational protection. Strategic political activity at both the national and international level has manipulated the values and beliefs underlying the global discourse on occupational health and safety. These dynamics challenged stronger rights in favor of a reactionary individualism that neither empowered workers nor protected health and safety. Contested politics thus reshaped the constitution of rights to make these rights safe for employer power and control.

The right to refuse that emerged in the 1970s in North America and was later adopted in global norms in no way entailed any expansion of individual rights into the realm of employment relations. It was more a contraction of individual rights. The underlying assumptions of the "individual employment rights" era should, therefore, be questioned. The individual employment rights narrative applied to occupational safety and health is a misrepresentation in labor scholarship.

Speaking of "individual rights" in employment is a misrepresentation without reference to the associational and collective dimensions of those protections. Because of the social nature of employment, one person's hazard simply becomes the next person's problem. There is insight to be gained from the *Meyers Industries* dissent by members of the NLRB. The dissent argued that a work-related right "is not in essence an individual right; it is a right shared by and created for employees as a group through the legislative process" and therefore any assertion of a right in the employment relationship is "literal group action."[3] *Authentic* individual rights in employment relations are not derogations of certain types of social action but rather expressions of social action. It's a questionable view that says exclusively individualized rights are protective of rights at work. They are not. Restricting the associational and literal group action dimensions of worker rights in labor and employment relations is more a basic restriction on all kinds of rights at work.

Beyond critical engagement, there is an important role for conceptualizing how best to use human rights principles in making concrete change, especially where global norms are silent on an issue of concern, or even limited or restrictive of rights. Although ILO international labor standards are an important part of international law, their jurisprudence does not in all circumstances embody or conform to basic human rights principles. This is the case with the right to refuse. Global human rights jurisprudence on many topics is outlined but not developed, thus necessitating additional work on the boundaries of particular subjects. On the right to refuse, if this area of law is to respect fundamental human rights principles, refusal rights should incorporate the human rights values of nondiscrimination, the protection against interference in the exercise of human rights, the participation of rights holders in the governance of their own human rights, protection of the right to control one's health and body, and the recognition of the interdependency of refusal rights with other human rights such as the freedom of association. Such an approach would consequently evaluate the right through a lens of *effectiveness*[4] and all refusal rights would be protected, as would other human rights, as the *first responsibility* of government.[5] Limiting the right to refuse could only happen where it was, after deliberation, deemed absolutely necessary in order to protect other human rights. The need to universally safeguard employer power in the employment relationship qualifies as no such right.

Given these basic human rights values and principles, refusal rights should be at the center of the fundamental human right to a safe and healthy working environment. Applying these human values and principles to international labor rights standard-setting and the ILO supervision of labor rights laws, however, requires that society focus on expanding the definition of workers' freedom of association and basic labor relations. One first step would be to move workers' freedom of association and collective bargaining policy away from its traditional foundation rooted in market-based industrial relations theory, toward a stronger human rights-based approach. Given the analysis outlined in this book, a strict industrial relations pluralist view of the freedom of association ultimately restricts human rights in real world practice. The human rights view thus does represent a new approach to industrial relations theory.

Very modest reforms in the direction of human rights based labor policy could easily be made in practice, independent of a radical reshaping of labor rights. One starting point is to develop a workers' self-help jurisprudence on safe and healthy working conditions under Section 7(b) of the International Covenant on Economic, Social and Cultural Rights. The UN Committee on Economic, Social and Cultural Rights should adopt a General Comment on Occupational Safety and Health that elaborates the universal protection of workers' self-help activity in the working environment as a fundamental human right. The CESCR should criticize the dominant interpretation of any ILO supervisory body that says worker safety and health can be balanced with nonhuman rights such as the perceived prerogatives of management control and private enterprise. Likewise, ILO supervision on workers' freedom of association should recognize the interconnections with a human right to safety and health. The vague and undeveloped treatment of workers' self-help rights on occupational safety and health must similarly be replaced with a clear understanding of the complementarities between the freedom of association and the exercise of the right to refuse unsafe work. The CESCR must move beyond simply arguing that national labor inspection services and a vaguely defined national occupational safety and health authority are adequate to meet the human rights obligations to safe and healthy work under ICESCR Section 7(b). When they elaborate the right to refuse unsafe work, the Committee should apply the same fundamental human rights principles they apply when elaborating other human rights issues, none of which mention the priority of management control over fundamental human rights concerns.

The failure of some critical ILO standards to conform to basic human rights principles must be addressed. The ILO Committee of Experts must modernize their global jurisprudence to interpret, at a minimum, the safety and health conventions, including Convention No. 155, in conformity with the principles embodied in the International Covenant on Economic, Social and Cultural Rights. The ILO's supervision of health and safety must recognize the real-world inequality in work and employment relations. Worker protections must be interpreted in accordance with the basic values and principles of fundamental human rights and social justice.

Such action may seem impossible to envision in light of the restrictive clauses throughout many ILO international labor norms. The Committee of Experts could assume, however, that no international convention may contravene basic universal human rights norms. Human rights principles must serve as a baseline for international labor standards. This requires accepting that many forms of employee dissent must be protected and that workers must hold liberties to define hazards in the working environment, beyond the occupational safety and health inspectorate. It ultimately requires recognizing worker freedom of association and occupational safety and health as two interconnected and interrelated human rights. This approach is also needed if refusal rights are to be made effective.

Specific action by the ILO could unfold in a number of ways. Regarding the freedom of association, the Committee of Experts must depart from their current rigid interpretation of trade union discrimination. It is not adequate to offer protection only to those workers engaged in formal unionization. The protection against acts of discrimination and retaliation must be extended to all workers engaged in concerted action, broadly defined to mean all labor action that holds an obvious mutual concern.

Protection of the working environment is the most obvious issue of mutual concern, and any question on the working environment is of obvious mutual concern, warranting legal protection as a result, independent of the constitution of any specific hazard.

Another strategy would be to expand the jurisprudence on the right to strike to cover worker self-help activity on questions of occupational health and safety. A model for this already exists because the right to strike is recognized despite not being outlined in the text of either of the core labor standards on the freedom of association. The right to strike is considered an "intrinsic corollary" of the right to organize. The strongest protection of the right to refuse could likewise be considered an "intrinsic corollary" of organizational activity and association, in turn warranting ILO and in turn international recognition.

A broader but still moderate reform strategy for the ILO would be to support a high-level rethinking of the general meaning of the limiting language "national conditions and practices" found in many global labor standards. Although such flexibility clauses have been negotiated within many international conventions, these provisions should not be used as a get-out-of-jail-free pass by national governments. There should be a clarification as to when stepping back from obligations via "national conditions" may occur, if ever. This clarification could be similar to how the concept of progressive realization has been clarified by the CESCR under the International Covenant on Economic, Social and Cultural Rights. Historically, flexibility was given a very low priority in discussions about how a country should regulate occupational safety and health. The director-general of the ILO in 1974, for example, reported a "wide agreement that flexibility should have no place in standards aimed at ensuring safety and health at work."[6] This is no longer the International Labour Organization's approach, however. There must be an ongoing dialog about the idea of "national conditions and practices" so that no corporation or national government can sidestep the protection of basic human rights.

This point raises another related issue regarding flexibility clauses in general. An ongoing discussion is also needed about the relationship between cultural differences and protecting universal human rights. The ILO Employers' Group is quick to argue that flexibility is needed in the application of international labor standards. Oddly, these arguments mirror those seeking respect for cultural differences in the face of various international norms. On the issue of workplace health and safety, however, the work being regulated is often located somewhere inside the supply chain of any one of the thousands of multinational corporations that now operate around the world. Is hazardous work a cultural value to be respected? Do we accept that the same legitimate flexibility needed to respect cultural differences must also be afforded to multinational corporations to disrespect the health and safety of workers? A more complex, better understanding is needed of the interface between cultural differences and universal human rights so that multinational companies cannot manipulate these important reservations for their own self-interested aims.

The limited language on refusal rights negotiated a generation ago in Convention No. 155 has now propagated worldwide. The ILO should recognize how these norms create procedural burdens to justice and undermine the protection of all occupational health and safety. Workers should be protected against acts of discrimination and retaliation regarding the working environment any time worker action is taken in good faith, independent of any workplace hazard threshold, and even if these actions are improper procedurally. Given the social inequalities at work and the numerous pressures within employment relations, this new global norm must be among the top strategies to assure workers are protected. The broad protection of workers against an employer's discriminatory and retaliatory acts—of all kinds—in this analysis is the cornerstone to protecting the fundamental human right to safety and health at work.

Fundamentally, there is a need for a more substantial rethinking of the role of labor rights in the working environment. To address the problem at the ground level, the ILO and the social partners must rethink the issue of worker representation in the working environment. Voluntaristic collective bargaining is the main form of worker representation advocated by global norms today. Although important, this voluntarism norm means that the priority is placed on the freedom to negotiate an agreement between unions and management. Negotiating in principle raises no direct issue but a strict interpretation of voluntary labor relations creates winners and losers that can deeply affect the human right to occupational safety and health. Many workers, for example, are not able to organize for bargaining, much less negotiate an agreement, meaning they are unable to secure proper representation in the working environment. When workers can negotiate, voluntarism in labor policy means that management may negotiate to limit rights, such as placing limits on the right to refuse or strike. Negotiations under a purely voluntaristic labor policy approach leave key human rights protections subject to raw power relations between the two parties. This is especially unfortunate given the strategic importance of workers' freedom of association to the protection of occupational safety and health. The current general model of labor relations promoted globally thus creates specific obstacles to the effective universal protection of worker representation in the working environment and, in turn, to the realization of the human right to occupational safety and health. Critics often argue that nation-state power is weakened by globalization and as a result, these choices are simple political expedients in an imperfect world. Given the power of strategic cultural frames, however, be it voluntarism in industrial relations law and policy or the more complex concoction of values documented in this book, one could question whether this weakness is simply a consequence of limited thinking.

Protecting worker health and safety ultimately means turning to the question of labor rights in the working environment. Such a debate must include but also extend beyond the question of pluralist collective bargaining rights. It must encompass a commitment to extend new forms of effective worker representation universally to workers regardless of their status, creating new mechanisms for labor rights in the work environment. Some strategies to this end might include requiring safety and health committees in all collective bargaining agreements; mandating, universally, new forms of worker and labor representation on questions of safety and health in the working environment; mandating universally a basic collective negotiation on health and safety; or mandating some form of local multi-stakeholder negotiation that would include both employees, including previously injured workers, and any affected communities broadly defined. These strategies would also need to be responsive to the great changes that have unfolded across the employment relationship over the previous generation. Precarious workers and subcontracted labor arrangements must undoubtedly also be included in any future worker representation regime extending association rights deeper into the governance of the working environment.

Given the mandate of the ILO to achieve lasting peace, something that it says can only occur if it is based on social justice, each of these suggestions would seem to be worthwhile endeavors for labor policymaking and worker activism. What must be criticized is the unspoken institutionalization of employment systems that by default damage human life and the environment while treating workers as nothing more than commodities, readily disposable. Unsafe and hazardous work is a consequence of a larger socioeconomic sickness. Reinterpreting key international labor standards or even the drafting of new global standards on labor rights in the working environment are movements in the right direction. The larger question remains whether these strategies are enough to create an economy capable of respecting human rights at work, protecting worker health and safety, and ensuring a sustainable working environment for future generations. What appears to be certain, however, is that without these important changes in an employment relations system, achieving these objectives is unlikely.

These are the challenges underlying the protection of occupational safety and health as a fundamental human right. What is needed is a radical reshaping of social consciousness on the advocacy of labor rights in the working environment. Social and institutional action must move beyond weak consultative voice mechanisms and protect authentic workers' self-help activity, representation, and governance of the working environment. Such efforts must be universal across the economy, protect workers independent of their employment status, and possibly even be federated to the extent that they could be more effective around communities, regions, work processes, occupations, or different economic sectors and industries. The most important point, however, is to ensure a fundamental change in the relationships between government, environment, and worker.

Underlying any change in course for the institutions of labor and employment must be a commitment to the idea of decommodifying labor. It is not enough to say workers should be treated as *more than* commodities. Workers should not be treated as commodities in any respect. Such a commitment requires a particularly active approach to regulating both labor and employment as well as the broader economic and social policy context within which labor and work exists. Without such a commitment to decommodifying labor and employment relations, there is little chance for the effective and sustainable protection of human rights in the working environment.

This book thus returns to where it began, to the treatment of human beings as commodities. How can one claim they have treated another person as anything other than a commodity if they coerce them for private profit to perform some act deemed a threat to their health and safety? What is it about work and the employment relationship that makes society believe it is okay for employers to take action against a person that would otherwise be considered abhorrent? Making a human being choose between hazard and hardship is the true essence of whether a society's laws, institutions, and economy treat labor as a commodity.

Kalmen Kaplansky, a grandfather of the Canadian human rights movement, noted the role of the ILO as standing in opposition to free market economics.[7] As the Canadian labor representative to the ILO who aided the drafting of Convention No. 111 on Discrimination in Employment and Occupation, actions that have been cited as a primary reason for the ILO's Nobel Peace Prize award in 1969, Kaplansky once described the ILO's original, founding raison d'être as being largely a response to capitalism and the false belief in the idea of market freedom:

> The economic doctrine of the Industrial Revolution was *laissez faire* liberalism and individualism, according to which all individuals in society had the same natural rights, and that even if all did not possess equal capability, each could at least understand his own interest so that the best that could be done to help him was to leave him to himself. As applied to economic life this meant freedom of work, free competition, free trade (both internal and external), and correspondingly the non-intervention of the state. But this doctrine of economic freedom, allied to the new inventions which had made the age of machine industry possible, created an upheaval in social relationships.[8]

The ILO's focus on ameliorating upheavals in social relationships at the hands of the market requires prescriptive standards. For the ILO to stay responsive to its mission it must embrace the role of crafting global norms to protect employee dissent in the working environment. Global capitalism as it functions today means production comes first, social and environmental concerns come second. We have, collectively, placed ourselves on an unsustainable path both in terms of meeting basic human needs and in the protection of the environment for future generations. Confronting these challenges obliges the recognition that no human being is a commodity to be bought and sold for a price. How the international labor and human rights systems respond to these challenges will in all likelihood determine their future relevance to workers and humanity.

NOTES

Introduction

1. For one overview of the debate on citizenship at work, see Michel Coutu and Gregor Murray, "Towards Citizenship at Work?" *Relations Industrielles / Industrial Relations* 60, no. 4 (2005): 617–30.

2. *Duane Carlson, Plaintiff, v. Arrowhead Concrete Works, Inc., Defendant*, 375 F. Supp. 2d 835, D. Minn.(2005).

3. *Maglich v. Miller-Dwan Medical Center*, State of Minnesota Office of Administrative Hearings 1-1901-11970-2(1999).

4. Leigh Holmwood, "ABC Wins Gizbert Appeal," *Guardian*, August 21, 2006.

5. International Transport Workers Federation, August 3, 2011, "Slovenian Crane Operators Strike over Health and Safety," http://www.itfglobal.org/news-online/index.cfm/newsdetail/6269.

6. "Trying to Pull Together: Africans Are Asking Whether China Is Making Their Lunch or Eating It," *Economist*, April 20, 2011.

7. Human Rights Watch, "You'll Be Fired if You Refuse: Labor Abuses in Zambia's Chinese State-Owned Copper Mines" (New York: Human Rights Watch, 2011), 54.

8. ILO Programme on HIV/AIDS and the World of Work, "Implementing the ILO Code of Practice on HIV/AIDS and the World of Work: An Education Training Manual" (Geneva: International Labour Office, 2003), module 5, 10.

9. "Prostitute to Sue Brothel over Gun," *The Age*, July 13, 2011.

10. "Troops Told 'Shoot to Kill' in New Orleans," *ABC News* September 2, 2005. Blanco said: "They have landed in New Orleans. These troops are fresh back from Iraq, well trained,

experienced, battle-tested and under my orders to restore order in the streets. They have M-16s and they are locked and loaded. These troops know how to shoot and kill and they are more than willing to do so if necessary and I expect they will."

11. *A Failure of Initiative: Final Report of the Select Bipartisan Committee to Investigate the Preparation for and Response to Hurricane Katrina. 2006.* Washington, D.C.: Government Printing Office.

12. Occupational Health and Safety Administration, Region 6 (Dallas), "Final Investigative Report. Section 11(c) Refusal to Work Complaint." Closed May 15, 2007, on file with author as Case No. 281.

13. "Gulf Rig Workers Could Have Called 'Time-Out'," *CNN Money*, May 27, 2010.

14. "In Gulf, It Was Unclear Who Was in Charge of Rig," *New York Times*, June 5, 2010.

15. T. R. Chouhan, *Bhopal: The Inside Story* (New York: Council on International and Public Affairs, 2004), 43, 47.

16. "The Nobel Peace Prize 1969 Presentation Speech," http://www.nobelprize.org/nobel_prizes/peace/laureates/1969/press.html.

17. Address by the President of the United States of America to the Delegates Attending the Twenty-sixth Session of the International Labour Conference, 1944.

18. Karl Polanyi, *The Great Transformation: The Political and Economic Origins of Our Time* (Boston: Beacon Press, 1957).

19. Ha-Joon Chang, "The Market, the State, and Institutions in Economic Development," in *Rethinking Development Economics*, ed. Ha-Joon Chang (New York: Anthem Press, 2003), 49–51.

20. Guy Standing, "The I.L.O.: An Agency for Globalization?" *Development and Change* 33, no. 3 (2008). See also Standing, *The Precariat: The New Dangerous Class* (New York: Bloomsbury USA, 2011).

21. Eddy Lee Gerry Rodgers, Lee Swepston, and Jasmien Van Daele, *The ILO and the Quest for Social Justice, 1919–2009* (Geneva: International Labour Office, 2009), 184–99. See also the oral history of Louis Emmerij at the UN Intellectual History Project, www.unhistory.org.

22. Standing, "The I.L.O.: An Agency for Globalization?" 359.

23. See also Standing, *Work after Globalization: Building Occupational Citizenship* (Cheltenham: Edward Elgar, 2009).

24. For example, Gary S. Fields, *Trade and Labour Standards: A Review of the Issues* (Paris: Organisation for Economic Co-operation and Development, 1995).

25. Jukka Takala, *Decent Work—Safe Work: Introductory Report to the XVIIth World Congress on Safety and Health at Work* (Geneva: International Labour Office, 2005), 5.

26. International Labour Office, "My Life, My Work, My Safe Work: Managing Risk in the Work Environment" (Geneva: International Labour Organization and the International Social Security Association, 2008), 4.

27. Ibid.

28. Pan American Health Organization, *Workers' Health in the Region of the Americas*, 41st Directing Council (CD 41/15) (Washington, D.C.: Pan American Health Organization, 1999), 244. See Antonio Giuffrida, Roberto F. Iunes, and William D. Savedoff, "Occupational Risks in Latin America and the Caribbean: Economic and Health Dimensions," *Health Policy and Planning* 17, no. 3 (2002).

29. Giuffrida, Antonio, Roberto F. Iunes, and William D. Savedoff. Economic and Health Effects of Occupational Hazards in Latin America and the Caribbean. Technical Papers Series No. Soc-121, edited by Sustainable Development Department. Washington, D.C.: Inter-American Development Bank, 2001.

30. Lisa Rosenstock, Mark Cullen, and Marilyn Fingerhut, "Occupational Health," in *Disease Control Priorities in Developing Countries,* ed. Dean T. Jamison et al. (New York: Oxford University Press, 2006), 1128.

31. Danielle Venn, *Legislation, Collective Bargaining and Enforcement: Updating the OECD Employment Protection Indicators* (Paris: Organisation for Economic Co-operation and Development, 2009), 9.

1. Human Rights and the Struggle to Define Hazards

1. John Gaventa, *Power and Powerlessness: Quiescence and Rebellion in an Appalachian Valley* (Urbana: University of Illinois Press, 1982), 73.

2. James Gray Pope, "Labor's Constitution of Freedom, 1920–1958," PhD diss.," Princeton University, 2004.

3. Ibid., 52.

4. Ibid.

5. Arturo Dizon Brion, "The Right to Refuse Unsafe Work in Ontario," LLM thesis, York University, 1995, 41–55.

6. Carl Gersuny, *Work Hazards and Industrial Conflict* (Hanover, N.H.: University Press of New England, 1981), 121.

7. Richard Brown, "The Right to Refuse Unsafe Work," *University of British Columbia Law Review* 17, no. 1 (1983).

8. Ibid, 14.

9. Ibid.

10. Ibid. 14. 4 L.A.C. (2d) 315. Brown provides a partial list of cases in note 30: *Re Mueller Ltd.* (1974) 7 L.A.C. (2d) 282; *Re Steel Company of Canada Ltd.* (1975) 8 L.A.C. (2d) 198; *Gibraltar Mines* [1975] W.L.A.C. 788; *Re Great Canadian Oil Sands Ltd* (1980) 22 L.A.C. (2d) 426.

11. Ibid., 15.

12. Ibid.

13. James A. Gross and Patricia Greenfield, "Arbitral Value Judgments in Health and Safety Disputes: Management Rights over Workers' Rights," *Buffalo Law Review* 34 (1985).

14. Brown, "Right to Refuse Unsafe Work," 19.

15. Figures cited here are from the Bureau of Labor Statistics. The 1966 figures are from *Handbook of Labor Statistics* (Washington, D.C.: United States Department of Labor, 1971), 314. The figures for 1967–74 are from *Handbook of Labor Statistics* (Washington, D.C.: United States Department of Labor, 1976), 301–8. The figures from 1975 are from *Work Stoppages, Summary 76–7* (Washington, D.C.: United States Department of Labor, 1975), 7.

16. Rachel Scott, *Muscle and Blood*, 1st ed. (New York: Dutton, 1974), 287.

17. Joseph A. Page and Peter N. Munsing, "Occupational Health and the Federal Government: The Wages Are Still Bitter," *Law and Contemporary Problems* 38 (1974).

18. Gersuny, *Work Hazards and Industrial Conflict,* 136. See also Health Research Group, *Job Safety and Health: Inadequate Enforcement and Stalled Review* (Washington, D.C.: Health Research Group, c. 1975).

19. Anthony Mazzocchi, unpublished labor education papers on file with author, 28.

20. Anthony Mazzocchi, "The Workers' Place in Enforcing OSHA," *Annals of the New York Academy of Sciences* 572 (December 1989).

21. Nicholas A. Ashford, *Crisis in the Workplace: Occupational Disease and Injury, a Report to the Ford Foundation* (Cambridge: MIT Press, 1976), 514.

22. Ibid., 514–15.

23. Ibid.

24. "The New Activism on Job Health: A Challenge to Business from Industrial Hygienists on Unions' Payrolls," *Business Week*, September 18, 1978.

25. Ibid.

26. James C. Oldham, "Organized Labor, the Environment, and the Taft-Hartley Act," *Environment Law Review* (1974). See footnote 9.

27. Ibid., 953.

28. "Urban Environment Conference Papers, 1971–1984," Walter P. Reuther Library of Labor and Urban Affairs Archives at Wayne State University.

29. Barbara Ehrenreich and Tom Ehrenreich, "Conscience of a Steelworker," *Nation*, September 25, 1971. Gilbert Pugliese's case was also documented in local newspapers. "Average Guy Takes a Poke at Pollution—He's Winning," *Cleveland Press*, September 23, 1971.

30. Oldham, "Organized Labor, the Environment, and the Taft-Hartley Act," 936, quoting Reuther.

31. Ibid.

32. Robert Gordon, "Shell no! OCAW and the Labor Environmental Alliance," *Environmental History* 3, no. 4 (1998), 469.

33. "The First Strike over Potential Hazards to Health," *San Francisco Examiner*, March 4, 1973.

34. Deborah Shapely, "Shell Strike: Ecologists Refine Relations with Labor," *Science*, April 13, 1973.

35. "Environmentalists Try to Win Labor Over: Using Workplace Safety and a Promise of New Jobs to Entice Labor's Support," *Business Week*, October 3, 1977.

36. Douglas W. Erlandson, c. 1979, "The Shell Strike of 1973," http://www.usw12-591.org/strike1973.html.

37. Robert Gordon, "Poisons in the Fields: The United Farm Workers, Pesticides, and Environmental Politics," *Pacific Historical Review* 68, no. 1 (1999): 51.

38. Ibid., 64.

39. Ibid., 70.

40. Laurie Mercier, *Anaconda: Labor, Community, and Culture in Montana's Smelter City* (Urbana: University of Illinois Press, 2001).

41. Oldham, "Organized Labor, the Environment, and the Taft-Hartley Act," 951–79.

42. "Universal Declaration of Human Rights, General Assembly Resolution 217A, at 71, U.N. GAOR, 3rd Sess., 1st plen. mtg., U.N. Doc A/810" (Dec. 12, 1948).

43. International Covenant on Economic, Social and Cultural Rights, 993 U.N.T.S. 3 (1966).

44. Matthew C. R. Craven, *The International Covenant on Economic, Social and Cultural Rights: A Perspective on Its Development* (Oxford: Clarendon Press, 1995).

45. Philip Alston, " 'Core Labour Standards' and the Transformation of the International Labour Rights Regime," *European Journal of International Law* 15, no. 3 (2004).

46. Tony Evans, "International Human Rights Law as Power/Knowledge," *Human Rights Quarterly* 27, no. 3 (August 2005): 1052–53.

47. U.N. Econ. & Soc. Council [ECOSOC], Committee on Economic, Social & Cultural Rights, *General Comment No. 14—The Right to the Highest Attainable Standard of Health (Art. 12 of the Covenant)* (Adopted August 11, 2000).

48. Ibid.

49. Ibid.

50. U. N. Economic and Social Council, *General Comment No. 19—The Right to Social Security (Art. 9 of the Covenant)* (Adopted November 23, 2007).

51. *General Comment No. 14—The Right to the Highest Attainable Standard of Health (Art. 12 of the Covenant)*.

52. "Universal Declaration of Human Rights, General Assembly Resolution 217A."

53. Malcolm Langford, "The Justiciability of Social Rights: From Practice to Theory," in *Social Rights Jurisprudence: Emerging Trends in International and Comparative Law*, ed. Malcolm Langford (New York: Cambridge University Press, 2008), 10, 29.

54. Matthew Craven, "Assessment of the Progress on Adjudication of Economic, Social and Cultural Rights," in *The Road to a Remedy: Current Issues in the Litigation of Economic, Social and*

Cultural Rights, ed. John Squires, Malcolm Langford, and Bret Thiele (Sydney: University of New South Wales Press, 2005), 29–30.

55. World Conference on Human Rights, June 14–25, 1993, "Vienna Declaration and Programme of Action, U.N. Doc. A/CONF.157/23" (July 12, 1993).

56. Johannes Morsink, *The Universal Declaration of Human Rights: Origins, Drafting, and Intent* (Philadelphia: University of Pennsylvania Press, 1999), 245.

57. Simone Weil, *The Need for Roots: Prelude to a Declaration of Duties toward Mankind* (New York: Putnam, 1952), 4.

58. James B. Atleson, *Values and Assumptions in American Labor Law* (Amherst: University of Massachusetts Press, 1983), 143.

59. Declaration of the United Nations Conference on the Human Environment. 1972. Adopted at the 21st plenary meeting in Stockholm on June 16.

2. Theoretical Perspectives on Individual Employment Rights

1. Atleson, *Values and Assumptions in American Labor Law*.

2. Ibid., 8.

3. Paul Frymer, *Black and Blue: African Americans, the Labor Movement, and the Decline of the Democratic Party* (Princeton: Princeton University Press, 2008), 29.

4. Nelson Lichtenstein, *State of the Union: A Century of American Labor* (Princeton: Princeton University Press, 2002).

5. Nelson Lichtenstein, "The Rights Revolution," *New Labor Forum* 12, no. 1 (2003).

6. Lichtenstein, *State of the Union*, 171.

7. Lichtenstein, "Rights Revolution."

8. Ibid.

9. Richard P. McIntyre, *Are Worker Rights Human Rights?* (Ann Arbor: University of Michigan Press, 2008).

10. Human Rights Watch, *Unfair Advantage: Workers' Freedom of Association in the United States under International Human Rights Standards* (New York: Human Rights Watch, 2000).

11. Jay Youngdahl, "Solidarity First: Labor Rights Are Not the Same as Human Rights," *New Labor Forum* 18, no. 1 (2009). Youngdahl cites Canadian philosopher Charles Taylor and his work in Charles Taylor, "Philosophy and the Human Sciences," *Philosophical Paper 2* (1985).

12. Kevin Kolben, "Labor Rights as Human Rights?" *Virginia Journal of International Law* 50, no. 2 (2010).

13. Michael J. Piore and Sean Safford, "Changing Regimes of Workplace Governance, Shifting Axes of Social Mobilization and the Challenge to Industrial Relations Theory," *Industrial Relations* 45, no. 3 (2006).

14. Ibid., 304.

15. Ibid., 300.

16. Jefferson Cowie and Nick Salvatore, "The Long Exception: Rethinking the Place of the New Deal in American History," *International Labor and Working-Class History* 74, no. 1 (2008).

17. Ibid., 6–7, 20–21.

18. David Montgomery, "The Mythical Man," *International Labor and Working-Class History* 71, no. 1 (2008): 56–62.

19. David Montgomery, *Workers' Control in America: Studies in the History of Work, Technology, and Labor Struggles* (Cambridge; New York: Cambridge University Press, 1979), 156–58.

20. John T. Dunlop, *Industrial Relations Systems*, rev. ed. (Boston: Harvard Business School Press, [1958] 1993).

21. Ibid., 109.

22. Ibid., 113.

23. Ibid., 125.

24. Ibid., 127.

25. Chris Carter, Stewart Clegg, and Martin Kornberger, *A Very Short, Fairly Interesting, and Reasonably Cheap Book about Studying Strategy* (Thousand Oaks, California: Sage Publications, 2008), 47.

26. John E. Kelly, *Rethinking Industrial Relations: Mobilization, Collectivism, and Long Waves* (New York: Routledge, 1998).

27. Ibid., 4.

28. Peter A. Hall and David W. Soskice, "An Introduction to Varieties of Capitalism," in *Varieties of Capitalism: The Institutional Foundations of Comparative Advantage*, ed. Peter A. Hall and David W. Soskice (New York: Oxford University Press, 2001), 29.

29. Peter Evans, "The Eclipse of the State? Reflections on Stateness in an Era of Globalization," *World Politics* 50, no. 1 (1997).

30. John Godard, "An Institutional Environments Approach to Industrial Relations," in *New Directions in the Study of Work and Employment: Revitalizing Industrial Relations as an Academic Enterprise*, ed. Charles J. Whalen (Cheltenham: Edward Elgar, 2008), 69.

31. Ibid., 70.

32. Ibid., 71.

33. Ibid.

34. Gaventa, *Power and Powerlessness*.

35. E. E. Schattschneider, *The Semisovereign People; A Realist's View of Democracy in America* (New York: Holt, Rinehart and Winston, 1960), 71.

36. Ibid., 105.

37. Peter Bachrach and Morton S. Baratz, "Two Faces of Power," *American Political Science Review* 56, no. 4 (1962).

38. Peter Bachrach and Morton S. Baratz, "Decisions and Nondecisions: An Analytic Framework," *American Political Science Review* 57, no. 3 (1963).

39. Schattschneider, *Semisovereign People*, 71.

40. Gaventa, *Power and Powerlessness*, 9.

41. Bachrach and Baratz, "Two Faces of Power."

42. Bachrach and Baratz, "Decisions and Nondecisions."

43. Steven Lukes, *Power: A Radical View*, 2nd ed. (New York: Palgrave Macmillan [1974], 2005).

44. Gaventa, *Power and Powerlessness*, 11. Quoting Peter Bachrach and Morton S. Baratz, *Power and Poverty: Theory and Practice* (New York,: Oxford University Press, 1970); Gaventa's emphasis.

45. Lukes, *Power*, 20–23.

46. Ibid., 24.

47. Cynthia Hardy, "The Nature of Unobtrusive Power," *Journal of Management Studies* 22, no. 4 (1985).

48. Ibid., 384, 387.

49. Ibid., 398, 392.

50. Bruce E. Kaufman, *Managing the Human Factor: The Early Years of Human Resource Management in American Industry* (Ithaca: Cornell University Press, 2008).

51. Ibid., 214.

52. Gaventa, *Power and Powerlessness*, 29.

53. Godard, "Institutional Environments Approach," 68–70.

54. Grounded theory method encourages researchers to try to analyze social processes without accepting predetermined concepts drawn from academic literature that could bias how an investigator understands the real world. In this approach "all is data" and concept "emergence" is

prioritized. This approach was first articulated in Barney G. Glaser, "The Constant Comparative Method of Qualitative Analysis," *Social Problems* 12, no. 4 (1965). The most cited articulation is Barney G. Glaser and Anselm L. Strauss, *The Discovery of Grounded Theory; Strategies for Qualitative Research* (New Brunswick, N.J.: Aldine Transaction, [1967] 2006). Variations have developed; see Anthony Bryant and Kathy Charmaz, *The SAGE Handbook of Grounded Theory* (Thousand Oaks, Calif.: Sage Publications, 2007).

55. Gaventa, *Power and Powerlessness*, 27.

56. John Logan, "The Union Avoidance Industry in the United States," *British Journal of Industrial Relations* 44, no. 4 (2006).

57. Robert B. Reich, *Supercapitalism: The Transformation of Business, Democracy, and Everyday Life* (New York: Alfred A. Knopf, 2007), 51.

58. Alex Carey and Andrew Lohrey, *Taking the Risk out of Democracy: Corporate Propaganda versus Freedom and Liberty* (Urbana-Champaign: University of Illinois Press, 1997).

59. Ibid., 18.

60. Ibid., 20.

61. Albert O. Hirschman, *The Rhetoric of Reaction: Perversity, Futility, Jeopardy* (Cambridge: Belknap Press, Harvard University Press, 1991), 11.

62. James A. Gross, *Broken Promise: The Subversion of U.S. Labor Relations Policy, 1947–1994* (Philadelphia: Temple University Press, 1995), 235.

63. Harold L. Wilensky, *Rich Democracies: Political Economy, Public Policy, and Performance* (Berkeley: University of California Press, 2002), 92.

64. Hazel Henderson, "Ecologists versus Economists," *Harvard Business Review* 51 (July–August 1973).

3. The Right to Refuse in International Labor Law

1. Brown, "The Right to Refuse Unsafe Work," 3.

2. Two examples are Gillian MacNaughton and Diane F. Frey, "Decent Work for All: A Holistic Human Rights Approach," *SSRN eLibrary* (2010), and Alston, " 'Core Labour Standards'."

3. International Labour Organization, "The Constitution of the International Labour Organization," (15 UNTS 40). Established in 1919, modified by the amendment of 1922 which entered into force on 4 June 1934; the Instrument of Amendment of 1945 which entered into force on 26 September 1946; the Instrument of Amendment of 1946 which entered into force on 20 April 1948; the Instrument of Amendment of 1953 which entered into force on 20 May 1954; the Instrument of Amendment of 1962 which entered into force on 22 May 1963; and the Instrument of Amendment of 1972 which entered into force on 1 November 1974.

4. Charles J. Morris, "NLRB Protection in the Nonunion Workplace: A Glimpse at a General Theory of Section 7 Conduct," *University of Pennsylvania Law Review* 137, no. 5 (1989): 1677.

5. International Labour Office, *Freedom of Association: Digest of Decisions and Principles of the Freedom of Association Committee of the Governing Body of the ILO*, 5th [rev.] ed. (Geneva: International Labour Office, 2006).

6. Ibid., paragraph 769.

7. This includes Conventions "Convention (No. 87) concerning Freedom of Association and Protection of the Right to Organise, 68 U.N.T.S. 17 (1950)" and "Convention (No. 98) concerning the Application of the Principles of the Right to Organise and to Bargain Collectively, 96 U.N.T.S. 258 (1951)."

8. ILO, *Freedom of Association: Digest*, paragraph 771. Emphasis added.

9. Ibid., paragraph 769.

10. Ibid., paragraph 779.

11. Ibid., paragraphs 780–81.

12. "Convention (No. 158) concerning Termination of Employment at the Initiative of the Employer, 1412 U.N.T.S. 23645 (1982)."

13. B. Gernigon, H. Guido, and A. Odero, *ILO Principles concerning the Right to Strike* (International Labour Organization, 2000), 11, note 5.

14. International Labour Office, *General Survey: Freedom of Association and Collective Bargaining. Report III, Part 4B* (Geneva: International Labour Office, 1994), paragraph 173.

15. Ibid., paragraph 170. See also Tonia Novitz, *International and European Protection of the Right to Strike: A Comparative Study of Standards Set by the International Labour Organization, the Council of Europe and the European Union* (Oxford: Oxford University Press, 2003).

16. International Labour Office, *General Survey: Freedom of Association*, paragraph 137.

17. Ibid.

18. Ibid., paragraph 171.

19. *NLRB v. Washington Aluminum Company*, 370 U.S. 9 (1962).

20. International Labour Office, *General Survey concerning the Occupational Safety and Health Convention, 1981 (No. 155), the Occupational Safety and Health Recommendation, 1981 (No. 164), and the Protocol of 2002 to the Occupational Safety and Health Convention, 1981* (98th Session, Report III, Part 1B, 2009). See Paragraph 148.

21. Ibid., paragraph 145.

22. International Labour Office, "Convention (No. 155) concerning Occupational Safety and Health and the Working Environment, 1331 U.N.T.S. 22345 (1981)."

23. Ibid.

24. Ibid.

25. Ibid.

26. International Labour Office, "Convention (No. 176) concerning Safety and Health in Mines, 2029 U.N.T.S. 207 (1995)."

27. International Labour Organization, "Recommendation (No. 172) concerning Safety in the Use of Asbestos" (1986).

28. International Labour Organization, "Recommendation (No. 177) concerning Safety in the Use of Chemicals at Work" (1990).

29. International Labour Office, *General Survey concerning the Occupational Safety and Health Convention, 1981*, 44.

30. Ibid., 49.

31. Ibid., 18.

32. Ibid., 19.

33. "Convention (No. 187) concerning the Promotional Framework for Occupational Safety and Health, 57553 U.N.T.S. 45739 (2006)."

34. International Labour Office, *General Survey concerning the Occupational Safety and Health Convention, 1981*, 21.

35. ILO, "Convention (No. 155) concerning Occupational Safety and Health and the Working Environment, 1331 U.N.T.S. 22345 (1981)." Article 5(e).

36. ILO, *General Survey concerning the Occupational Safety and Health Convention, 1981*, 25.

37. Ibid., 24.

38. Ibid., paragraph 149.

39. Labor Management Relations Act 1947. 29 U.S.C. §§ 141 et seq.

40. *Alleluia Cushion Co., Inc. and Jack G. Henley*, 221 NLRB 162 999–1007(1975).

41. Ibid.

42. Ibid.

43. *Dawson Cabinet Company, Inc. and Lois Gastineau*, 228 NLRB 47 290–93(1977).

44. *Air Surrey Corporation and Randy Patton*, 229 NLRB 155 1064–73(1977).

45. *Steere Dairy, Inc. and David L. Watkins*, 237 NLRB 219 1350–54(1978).

46. *Ontario Knife Company and Angel L. Cobado*, 247 NLRB 168 1288–98(1980).

47. *Pink Moody, Inc. and Reynaldo Salinas*, 237 NLRB 7 39–44(1978).

48. *General Nutrition Center, Inc. and Patricia Roach*, 221 NLRB 130 850–61(1975).

49. *Diagnostic Center Hospital Corp. of Texas and International Brotherhood of Teamsters, Chauf-feurs, Warehousemen and Helpers of America, Local Union No. 988 and Yolanda Garza de Birdwell*, 228 NLRB 143 1215–34(1977).

50. Ibid., 1217.

51. *Alleluia Cushion Co., Inc. and Jack G. Henley*, 1000.

52. The first of these cases was *Marshall v. Daniel Construction Co.*, 563 F. 2d 707 (CA5)(1977). The second case was *Marshall v. Certified Welding Corp.*, No. 77–2048 (CA10)(1978). The case that was decided by the Supreme Court was *Whirlpool Corp. v. Marshall*, 445 U.S. 1(1980).

53. *Whirlpool Corp. v. Marshall*.

54. Ibid., 10.

55. Ibid., 21.

56. See *Meyers Industries, Inc. and Kenneth P. Prill*, 268 73. In 1985 the U.S. Court of Appeals for the District of Columbia Circuit remanded the case for erroneously assuming the statute mandated the Board's interpretation of concerted activities. The case was clarified by the NLRB in *Meyers Industries, Inc. and Kenneth P. Prill*, 281 NLRB 118 882–89(1986).

57. Kenneth Lasch Smukler, "Individual Safety Protests in the Nonunion Workplace: Hazardous Decisions under Hazardous Conditions," *Dickinson Law Review* 89 (1984–85).

58. *Meyers Industries, Inc. and Kenneth P. Prill*, dissenting opinion, 499.

59. Brown, "The Right to Refuse Unsafe Work," 5.

60. *Systems with Reliability, Inc. and Duane L. Albaugh*, 322 NLRB 132 757–62(1996), 760. Quotation in this case is from *Eastex, Inc. v. N.L.R.B.*, 437 U.S. 556(1978), 564–67.

61. Charles Craypo and Bruce Nissen, *Grand Designs: The Impact of Corporate Strategies on Workers, Unions, and Communities* (Ithaca: ILR Press, 1993).

62. Gil Troy, *The Reagan Revolution: A Very Short Introduction* (Oxford: Oxford University Press, 2009), 114.

63. *Council Directive 89/391/EEC of 12 June 1989 on the Introduction of Measures to Encourage Improvements in the Safety and Health of Workers at Work*.

64. International Labour Office, *ILO Standards-Related Activities in the Area of Occupational Safety and Health: An In-depth Study for Discussion with a View to the Elaboration of a Plan of Action for Such Activities*. Sixth item on the agenda of the International Labour Conference, Report VI, 91st Session. Geneva: International Labour Office, 2003), 13.

65. *Stockholm Convention on Persistent Organic Pollutants (entered into force 17 May 2004)*, 2256 UNTS 119.

66. *Rotterdam Convention on the Prior Informed Consent Procedure for Certain Hazardous Chemicals (entered into force 24 February 2004)*, 2244 UNTS 337.

67. *Basel Convention on the Control of Transboundary Movements of Hazardous Wastes and Their Disposal (entered into force 5 May 1992)*, 1673 UNTS 57.

68. *ILO Standards-Related Activities in the Area of Occupational Safety and Health*, 12–13.

69. Ibid., 13.

4. How Effective Are Convention 155 Refusal Rights?

1. *General Survey concerning the Occupational Safety and Health Convention*, 5.

2. Ibid., 6.

3. Ibid.

4. Ibid.

5. Government of Canada, "Reply Submitted in Response to the 2009 General Survey of the International Labor Organization" (2009).

6. Eric Tucker, "Diverging Trends in Worker Health and Safety Protection and Participation in Canada, 1985–2000," *Relations Industrielles / Industrial Relations* 58, no. 3 (2003).

7. Jane Jenson and Susan D. Phillips, "Redesigning the Canadian Citizenship Regime: Remaking the Institutions of Representation," in *Citizenship, Markets, and the State*, ed. Klaus Eder, Colin Crouch, and Damian Tambini (New York: Oxford University Press, 2001).

8. Robert Hebdon, "Industrial Conflict under Ontario's No-Strike Laws" (University of Toronto, 1992), 274. See also Robert Hebdon and Douglas Hyatt, "The Effects of Industrial Relations Factors on Health and Safety Conflict," *Industrial & Labor Relations Review* 51, no. 4 (July 1998).

9. Eric Tucker, "The Persistence of Market Regulation of Occupational Health and Safety: The Stillbirth of Voluntarism," in *Essays in Labour Relations Law: Papers Presented at the Conference on Government and Labour Relations: The Death of Voluntarism; School of Management, University of Lethbridge, September 6–8, 1984*, ed. G. England (Don Mills, Ontario: CCH Canadian, 1984), 234–35.

10. Marc Renaud and Chantal St-Jacques, "The Right to Refuse in Québec: Five-Year Evolution of a New Mode of Expressing Risk," *International Journal of Health Services* 18, no. 3 (1988).

11. Tucker, "Diverging Trends," 415.

12. Vivienne Walters, "State Mediation of Conflicts over Work Refusals: The Role of the Ontario Labour Relations Board," *International Journal of Health Services* 21, no. 4 (1991): 728.

13. Garry C. Gray, "A Socio-Legal Ethnography of the Right to Refuse Dangerous Work," *Studies in Law, Politics, and Society* 24 (2002).

14. Renaud and St-Jacques, "Right to Refuse in Québec," 413.

15. *Bootlegger Inc. v. Couture*, 500-05-008894-832, decision rendered January 24, 1984, Droit du travail express, number 84 T-171 (1984); *Hôtel-Dieu de Québec v. Lévesque*, Labor Court, Québec, 200-28-000576-832, decision rendered April 12, 1984, Droit du travail express, number 84-T-457 (1984).

16. Robert Sass, "The Need to Broaden the Legal Concept of Risk in Workplace Health and Safety," *Canadian Public Policy–Analyse de Politiques* XII, no. 2 (1986).

17. Renaud and St-Jacques, "Right to Refuse in Québec."

18. Brion, "Right to Refuse Unsafe Work in Ontario," 13.

19. Brown, "Right to Refuse Unsafe Work," 29. See also Richard Fidler, "The Occupational Health and Safety Act and the Internal Responsibility System," *Osgoode Hall Law Journal* 24 (1986).

20. *Robert Pharand, Peter Digiglio and John Tolin, et al, Applicants, v. Inco Metals Co., Respondent*, 1297-79-U [1980] OLRB Rep. July 981(1980).

21. John Mark Lawrence Harcourt, "The Right to Refuse Unsafe Work: Arbitration and Labour Relations Board Decisions" (PhD diss., University of Alberta, 1995), 130. See also Mark Harcourt and Sondra Harcourt, "When Can an Employee Refuse Unsafe Work and Expect to Be Protected from Discipline? Evidence from Canada," *Industrial and Labor Relations Review* 53, no. 4 (2000).

22. Vivienne Walters, "Occupational Health and Safety Legislation in Ontario: An analysis of Its Origins and Content," *Canadian Review of Sociology and Anthropology* 20, no. 4 (1983), 426.

23. *Occupational Safety and Health Act, 29 U.S.C. 660(c), as amended; Public Law 91-596*. Although Section 502 of the Taft-Hartley Act of 1947 outlined refusal rights, OSHA 11(c) was the first refusal protection adopted outside an industrial relations statute.

24. U.S. General Accounting Office, "Whistleblowers: Management of the Program to Protect Trucking Company Employees Against Reprisal. Report GAO/GGD-88-123. September 1988" (Washington, D.C., 1988), 11–12.

25. Risa L. Lieberwitz, "Whistleblowing in the United States" Colloque International, *Les normes de RSE: Mise en œurve, contrôle et sanctions,* October 27–29, 2010, COMPTRASEC, CNRS, Université Montresquieu Bordeaux IV, France (conference paper, 2010), 12.

26. Office of the Inspector General, U.S. Department of Labor, "Nationwide Audit of OSHA's Section 11(c) Discrimination Investigations. Report No. 05-97-107-10-105. March 31, 1997" (Washington, D.C., 1997), 34.

27. Ibid.

28. Office of Inspector General, U.S. Department of Labor, "Complainants Did Not Always Receive Appropriate Investigations under the Whistleblower Protection Program. Report No. 02-10-202-10-105" (Washington, D.C., 2010), 22.

29. U.S. Government Accountability Office, "Whistleblower Protection Program: Better Data and Improvised Oversight Would Help Ensure Program Quality and Consistency. Report GAO-09-106. January 2009" (Washington, D.C., 2009), 25–27. See also "Whistleblower Protection: Sustained Management Attention Needs to Address Long-Standing Program Weaknesses. Report GAO-10-722. August 2010" (Washington, D.C., 2010).

30. Ibid, 37–39.

31. Ibid.

32. Occupational Health and Safety Administration, Region 4 (Atlanta), "Final Investigative Report. Section 11(c) Refusal to Work Complaint" (closed May 22, 2006, on file with author as Case No. 76).

33. "Census of Fatal Occupational Injuries, 2004–2008." Washington, D.C.: U.S. Department of Labor.

34. Bureau of Labor Statistics, "Union Members Survey. 2010." Washington, D.C.: U.S. Department of Labor.

35. U.S. Government Accountability Office, "Whistleblower Protection Program: Better Data and Improved Oversight Would Help Ensure Program Quality and Consistency. Report GAO-09-106. January 2009." See also T. McGarity et al., "Workers at Risk: Regulatory Dysfunction at OSHA," Center for Progressive Regulation (2010). Office of the Inspector General, U.S. Department of Labor, "Complainants Did Not Always Receive Appropriate Investigations" note 28.

36. Occupational Health and Safety Administration, Region 4 (Atlanta), "Final Investigative Report. Section 11(c) Refusal to Work Complaint." (closed March 28, 2005, on file with author as Case No. 06).

37. OSHA Region 4 (Atlanta), "Final Investigative Report. Section 11(c) Refusal to Work Complaint" (closed February 13, 2006, on file with author as Case No. 71).

38. OSHA Region 4 (Atlanta), "Final Investigative Report. Section 11(c) Refusal to Work Complaint" (closed April 24, 2006, on file with author as Case No. 54).

39. OSHA Region 4 (Atlanta), "Final Investigative Report. Section 11(c) Refusal to Work Complaint" (closed June 29, 2006, on file with author as Case No. 70).

40. OSHA Region 4 (Atlanta), "Final Investigative Report. Section 11(c) Refusal to Work Complaint" (closed November 15, 2005, on file with author as Case No. 36).

41. Occupational Health and Safety Administration, Region 5 (Chicago), "Final Investigative Report. Section 11(c) Refusal to Work Complaint" (closed June 13, 2006, on file with author as Case No. 144).

5. Ideological Origins of the Global Framework

1. John Scott and Gordon Marshall, *A Dictionary of Sociology*, 3rd ed. (Oxford: Oxford University Press, 2005).

2. For a more in-depth analysis of the relationship between worker health and safety standards and the global trade debate, see Howard D. Samuel, "International Occupational Health Standards: An American Perspective," *American Journal of Industrial Medicine* 6 (1984).

3. According to the official filing of the notice to withdraw from ILO membership in 1975, the United States expressed in writing two reasons for its departure, disappointment with the condemnation of Israel at the ILO without an investigation and a lax attitude by the organization in seeking compliance with labor standards by the Soviet Union and its allies.

4. Alfred Robens, *Ten Year Stint* (London: Cassell & Company, 1972), 1.

5. Ibid., 9–10. His appointment was denounced by many trade unionists. Mineworkers and the colliery managers association feared an outside chairman would restructure the industry in a way that would ultimately harm workers and the nation. Alfred Robens's first act as chairmen of the National Coal Board was to tour every coal field, to, in his words, "give me a chance to assess the quality of the people occupying these posts, to get their views on the prospects of the industry, and to establish myself as the future Chairman." Robens later noted in detail his lessons learned from the tour: "My tour of the coalfields and discussions with experts both inside the industry and among our customers and suppliers had, long before I finally took over the Chairmanship, convinced me that what the Coal Board needed was a massive sales campaign, backed up by the greatest mechanization drive the industry had ever seen and a complete administrative reorganization. The need for the sales drive was obvious. Coal had been losing business for several years, stocks had been piling up at the pithead, and competition from fuel oil was intense. On the production side, I could see that new machines capable of carrying the industry to unheard-of heights of productivity were already available. What was needed was determined and sustained effort to bring them rapidly into the pits and with goodwill on the part of the men. I could see that this was something the unions would support wholeheartedly and, to this day, there has been no Ludditism in the industry."

6. Ibid., 310.

7. Martin Johnes and the individual sources, Iain McLean, 1999, "The Last Day before Half-Term," http://www.nuffield.ox.ac.uk/politics/aberfan/chap1.htm.

8. Iain McLean, "Heartless Bully Who Added to Agony of Aberfan," *Observer*, January 5, 1997. Quote from Prime Minister Harold Wilson.

9. Tribunal Appointed to Inquire into the Disaster at Aberfan on October 21st, 1966, *Report of the Tribunal Appointed to Inquire into the Disaster at Aberfan on October 21st, 1966* (London: Her Majesty's Stationery Office, 1967). See also Robens, *Ten Year Stint*, 256.

10. *Report of the Tribunal.*

11. McLean, "Heartless Bully Who Added to Agony of Aberfan."

12. Ibid.

13. Chairman Committee on Safety and Health at Work; Lord Robens, *Safety and Health at Work, Report of the Committee, 1970–1972* (presented to Parliament by the Secretary of State for Employment by Command of Her Majesty) (London: Her Majesty's Stationery Office, 1972), xiv.

14. R.C. Browne, "Safety and Health at Work: The Robens Report," *British Journal of Industrial Medicine* 30, no. 1 (1973): 87.

15. The Robens Committee visited the United States in May 1971 shortly after the passage of the U.S. Occupational Safety and Health Act of 1970.

16. Browne, "Safety and Health at Work: The Robens Report," 87–88.

17. Committee on Safety and Health at Work; Lord Robens, *Safety and Health at Work, Report of the Committee, 1970–1972*, 7.

18. Browne, "Safety and Health at Work: The Robens Report," 88.

19. Committee on Safety and Health at Work; Lord Robens, *Safety and Health at Work, Report of the Committee, 1970–1972*, 5.

20. See Ashford, *Crisis in the Workplace: Occupational Disease and Injury, A Report to the Ford Foundation*, 514.

21. Institute of Electrical and Electronics Engineers Canada, 1977, "McNaughton Medal Winner Biographies," http://www.ieee.ca/awards/bios.htm.

22. Robert Sass, "Interview with the Author" (Saskatoon, February 2010).

23. Michael Useem, *The Inner Circle: Large Corporations and the Rise of Business Political Activity in the U.S. and U.K* (New York: Oxford University Press, 1984), 194.

24. John Porter, *The Vertical Mosaic: An Analysis of Social Class and Power in Canada* (Toronto: University of Toronto Press, 1968), 299–307.

25. Ibid.

26. Ibid.

27. Ibid.

28. Royal Commission on the Health and Safety of Workers in the Mines, James M. Ham, Commissioner, *Report of the Royal Commission on the Health and Safety of Workers in the Mines* (Toronto: Ministry of the Attorney General, 1976), preface.

29. Ibid., 249

30. Ibid., 250.

31. Ibid.

32. Ibid., 178.

33. Ibid.

34. Economics and Research Branch, Labour Canada, *Safety Enforcement Policies and Practices in Canada* (Ottawa: Department of Labour, 1975), 28.

35. Ibid., 34.

36. Ibid., 42.

37. Dennis Gruending, "Encyclopedia of Saskatchewan: Blakeney, Allan E. (1925–)," http://esask.uregina.ca/entry/blakeney_allan_e_1925-.html.

38. "A Rights-Based Approach to Workplace Health and Safety" (unpublished paper on file with author, undated), 2.

39. Ibid., 3.

40. Robert Sass, "The Work Environment Board and the Limits of Social Democracy in Canada," *International Journal of Health Services* 23, no. 2 (1993): 280.

41. "A Rights-Based Approach to Workplace Health and Safety," 5.

42. Ibid., 13.

43. Sass, "Interview with the Author."

44. The language protecting the right to refuse was under Section 26. See Saskatchewan Labour Occupational Health and Safety Branch, *Manual for Occupational Health Committees* (Saskatoon: Saskatchewan Labour, 1978), 8.

SECTION 26—RIGHT OF WORKER TO REFUSE DANGEROUS ACTS

(1) A worker may refuse to do any particular act or series of acts at work which he has reasonable grounds to believe are unusually dangerous to his health or safety or the health and safety of any other person at the place of employment until the occupational health committee or occupational health officers has investigated the matter and advised him otherwise.

(2) No discriminatory action shall be taken against any worker by reason of the fact that he has exercised the right conferred upon him by subsection (1).

(3) Where discriminatory action shall be taken against any worker who has exercised the right conferred upon him by subsection (1), there shall be a presumption in favour of the worker that the discriminatory action was taken against him for that reason, and the onus shall be upon the employer to establish that the worker was discriminated against for good and sufficient other reason.

45. Sass, "Rights-Based Approach to Workplace Health and Safety," 18.

46. Ibid., 15.

47. Sass, "Interview with the Author."

48. Ibid.

49. Sass, "Rights-Based Approach to Workplace Health and Safety," 15.

50. Bruce G. Doern, "The Political Economy of Regulating Occupational Health: The Ham and Beaudry Reports," *Canadian Public Administration–Administration Publique du Canada* 20, no. 1 (1977).

51. Walters, "Occupational Health and Safety Legislation in Ontario."

52. Ibid., 427.

53. Ibid.

54. Ibid., 429.

55. Ontario New Democratic Party Task Force on Occupational Safety and Health, *Not Yet Healthy, Not Yet Safe* (Toronto: Ontario New Democratic Party, 1983).

56. Ibid., 1.

57. Ibid., 1–2.

58. Ibid., 3.

59. Ibid. For detailed stories, see 17–20.

60. Ontario New Democratic Party Task Force on Occupational Safety and Health, *Not Yet Healthy, Not Yet Safe*, 20.

61. Ibid., 2. Quote is from Ron Rowbottom, occupational health and safety coordinator, Simcoe Can Workers' Union, Local 535.

62. Ibid., 2.

63. NDP Special Task Force on Occupational Health and Safety in the Federal Workplace, *Graveyard Shifts: Life and Death on the Job in Canada* (Ottawa: New Democratic Party, 1982).

64. Second Task Force on Occupational Health and Safety, *Still Not Healthy, Still Not Safe* (Toronto: Ontario New Democratic Party, 1986).

65. Robert Sass, "The Corruption of Occupational Health and Safety in Canada: The Triumph of the Internal Responsibility System (IRS) as Public Policy" (unpublished paper on file with author, undated).

66. Ibid.

67. Colin Aykroyd, "An Examination of the Right to Refuse Unsafe Work," *Labor Research Bulletin* (Research and Planning Branch, Province of British Columbia, Ministry of Labour) 6, no. 6 (1978): 12.

6. Negotiating "Safe" Rights versus Seeking Social Justice

1. John Mainwaring, *A Review of International Labour Conventions* (Ottawa: International Labour Affairs Branch, Labour Canada, 1974), 4, 30. See also John Mainwaring, *Canada as an ILO Member: Performance and Potential*, a paper presented to the International Affairs Seminar of the Canadian Labour Congress (Ottawa: International Labour Affairs Branch, Labour Canada, 1968).

2. John Mainwaring, *The International Labour Organization: A Canadian View* (Ottawa: Labour Canada, 1986), 154.

3. International Labour Office, *ILO Governing Body Spring Session Decisions*. Press release, March 1, 1974 (Geneva: International Labour Office, 1974).

4. International Labour Office, *Making Work More Human, Working Conditions and Environment, Report of the Director-General to the 60th International Labour Conference* (Geneva: International Labour Office, 1975), 2.

5. *ILO Governing Body Spring Session Decisions*.

6. Ibid.

7. ILO, *Making Work More Human, Working Conditions and Environment*, 13.

8. Ibid., 76.

9. Mainwaring, *International Labour Organization: A Canadian View*, 153.

10. International Labour Organization Governing Body, *Draft Minutes of the 208th Session*. November 14–17 (Geneva: International Labour Office, 1978).

11. International Labour Office, "Individual Country Responses to Question 9 of the 2009 General Survey concerning the Occupational Safety and Health Convention, 1981 (No. 155), the Occupational Safety and Health Recommendation, 1981 (No. 164), and the Protocol of 2002 to the Occupational Safety and Health Convention, 1981." (Unpublished, on file with author).

12. International Labour Office, *Proposed Conclusions on Safety and Health and the Working Environment* (Report VII (a) (2) for the 66th Session of the International Labour Conference (Geneva: International Labour Office, 1980), 78.

13. Ibid., 80.

14. International Labour Office, *Record of Proceedings of the 66th Session of the International Labour Conference* (Geneva: International Labour Organization, 1980), 14/7.

15. The term new international economic order was advanced by a group of Third World governments in the 1970s who advocated more equitable terms of international trade and development.

16. Steve Charnovitz, "The Influence of International Labour Standards on the World Trading Regime," *International Labour Review* 126, no. 5 (1987).

17. International Labour Office, *Record of Proceedings of the 66th Session of the International Labour Conference*, 14/7 (Marshall).

18. Ibid.

19. Ibid.

20. Ibid.

21. Ibid., 35/1.

22. Ibid., 35/2.

23. Ibid., 35/1.

24. Ibid., 35/2.

25. International Labour Office, *Safety and Health and the Working Environment*. Report VI (1) to the 67th International Labour Conference (Geneva: International Labour Office, 1981), 56.

26. ILO, *Record of Proceedings of the 66th Session of the International Labour Conference*, 35/9–10.

27. Ibid., 35/14.

28. Ibid.

29. Ibid., 35/14–35/17.

30. ILO, *Record of Proceedings of the 66th Session of the International Labour Conference*, 35/15. The reason for the large number of votes is the ILO's traditional weighting of the votes of the members of the committee to assure tripartite voting between government, employer, and worker delegates.

31. Ibid., 42/1.

32. Ibid.

33. Ibid., 42/2–42/3.

34. International Labour Organization, *Record of Proceedings of the 67th Session of the International Labour Conference* (Geneva: International Labour Organization, 1981), 25/1.

35. Ibid.

36. Ibid., 25/2.

37. ILO, *Safety and Health and the Working Environment*, 64.

38. ILO, *Record of Proceedings of the 67th Session of the International Labour Conference*, 25/5.

39. Ibid.

40. Ibid., 25/5–25/6.

41. Ibid., 25/10.

42. Ibid.

43. Ibid., 25/11.

44. Ibid.

45. ILO, *General Survey concerning the Occupational Safety and Health Convention, 1981.*

46. ILO, *Record of Proceedings of the 67th Session of the International Labour Conference*, 30/1–30/2.

47. Ibid.,

48. Ibid., 30/2.

49. Ibid., 30/4.

50. Ibid., 30/3.

Conclusion

1. ILO, *General Survey concerning the Occupational Safety and Health Convention, 1981*, 29.

2. Ibid., 82.

3. *Meyers Industries, Inc. and Kenneth P. Prill.*

4. "Universal Declaration of Human Rights, General Assembly Resolution 217A, at 71, U.N. GAOR, 3rd Sess., 1st plen. mtg., U.N. Doc A/810," Article 8.

5. World Conference on Human Rights, "Vienna Declaration and Programme of Action, U.N. Doc. A/CONF.157/23," Article 1.

6. International Labour Office, *Making Work More Human, Working Conditions and Environ-ment, Report of the Director-General to the 60th International Labour Conference*.

7. Ross Lambertson, "'The Dresden Story': Racism, Human Rights, and the Jewish Labour Committee of Canada," *Labour/Le Travail* 47 (Spring 2001). See also Ross Lambertson, *Repression and Resistance: Canadian Human Rights Activists, 1930–1960* (Toronto: University of Toronto Press, 2005).

8. Antony Evelyn Alcock, *History of the International Labor Organization*, 1st American ed. (New York: Octagon Books, 1971).

BIBLIOGRAPHY

Address by the President of the United States of America to the Delegates Attending the Twenty-Sixth Session of the International Labour Conference. 1944.

Air Surrey Corporation and Randy Patton, 229 NLRB 155 1064–73 (1977).

Alcock, Antony Evelyn. *History of the International Labor Organization*. 1st American ed. New York: Octagon Books, 1971.

Alleluia Cushion Co., Inc. and Jack G. Henley, 221 NLRB 162 999–1007 (1975).

Alston, Philip. "'Core Labour Standards' and the Transformation of the International Labour Rights Regime." *European Journal of International Law* 15, no. 3 (2004): 457.

Ashford, Nicholas A. *Crisis in the Workplace: Occupational Disease and Injury, a Report to the Ford Foundation*. Cambridge: MIT Press, 1976.

Atleson, James B. *Values and Assumptions in American Labor Law*. Amherst: University of Massachusetts Press, 1983.

"Average Guy Takes a Poke at Pollution—He's Winning." *Cleveland Press*, September 23, 1971.

Aykroyd, Colin. "An Examination of the Right to Refuse Unsafe Work." Research and Planning Branch, Province of British Columbia, Ministry of Labour. *Labor Research Bulletin* 6, no. 6 (1978): 10–18.

Bachrach, Peter, and Morton S. Baratz. "Decisions and Nondecisions: An Analytic Framework." *American Political Science Review* 57, no. 3 (1963): 632–42.

———. *Power and Poverty; Theory and Practice*. New York: Oxford University Press, 1970.

———. "Two Faces of Power." *American Political Science Review* 56, no. 4 (1962): 947–52.

Basel Convention on the Control of Transboundary Movements of Hazardous Wastes and Their Disposal (Entered into Force 5 May 1992), 1673 UNTS 57.

Bootlegger Inc. v. Couture, 500-05-008894-832, decision rendered January 24, 1984, Droit du travail express, number 84 T-171 (1984).

Brion, Arturo Dizon. "The Right to Refuse Unsafe Work in Ontario." LLM thesis, York University, 1995.

Brown, Richard. "The Right to Refuse Unsafe Work." *University of British Columbia Law Review* 17, no. 1 (1983): 1–34.

Browne, R. C. "Safety and Health at Work: The Robens Report." *British Journal of Industrial Medicine* 30, no. 1 (1973): 87–94.

Bryant, Anthony, and Kathy Charmaz. *The Sage Handbook of Grounded Theory*. Thousand Oaks, CA: Sage Publications 2007.

Bureau of Labor Statistics. *Handbook of Labor Statistics*. Washington, D.C.: United States Department of Labor, 1971.

———. *Handbook of Labor Statistics*. Washington, D.C.: United States Department of Labor, 1976.

———. *Union Members Survey*. 2010. Washington, D.C.: U.S. Department of Labor.

———. *Work Stoppages, Summary 76–7*. Washington, D.C.: United States Department of Labor, 1975.

Carey, Alex, and Andrew Lohrey. *Taking the Risk Out of Democracy: Corporate Propaganda versus Freedom and Liberty*. Urbana-Champaign: University of Illinois Press, 1997.

Carter, Chris, Stewart Clegg, and Martin Kornberger. *A Very Short, Fairly Interesting, and Reasonably Cheap Book about Studying Strategy*. Thousand Oaks: Sage Publications, 2008.

Census of Fatal Occupational Injuries, 2004–2008. Washington, D.C.: U.S. Department of Labor.

Chang, Ha-Joon. "The Market, the State, and Institutions in Economic Development." In *Rethinking Development Economics*, edited by Ha-Joon Chang. New York: Anthem Press, 2003.

Charnovitz, Steve. "The Influence of International Labour Standards on the World Trading Regime." *International Labour Review* 126, no. 5 (1987): 565–84.

Chouhan, T. R. *Bhopal: The Inside Story*. New York: Council on International and Public Affairs, 2004.

Committee on Safety and Health at Work; Lord Robens, Chairman. *Safety and Health at Work, Report of the Committee, 1970–1972*. Presented to Parliament by the Secretary of State for Employment. London: Her Majesty's Stationery Office, 1972.

"Convention (No. 87) concerning Freedom of Association and Protection of the Right to Organise, 68 U.N.T.S. 17 (1950)."

"Convention (No. 98) concerning the Application of the Principles of the Right to Organise and to Bargain Collectively, 96 U.N.T.S. 258 (1951)."

"Convention (No. 155) concerning Occupational Safety and Health and the Working Environment, 1331 U.N.T.S. 22345 (1981)."

"Convention (No. 158) concerning Termination of Employment at the Initiative of the Employer, 1412 U.N.T.S. 23645 (1982)."

"Convention (No. 176) concerning Safety and Health in Mines, 2029 U.N.T.S. 207 (1995)."

"Convention (No. 187) concerning the Promotional Framework for Occupational Safety and Health, 57553 U.N.T.S. 45739 (2006)."

Council Directive 89/391/EEC of 12 June 1989 on the Introduction of Measures to Encourage Improvements in the Safety and Health of Workers at Work.

Coutu, Michel, and Gregor Murray. "Towards Citizenship at Work?" *Relations Industrielles / Industrial Relations* 60, no. 4 (2005): 617–30.

Cowie, Jefferson, and Nick Salvatore. "The Long Exception: Rethinking the Place of the New Deal in American History." *International Labor and Working-Class History* 74, no. 1 (2008): 3–32.

Craven, Matthew. "Assessment of the Progress on Adjudication of Economic, Social and Cultural Rights." In *The Road to a Remedy: Current Issues in the Litigation of Economic, Social and Cultural Rights*, edited by John Squires, Malcolm Langford and Bret Thiele, 27–42. Sydney: University of New South Wales Press, 2005.

Craven, Matthew C.R. *The International Covenant on Economic, Social and Cultural Rights: A Perspective on Its Development.* Oxford: Clarendon Press, 1995.

Craypo, Charles, and Bruce Nissen. *Grand Designs: The Impact of Corporate Strategies on Workers, Unions, and Communities.* Ithaca: ILR Press, 1993.

Dawson Cabinet Company, Inc. and Lois Gastineau, 228 NLRB 47 290–93 (1977).

Declaration of the United Nations Conference on the Human Environment. 1972. Adopted at the 21st plenary meeting in Stockholm on June 16.

Diagnostic Center Hospital Corp. of Texas and International Brotherhood of Teamsters, Chauffeurs, Warehousemen and Helpers of America, Local Union No. 988 and Yolanda Garza De Birdwell, 228 NLRB 143 1215–34 (1977).

Doern, Bruce G. "The Political Economy of Regulating Occupational Health: The Ham and Beaudry Reports." *Canadian Public Administration-Administration Publique du Canada* 20, no. 1 (1977): 1–35.

Duane Carlson, Plaintiff, v. Arrowhead Concrete Works, Inc., Defendant, 375 F. Supp. 2d 835, D. Minn. (2005).

Dunlop, John T. *Industrial Relations Systems.* Harvard Business School Press Classics. Revised ed. Boston: Harvard Business School Press [1958], 1993.

Eastex, Inc. v. N.L.R.B., 437 U.S. 556 (1978).

Economics and Research Branch, Labour Canada. *Safety Enforcement Policies and Practices in Canada.* Ottawa: Department of Labour, 1975.

Ehrenreich, Barbara, and Tom Ehrenreich. "Conscience of a Steelworker." *Nation,* September 25, 1971.

"Environmentalists Try to Win Labor Over: Using Workplace Safety and a Promise of New Jobs to Entice Labor's Support." *Business Week,* October 3, 1977.

Erlandson, Douglas W. c. 1979. "The Shell Strike of 1973." http://www.usw12-591.org/strike1973.html.

Evans, Peter. "The Eclipse of the State? Reflections on Stateness in an Era of Globalization." *World Politics* 50, no. 1 (1997): 62–87.

Evans, Tony. "International Human Rights Law as Power/Knowledge." *Human Rights Quarterly* 27, no. 3 (August 2005): 1046–68.

A Failure of Initiative: Final Report of the Select Bipartisan Committee to Investigate the Preparation for and Response to Hurricane Katrina. 2006. Washington, DC: Government Printing Office.

Fidler, Richard. "The Occupational Health and Safety Act and the Internal Responsibility System." *Osgoode Hall Law Journal* 24 (1986): 315–52.

Fields, Gary S. *Trade and Labour Standards: A Review of the Issues*. Paris: Organisation for Economic Co-operation and Development, 1995.

"The First Strike over Potential Hazards to Health." *San Francisco Examiner*, March 4, 1973.

Frymer, Paul. *Black and Blue: African Americans, the Labor Movement, and the Decline of the Democratic Party*. Princeton: Princeton University Press, 2008.

Gaventa, John. *Power and Powerlessness: Quiescence and Rebellion in an Appalachian Valley*. Urbana: University of Illinois Press, 1982.

General Nutrition Center, Inc. and Patricia Roach, 221 NLRB 130 850–61 (1975).

Gernigon, B., H. Guido, and A. Odero. *ILO Principles concerning the Right to Strike*. International Labour Organization, 2000.

Gerry Rodgers, Eddy Lee, Lee Swepston, and Jasmien Van Daele. *The ILO and the Quest for Social Justice, 1919–2009*. Geneva: International Labour Office, 2009.

Gersuny, Carl. *Work Hazards and Industrial Conflict*. Hanover, N.H.: University Press of New England, 1981.

Giuffrida, Antonio, Roberto F. Iunes, and William D. Savedoff. *Economic and Health Effects of Occupational Hazards in Latin America and the Caribbean*. Technical Papers Series No. Soc-121, edited by Sustainable Development Department. Washington, D.C.: Inter-American Development Bank, 2001.

———. "Occupational Risks in Latin America and the Caribbean: Economic and Health Dimensions." *Health Policy and Planning* 17, no. 3 (2002): 235–46.

Glaser, Barney G. "The Constant Comparative Method of Qualitative Analysis." *Social Problems* 12, no. 4 (1965): 436–45.

Glaser, Barney G., and Anselm L. Strauss. *The Discovery of Grounded Theory; Strategies for Qualitative Research*. New Brunswick, N.J.: Aldine Transaction [1967], 2006.

Godard, John. "An Institutional Environments Approach to Industrial Relations." In *New Directions in the Study of Work and Employment: Revitalizing Industrial Relations as an Academic Enterprise*, edited by Charles J. Whalen, 68–86. Cheltenham: Edward Elgar, 2008.

Gordon, Robert. "Poisons in the Fields: The United Farm Workers, Pesticides, and Environmental Politics." *Pacific Historical Review* 68, no. 1 (1999): 51–77.

———. "Shell No! OCAW and the Labor Environmental Alliance." *Environmental History* 3, no. 4 (1998): 460–87.

Government of Canada. "Reply Submitted in Response to the 2009 General Survey of the International Labor Organization." 2009.

Gray, Garry C. "A Socio-Legal Ethnography of the Right to Refuse Dangerous Work." *Studies in Law, Politics, and Society* 24 (2002): 133–69.

Gross, James A. *Broken Promise: The Subversion of U.S. Labor Relations Policy, 1947–1994*. Philadelphia: Temple University Press, 1995.

Gross, James A., and Patricia Greenfield. "Arbitral Value Judgments in Health and Safety Disputes: Management Rights over Workers' Rights." *Buffalo Law Review* 34 (1985): 645.

Gruending, Dennis. "Encyclopedia of Saskatchewan: Blakeney, Allan E. (1925–)." http://esask.uregina.ca/entry/blakeney_allan_e_1925-.html.

"Gulf Rig Workers Could Have Called 'Time-Out'." *CNN Money*, May 27, 2010.

Hall, Peter A., and David W. Soskice. "An Introduction to Varieties of Capitalism." In *Varieties of Capitalism: The Institutional Foundations of Comparative Advantage*, edited by Peter A. Hall and David W. Soskice. New York: Oxford University Press, 2001.

Harcourt, John Mark Lawrence. "The Right to Refuse Unsafe Work: Arbitration and Labour Relations Board Decisions." PhD diss., University of Alberta, 1995.

Harcourt, Mark, and Sondra Harcourt. "When Can an Employee Refuse Unsafe Work and Expect to Be Protected from Discipline? Evidence from Canada." *Industrial and Labor Relations Review* 53, no. 4 (2000): 684–703.

Hardy, Cynthia. "The Nature of Unobtrusive Power." *Journal of Management Studies* 22, no. 4 (1985): 384–99.

Health Research Group. *Job Safety and Health: Inadequate Enforcement and Stalled Review*. Washington D.C.: Health Research Group, c. 1975.

Hebdon, Robert. "Industrial Conflict under Ontario's No-Strike Laws." University of Toronto, 1992.

Hebdon, Robert, and Douglas Hyatt. "The Effects of Industrial Relations Factors on Health and Safety Conflict." *Industrial and Labor Relations Review* 51, no. 4 (July 1998): 579–93.

Henderson, Hazel. "Ecologists versus Economists." *Harvard Business Review* 51 (July-August 1973): 28–36, 152–57.

Hirschman, Albert O. *The Rhetoric of Reaction: Perversity, Futility, Jeopardy*. Cambridge: Belknap Press, Harvard University Press, 1991.

Holmwood, Leigh. "ABC Wins Gizbert Appeal." *Guardian*, August 21, 2006.

Hôtel-Dieu de Québec v. Lévesque, Labor Court, Québec, 200-28-000576-832, decision rendered April 12, 1984, Droit du travail express, number 84-T-457 (1984).

Human Rights Watch. *Unfair Advantage: Workers' Freedom of Association in the United States under International Human Rights Standards*. New York: Human Rights Watch, 2000.

——. "You'll Be Fired if You Refuse: Labor Abuses in Zambia's Chinese State-Owned Copper Mines." New York: Human Rights Watch, 2011.

ILO Programme on HIV/AIDS and the World of Work. "Implementing the ILO Code of Practice on HIV/AIDS and the World of Work: An Education Training Manual." Geneva: International Labour Office, 2003.

"In Gulf, It Was Unclear Who Was in Charge of Rig." *New York Times*, June 5, 2010.

Institute of Electrical and Electronics Engineers Canada. 1977. "Mcnaughton Medal Winner Biographies." http://www.ieee.ca/awards/bios.htm.

International Covenant on Economic, Social and Cultural Rights, 993 U.N.T.S. 3 (1966).

International Labour Office. *Freedom of Association: Digest of Decisions and Principles of the Freedom of Association Committee of the Governing Body of the ILO*. 5th [rev.] ed. Geneva: International Labour Office, 2006.

——. *General Survey concerning the Occupational Safety and Health Convention, 1981 (No. 155), the Occupational Safety and Health Recommendation, 1981 (No. 164), and the Protocol of 2002 to the Occupational Safety and Health Convention, 1981*. 98th Session, Report III, Part 1B, 2009.

——. *General Survey: Freedom of Association and Collective Bargaining. Report Iii, Part 4b*. Geneva: International Labour Office, 1994.

——. *ILO Governing Body Spring Session Decisions*. Press release, March 1, 1974. Geneva: International Labour Office, 1974.

——. *ILO Standards-Related Activities in the Area of Occupational Safety and Health: An in-Depth Study for Discussion with a View to the Elaboration of a Plan of Action for Such Activities*. Sixth item on the agenda of the International Labour Conference, Report VI, 91st Session. Geneva: International Labour Office, 2003.

——. "Individual Country Responses to Question 9 of the 2009 General Survey concerning the Occupational Safety and Health Convention, 1981 (No. 155), the Occupational Safety and Health Recommendation, 1981 (No. 164), and the Protocol of 2002 to the Occupational Safety and Health Convention, 1981." Unpublished. On file with author.

——. *Making Work More Human, Working Conditions and Environment, Report of the Director-General to the 60th International Labour Conference*. Geneva: International Labour Office, 1975.

——. "My Life, My Work, My Safe Work: Managing Risk in the Work Environment." Geneva: International Labour Organization and the International Social Security Association, 2008.

——. *Proposed Conclusions on Safety and Health and the Working Environment*. Report VII (a) (2) for the 66th Session of the International Labour Conference. Geneva: International Labour Office, 1980.

——. *Record of Proceedings of the 66th Session of the International Labour Conference*. Geneva: International Labour Organization, 1980.

——. *Record of Proceedings of the 67th Session of the International Labour Conference*. Geneva: International Labour Organization, 1981.

——. *Safety and Health and the Working Environment*. Report VI (1) to the 67th International Labour Conference. Geneva: International Labour Office, 1981.

International Labour Organization. "The Constitution of the International Labour Organization." 15 UNTS 40. Established in 1919, modified by the amendment of 1922 which entered into force on 4 June 1934; the Instrument of Amendment of 1945 which entered into force on 26 September 1946; the Instrument of Amendment of 1946 which entered into force on 20 April 1948; the Instrument of Amendment of 1953 which entered into force on 20 May 1954; the Instrument of Amendment of

1962 which entered into force on 22 May 1963; and the Instrument of Amendment of 1972 which entered into force on 1 November 1974.

——. "Recommendation (No. 172) concerning Safety in the Use of Asbestos." 1986.

——. "Recommendation (No. 177) concerning Safety in the Use of Chemicals at Work." 1990.

International Labour Organization Governing Body. *Draft Minutes of the 208th Session.* November 14–17. Geneva: International Labour Office, 1978.

International Transport Workers Federation. August 3, 2011. "Slovenian Crane Operators Strike over Health and Safety." http://www.itfglobal.org/news-online/index.cfm/newsdetail/6269.

Jenson, Jane, and Susan D. Phillips. "Redesigning the Canadian Citizenship Regime: Remaking the Institutions of Representation." In *Citizenship, Markets, and the State,* edited by Klaus Eder, Colin Crouch, and Damian Tambini, 69–89: Oxford: Oxford University Press, 2001.

Kaufman, Bruce E. *Managing the Human Factor: The Early Years of Human Resource Management in American Industry.* Ithaca: Cornell University Press, 2008.

Kelly, John E. *Rethinking Industrial Relations: Mobilization, Collectivism, and Long Waves.* New York: Routledge, 1998.

Kolben, Kevin. "Labor Rights as Human Rights?" *Virginia Journal of International Law* 50, no. 2 (2010): 450–84.

Labor Management Relations Act. 1947. 29 U.S.C. §§ 141 et seq.

Lamberston, Ross. "'The Dresden Story': Racism, Human Rights, and the Jewish Labour Committee of Canada." *Labour/Le Travail* 47 (Spring 2001): 43–82.

Lambertson, Ross. *Repression and Resistance: Canadian Human Rights Activists, 1930–1960.* Toronto: University of Toronto Press, 2005.

Langford, Malcolm. "The Justiciability of Social Rights: From Practice to Theory." In *Social Rights Jurisprudence: Emerging Trends in International and Comparative Law,* edited by Malcolm Langford, 3–45. Cambridge; New York: Cambridge University Press, 2008.

Lichtenstein, Nelson. "The Rights Revolution." *New Labor Forum* 12, no. 1 (2003): 61–73.

——. *State of the Union: A Century of American Labor.* Princeton: Princeton University Press, 2002.

Lieberwitz, Risa L. "Whistleblowing in the United States." Colloque International, *Les normes de RSE: Mise en œurve, contrôle et sanctions,* 27–29 October 2010, COMPTRASEC, CNRS, Université Montresquieu Bordeaux IV, France. Conference paper, 2010.

Logan, John. "The Union Avoidance Industry in the United States." *British Journal of Industrial Relations* 44, no. 4 (2006): 651–75.

Lukes, Steven. *Power: A Radical View.* 2nd ed. New York: Palgrave Macmillan [1974], 2005.

MacNaughton, Gillian, and Diane F. Frey. "Decent Work for All: A Holistic Human Rights Approach." *SSRN eLibrary* (2010).

Maglich v. Miller-Dwan Medical Center, State of Minnesota Office of Administrative Hearings 1-1901-11970-2 (1999).

Mainwaring, John. *Canada as an ILO Member: Performance and Potential.* Paper presented to the International Affairs Seminar of the Canadian Labour Congress. Ottawa: International Labour Affairs Branch, Labour Canada, 1968.

——. *The International Labour Organization: A Canadian View.* Ottawa: Labour Canada, 1986.

——. *A Review of International Labour Conventions.* Ottawa: International Labour Affairs Branch, Labour Canada, 1974.

Marshall v. Certified Welding Corp., No. 77-2048 (CA10) (1978).

Marshall v. Daniel Construction Co., 563 F. 2d 707 (CA5) (1977).

Mazzocchi, Anthony. "The Workers' Place in Enforcing OSHA." *Annals of the New York Academy of Sciences* 572 (December 1989): 155–56.

——. Unpublished labor education papers on file with author.

McGarity, T., R. Steinzor, S. Shapiro, and M. Shudtz. "Workers at Risk: Regulatory Dysfunction at OSHA." Center for Progressive Regulation (2010).

McIntyre, Richard P. *Are Worker Rights Human Rights?* Ann Arbor: University of Michigan Press, 2008.

McLean, Iain. "Heartless Bully Who Added to Agony of Aberfan." *Observer*, January 5 (1997), 12.

McLean, Iain, Martin Johnes, and the individual sources. 1999. "The Last Day before Half-Term." http://www.nuffield.ox.ac.uk/politics/aberfan/chap1.htm.

Mercier, Laurie. *Anaconda: Labor, Community, and Culture in Montana's Smelter City.* Urbana: University of Illinois Press, 2001.

Meyers Industries, Inc. and Kenneth P. Prill, 268 73.

Meyers Industries, Inc. and Kenneth P. Prill, 281 NLRB 118 882–89 (1986).

Montgomery, David. "The Mythical Man." *International Labor and Working-Class History* 71, no. 1 (2008): 56–62.

——. *Workers' Control in America: Studies in the History of Work, Technology, and Labor Struggles.* Cambridge; New York: Cambridge University Press, 1979.

Morris, Charles J. "NLRB Protection in the Nonunion Workplace: A Glimpse at a General Theory of Section 7 Conduct." *University of Pennsylvania Law Review* 137, no. 5 (1989): 1673–1754.

Morsink, Johannes. *The Universal Declaration of Human Rights: Origins, Drafting and Intent.* Philadelphia: University of Pennsylvania Press, 1999.

NDP Special Task Force on Occupational Health and Safety in the Federal Workplace. *Graveyard Shifts: Life and Death on the Job in Canada.* Ottawa: New Democratic Party, 1982.

"The New Activism on Job Health: A Challenge to Business from Industrial Hygienists on Unions' Payrolls." *Business Week*, September 18, 1978, 146.

NLRB v. Washington Aluminum Company, 370 U.S. 9 (1962).

"Nobel Peace Prize 1969 Presentation Speech." Awarded to the International Labour Organization, 1969. http://www.nobelprize.org/nobel_prizes/peace/laureates/1969/press.html.

Novitz, Tonia. *International and European Protection of the Right to Strike: A Comparative Study of Standards Set by the International Labour Organization, the Council of Europe and the European Union.* Oxford: Oxford University Press, 2003.

Occupational Health and Safety Administration, Region 4 (Atlanta). "Final Investigative Report. Section 11(C) Refusal to Work Complaint." Closed May 22, 2006, on file with author as Case No. 76.

——. "Final Investigative Report. Section 11(C) Refusal to Work Complaint." Closed March 28, 2005, on file with author as Case No. 06.

——. "Final Investigative Report. Section 11(C) Refusal to Work Complaint." Closed June 29, 2006, on file with author as Case No. 70.

——. "Final Investigative Report. Section 11(C) Refusal to Work Complaint." Closed February 13, 2006, on file with author as Case No. 71.

——. "Final Investigative Report. Section 11(C) Refusal to Work Complaint." Closed April 24, 2006, on file with author as Case No. 54.

——. "Final Investigative Report. Section 11(C) Refusal to Work Complaint." Closed November 15, 2005, on file with author as Case No. 36.

Occupational Health and Safety Administration, Region 5 (Chicago). "Final Investigative Report. Section 11(C) Refusal to Work Complaint." Closed June 13, 2006, on file with author as Case No. 144.

Occupational Health and Safety Administration, Region 6 (Dallas). "Final Investigative Report. Section 11(C) Refusal to Work Complaint." Closed May 15, 2007, on file with author as Case No. 281.

Occupational Health and Safety Branch, Saskatchewan Labour. *Manual for Occupational Health Committees*. Saskatoon: Saskatchewan Labour, 1978.

Occupational Safety and Health Act, 29 U.S.C. 660(C), as Amended; Public Law 91–596.

Office of the Inspector General, U.S. Department of Labor. "Complainants Did Not Always Receive Appropriate Investigations under the Whistleblower Protection Program. Report No. 02-10-202-10-105." Washington, D.C., 2010.

——. "Nationwide Audit of OSHA's Section 11(C) Discrimination Investigations. Report No. 05-97-107-10-105. March 31, 1997." Washington, D.C., 1997.

Oldham, James C. "Organized Labor, the Environment, and the Taft-Hartley Act." *Environment Law Review* (1974): 936–1026.

Ontario Knife Company and Angel L. Cobado, 247 NLRB 168 1288–98 (1980).

Ontario New Democratic Party Task Force on Occupational Safety and Health. *Not Yet Healthy, Not Yet Safe*. Toronto: Ontario New Democratic Party, 1983.

Page, Josephe A., and Peter N. Munsing. "Occupational Health and the Federal Government: The Wages Are Still Bitter." *Law and Contemporary Problems* 38 (1974): 651–68.

Pan American Health Organization. *Workers' Health in the Region of the Americas*. 41st Directing Council (CD 41/15). Washington, D.C.: Pan American Health Organization, 1999.

Pink Moody, Inc. and Reynaldo Salinas, 237 NLRB 7 39–44 (1978).

Piore, Michael J., and Sean Safford. "Changing Regimes of Workplace Governance, Shifting Axes of Social Mobilization and the Challenge to Industrial Relations Theory." *Industrial Relations* 45, no. 3 (2006): 299–325.

Polanyi, Karl. *The Great Transformation: The Political and Economic Origins of Our Time*. Boston: Beacon Press, 1957.

Pope, James Gray. "Labor's Constitution of Freedom, 1920–1958." PhD diss. Princeton University, 2004.

Porter, John. *The Vertical Mosaic: An Analysis of Social Class and Power in Canada*. Studies in the Structure of Power: Decision-Making in Canada, 2. Toronto: University of Toronto Press, 1968.

Porter, Michael E. *Competitive Strategy: Techniques for Analyzing Industries and Competitors, with a New Introduction*. New York: Free Press, 1998.

"Prostitute to Sue Brothel over Gun." *The Age*, July 13, 2011.

Reich, Robert B. *Supercapitalism: The Transformation of Business, Democracy, and Everyday Life*. New York: Alfred A. Knopf, 2007.

Renaud, Marc, and Chantal St-Jacques. "The Right to Refuse in Québec: Five-Year Evolution of a New Mode of Expressing Risk." *International Journal of Health Services* 18, no. 3 (1988): 401–17.

Robens, Alfred. *Ten Year Stint*. London: Cassell & Company, 1972.

Robert Pharand, Peter Digiglio, and John Tolin, et al., Applicants, v. Inco Metals Co., Respondent, 1297-79-U [1980] OLRB Rep. July 981 (1980).

Rosenstock, Lisa, Mark Cullen, and Marilyn Fingerhut. "Occupational Health." In *Disease Control Priorities in Developing Countries*, edited by Dean T. Jamison, Joel G. Breman, Anthony R. Measham, George Alleyne, Mariam Claeson, David B. Evans, Prabhat Jha, Anne Mills, and Philip Musgrove, 1127–45. New York: Oxford University Press, 2006.

Rotterdam Convention on the Prior Informed Consent Procedure for Certain Hazardous Chemicals (Entered into Force 24 February 2004), 2244 UNTS 337.

Royal Commission on the Health and Safety of Workers in the Mines, James M. Ham, Commissioner. *Report of the Royal Commission on the Health and Safety of Workers in the Mines*. Toronto: Ministry of the Attorney General, 1976.

Samuel, Howard D. "International Occupational Health Standards: An American Perspective." *American Journal of Industrial Medicine* 6 (1984): 67–73.

Sass, Robert. "The Corruption of Occupational Health and Safety in Canada: The Triumph of the Internal Responsibility System (IRS) as Public Policy." Unpublished paper on file with author, undated.

——. "The Need to Broaden the Legal Concept of Risk in Workplace Health and Safety." *Canadian Public Policy–Analyse De Politiques* XII, no. 2 (1986): 286–93.

——. "A Rights-Based Approach to Workplace Health and Safety." Unpublished paper on file with author, undated.

——. "The Work Environment Board and the Limits of Social Democracy in Canada." *International Journal of Health Services* 23, no. 2 (1993): 279–300.

Schattschneider, E. E. *The Semisovereign People: a Realist's View of Democracy in America*. New York: Holt, Rinehart and Winston, 1960.

Scott, John, and Gordon Marshall. *A Dictionary of Sociology*. 3rd ed. Toronto: Oxford University Press, 2005.

Scott, Rachel. *Muscle and Blood*. 1st ed. New York: Dutton, 1974.

Second Task Force on Occupational Health and Safety. *Still Not Healthy, Still Not Safe*. Toronto: Ontario New Democratic Party, 1986.

Shapely, Deborah. "Shell Strike: Ecologists Refine Relations with Labor." *Science* 13 (April 1973): 166.

Smukler, Kenneth Lasch. "Individual Safety Protests in the Nonunion Workplace: Hazardous Decisions under Hazardous Conditions." *Dickinson Law Review* 89 (1984–85): 207–31.

Standing, Guy. "The I.L.O.: An Agency for Globalization?" *Development and Change* 33, no. 3 (2008): 355–83.

——. *The Precariat: The New Dangerous Class*. New York: Bloomsbury USA, 2011.

——. *Work after Globalization: Building Occupational Citizenship*. Cheltenham: Edward Elgar, 2009.

Steere Dairy, Inc. and David L. Watkins, 237 NLRB 219 1350–54 (1978).

Stockholm Convention on Persistent Organic Pollutants (Entered into Force 17 May 2004), 2256 UNTS 119.

Systems with Reliability, Inc. and Duane L. Albaugh, 322 NLRB 132 757–62 (1996).

Takala, Jukka. *Decent Work—Safe Work: Introductory Report to the XVIIth World Congress on Safety and Health at Work*. Geneva: International Labour Office, 2005.

Taylor, Charles. "Philosophy and the Human Sciences." *Philosophical Paper 2* (1985): 187–210.

Tribunal Appointed to Inquire into the Disaster at Aberfan on October 21st, 1966. *Report of the Tribunal Appointed to Inquire into the Disaster at Aberfan on October 21st, 1966*. London: Her Majesty's Stationery Office, 1967.

"Troops Told 'Shoot to Kill' in New Orleans." *ABC News*, September 2, 2005.

Troy, Gil. *The Reagan Revolution: A Very Short Introduction*. Oxford: Oxford University Press, 2009.

"Trying to Pull Together: Africans Are Asking Whether China Is Making Their Lunch or Eating It." *Economist*, April 20, 2011.

Tucker, Eric. "Diverging Trends in Worker Health and Safety Protection and Participation in Canada, 1985–2000." *Relations Industrielles / Industrial Relations* 58, no. 3 (2003): 395–424.

——. "The Persistence of Market Regulation of Occupational Health and Safety: The Stillbirth of Voluntarism." In *Essays in Labour Relations Law: Papers Presented at the Conference on Government and Labour Relations: The Death of Voluntarism; School of Management, University of Lethbridge, September 6–8, 1984*, edited by G. England. CCH Canadian, 1984.

U.N. Economic and Social Council [ECOSOC], Committee on Economic, Social & Cultural Rights. *General Comment No. 14—the Right to the Highest Attainable Standard of Health (Art. 12 of the Covenant)*. Adopted August 11, 2000.

——. *General Comment No. 19—the Right to Social Security (Art. 9 of the Covenant)*. Adopted November 23, 2007.

U.S. General Accounting Office. "Whistleblowers: Management of the Program to Protect Trucking Company Employees against Reprisal. Report GAO/Ggd-88-123. September 1988." Washington, D.C., 1988.

U.S. Government Accountability Office. "Whistleblower Protection Program: Better Data and Improvised Oversight Would Help Ensure Program Quality and Consistency. Report GAO-09-106. January 2009." Washington, D.C., 2009.

———. "Whistleblower Protection: Sustained Management Attention Needs to Address Long-Standing Program Weaknesses. Report GAO-10-722. August 2010." Washington, D.C., 2010.

"Universal Declaration of Human Rights, General Assembly Resolution 217a, at 71, U.N. GAOR, 3rd Sess., 1st Plen. Mtg., U.N. Doc a/810." Dec. 12, 1948.

"Urban Environment Conference Papers, 1971–1984." Walter P. Reuther Library of Labor and Urban Affairs Archives at Wayne State University.

Useem, Michael. *The Inner Circle: Large Corporations and the Rise of Business Political Activity in the U.S. and U.K.* New York: Oxford University Press, 1984.

Venn, Danielle. *Legislation, Collective Bargaining and Enforcement: Updating the OECD Employment Protection Indicators*. Paris: Organisation for Economic Co-operation and Development, 2009.

Walters, Vivienne. "Occupational Health and Safety Legislation in Ontario: An Analysis of Its Origins and Content." *Canadian Review of Sociology and Anthropology* 20, no. 4 (1983): 413–34.

———. "State Mediation of Conflicts over Work Refusals: The Role of the Ontario Labour Relations Board." *International Journal of Health Services* 21, no. 4 (1991): 717–29.

Weil, Simone. *The Need for Roots; Prelude to a Declaration of Duties toward Mankind*. New York: Putnam, 1952.

Whirlpool Corp. v. Marshall, 445 U.S. 1 (1980).

Wilensky, Harold L. *Rich Democracies: Political Economy, Public Policy, and Performance*. Berkeley: University of California Press, 2002.

World Conference on Human Rights, June 14–25, 1993. "Vienna Declaration and Programme of Action, U.N. Doc. A/Conf.157/23." July 12, 1993.

Youngdahl, Jay. "Solidarity First: Labor Rights Are Not the Same as Human Rights." *New Labor Forum* 18, no. 1 (Winter 2009): 31–37.

Index

Note: Page numbers followed by *t* and n indicate tables and notes.